A FRIENDS MEETING OF THE OLDEN TIME

OUR QUAKER FRIENDS

OF YE OLDEN TIME

BEING IN PART A TRANSCRIPT OF THE MINUTE BOOKS OF CEDAR CREEK MEETING, HANOVER COUNTY, AND THE SOUTH RIVER MEETING, CAMPBELL COUNTY, VA.

Compiled By
JAMES P. BELL

Originally Published
Lynchburg, Virginia
1905

Reprinted
Genealogical Publishing Co., Inc.
Baltimore, 1976

Reprinted for Clearfield Company, Inc. by
Genealogical Publishing Co. Inc.
Baltimore, MD 1991

Library of Congress Cataloging in Publication Data

Bell, James Pinkney Pleasant.
Our Quaker Friends of ye olden time.
Reprint of the 1905 ed. published by J. P. Bell Co., Lynchburg, Va.
1. Hanover Co., Va.—Genealogy. 2. Campbell Co., Va.—Genealogy. 3. Registers of births, etc.—Hanover Co., Va. 4. Registers of births, etc.—Campbell Co., Va. I. Title.

F232.H3B44 1976 929'.3755'462 76-22486
ISBN 0-8063-0732-3

Reprinted from a volume in the Library of
the Maryland Historical Society
Baltimore, Maryland

Made in the United States of America

PUBLISHER'S NOTICE.

My maternal ancestors, the Terrell family, were Quakers, and sometimes in my early childhood I attended their meetings for worship, held in the old Meetinghouse at Golansville, in Caroline County, Va., and still retaining a love for these good people, I have for some time past contemplated publishing a book giving an account of their religious belief, and manner of conducting their meetings.

Through a member of the Society of Friends, in Richmond, Va., I have obtained extracts from some of their old Minute books, which I hope will be of interest to my readers; I also make extracts from The Southern Friend (a religious journal published in Richmond during the Civil War).

"Southern Heroes," a book published since the war, setting forth the stand taken by Friends, who would endure persecution rather than go forth to slay their fellow man.

I also have a little tract issued by the New York Yearly Meeting, entitled: "A Brief View of the Doctrines of Friends," which I shall use.

The Quakers have done much for the Christian world in preaching that the baptism of the Holy Spirit is essential to salvation, and that at all times, and under all circumstances, they should seek to be guided by the Holy Spirit; hence, when they assemble for worship, they wait in silence before the Lord until they shall feel that he has given them a message to deliver to the people. It was this belief in the guidance of the Holy Spirit and this silent waiting before the Lord that gave rise to the saying that the "Quakers are waiting for the Spirit to move them."

There is a depth of meaning to this waiting before the Lord that only the true spiritually minded can comprehend. True worship is the communion of the soul with its Maker.

"Friends" have done much for the bettering of the world in liberating their slaves and in aiding in every way possible the abolition of slavery. Also their faithful testimony against Oaths has made the Courts accept the "Affirmation" as binding the same as the oath, and all who have conscientious scruples against taking an oath can take the "affirmation."

My readers will be interested in reading over the "Marriage Certificates" to see that the Quakers really marry themselves, or as they say, "take each other in marriage." First, consent of the parents or guardians must be obtained; then the consent of the Meeting. In olden times the man and woman had to go before the men's meeting, and then before the women's (Monthly Meeting) and "declare their intentions," as it was called. But now they send in their "intentions" in writing, and the Monthly Meeting appoints a committee to visit them, and ascertain whether they are free from any other engagements and have full consent of parents or guardians. "No obstruction appearing," they can be married as soon as they may desire, after the favorable report of the committee.

The Monthly Meeting that accepts the report of the Committee appoints another Committee to attend the marriage, to see that it is conducted in the proper manner, and report to the next Monthly Meeting.

In reading the Disownments, you will discover that most of them were for "marrying out," that was, marrying one of another demonination, or being married by an "hireling priest," as the ministers of other churches were called. The Quakers began after a while to see that this was a serious loss to the Church, and now they are allowed to marry those of other churches, if they are married by "Friends' Ceremony."

The members are still dealt with and disowned for drunkeness, immorality, or for engaging in clandestine trade, and are advised against hazardous or speculative trade, or engaging in any business beyond their ability to manage.

The reader will also notice that before granting a Certificate of Removal, the Monthly Meeting saw to it that the business affairs of the applicant were properly adjusted and settled before the certificate was granted, that their business affairs should not bring discredit upon the Meeting.

The Friends not only liberated their own slaves, but also used every effort for the abolition of slavery. They did not allow their members to hire a slave, or take the position of overseer of slaves. The Quakers in North Carolina and Virginia were at one time a large body, but the bitter feeling against them, because of their anti-slavery views caused them to seek homes in the free States, and soon many of the meetings were so depleted that they had to be "laid down." Doubtless many of my readers in the Western States will say, as they read these pages, "Yes, my ancestors came from Virginia."

*J. P. BELL,
Of J. P. Bell Company,
Lynchburg, Va.

* Quaker name: James Pinkney Pleasant Bell.

TABLE OF CONTENTS.

BIRTHS AND DEATHS

A RECORD OF BIRTHS AND DEATHS AMONGST FRIENDS TAKEN FROM THE OLD RECORD BOOK OF CEDAR CREEK MEETING, HANOVER COUNTY, VIRGINIA.

Children of Richard and Ann Bloxsom of Louisa County.

	BORN. Mo. Day. Year.
Sarah	12-14-1764
William	8-24-1766
Richard	12-18-1767
Obadiah	4-10-1770
Gregory	10-17-1771
Gideon	9-17-1772
Ann	11- 7-1774
Mary	9- 7-1776
Elizabeth	11-17-1779

Children of William and Mary Ballard.

Thomas	11-12-1735
Frances	12-12-1737
Byrum	2-27-1740
Delphin	1- 5-1742
Moorman	3-16-1747
David	4- 9-1750

Children of George and Cicely Bell of Louisa County.

Robert	2-15-1764
George	7-13-1767
Nathan	4- 5-1769
Ashley	12- 2-1770
Anthony	7-22-1773
Pleasant	12-21-1777

Children of Benjamin and Tace Bates of Hanover County.

Lucy	5- 6-1795
Micajah	6-12-1797
Martha	3-17-1800

	BORN. Mo. Day. Year.
Tace Crew	10-11-1803
William Savery	4- 7-1806
Fleming	3- 1-1808

Children of Fleming and Unity Bates of Hanover County.

Benjamin Spence	8-14-1804
Margaret	3-12-1806
Deborah	7-24-1807
Lemuel	11- 4-1808
Unity	3- 6-1810
Hannah	6-15-1811
Fleming	10-25-1812
Edward	5-11-1814

Children of Philip and Susana Brooks of Hanover County. (from Culpeper).

Sarah	11-22-1802

Children of Menoah and Anne Chiles of Caroline County.

John	5- 3-1747
Anne	9- 6-1750
Henry	5-11-1752
Patty	3- 9-1757
Samuel	12-12-1759

Children of Joseph and Agnes Crew of Hanover County.

Armisby	8-31-1745
Mary	1-26-1749
Micajah Crew	7-22-1750
Nicholas	3-26-1752
Agatha	3-19-1753
Sukey	7-16-1754
Joseph	———

Children of Thomas and Judith Cheadle of Caroline County.

Molly	8-13-1748
John	8-27-1749
George	10-19-1750
Thomas	10- 7-1753

Children of Micajah and Judith Clark of Louisa County.

	BORN. Mo. Day. Year.
Christopher	2-20-1737
Robert	6-15-1738
Mourning	6- 6-1740
Micajah	12-27-1741
John	10-26-1743
Edward	10-12-1745

Children of Boling and Winifred Clarke of Louisa County.

Christopher	2-29-1743
Elizabeth	11-12-1744

Children of Frances and Christianna Clarke.

Molley	9-17-1747
Betty	11-22-1748
Nicholas	2- 6-1750
Francis	2- 7-1753

Children of John and Anne Clarke.

Thomas	7-30-1746
Francis	8- 5-1748
John	11- 3-1750

Children of James and Judith Crew of Hanover County.

Unity	8-31-1760
Littleberry	12-18-1762
Jesse	1-18-1765
Obadiah	3-31-1767
Sarah	7-16-1769
Judith	2- 1-1772
James	1- 5-1774
Dorothy	6-27-1776
Benjamin	5-21-1779
Mary	7-20-1781

Children of Micajah and Margaret Crew.

Tace	8-30-1776
Lemuel	8- 5-1778

	BORN. Mo. Day. Year.
Unity	9-25-1780
Walter	12-28-1784
Talitha	2-10-1788
Margaret	5-31-1790
Susanna	10-15-1792
Deborah D.	11-25-1794

Children of Pleasant and Amy Cobb of Caroline County.

Thomas	4-21-1786
Rebecca	10-20-1787
Mary	3-18-1789
Rhoda	9-30-1790
Abigal	3-28-1792
Elizabeth	11-19-1793
Pleasant	12-13-1795
Joseph	6-21-1797
Anselm	4-16-1799
Joanna	6-17-1803
Robert	2-16-1806

Children of Samuel and Ann Couch of Goochland County.

Daniel	———
Ann Wolston	———
Margaret	———
James	———
Deborah	———
Rebecca	2-26-1796
Mary Younghusband	———

Children of Littlebury and Huldah Crew of Hanover County.

James	9-22-1798
Benjamin	11-16-1799
John	4-30-1801
Milley	9-21-1802

Children of James and Charlotte Cowgill of Hanover Co. (Culpeper)

Rachel	18-18-1794
Abigal	10-16-1796

	BORN. Mo. Day. Year.
John	8-21-1798
James	5-24-1801

Children of Jesse and Peggy Crew of Hanover County.

Lancelot	8-19-1807
Elizabeth Ladd	9-29-1808
Judith	10-15-1809
Owen Milton	6-29-1811
Obadiah	11- 5-1812

Children of Walter and Sarah Bacon Crew of Hanover County.

Jane Temperance	1-17-1821
Margaret Talitha	8-31-1822
Mary Rice	9-24-1824
William Rice	12-12-1826
Sarah Bacon	4- 1-1828
Susan Unity	3-27-1830
Walter Fleming	1-14-1832
Deborah Tace	9-14-1833
Micajah Lemuel	6-13-1835
Samuel Izard	10-16-1837
Ann Eliza	12-16-1839
Martha Louis	11- 9-1841
Lucy Bell	8-18-1844
Nathaniel Edmond	8-10-1848

Children of Nathaniel C. and Deborah D. Crew Crenshaw.

John Bacon	5- 2-1820

Children of Nathaniel C. and Mary Y. Crenshaw.

Edmund Austin	2- 4-1827

Children of Nathaniel C. and Jane Denson Pretlow Crenshaw.

Elizabeth Ann	5-21-1830
Mary Jane	7- 5-1833

Children of John Bacon and Rachel Hoge Crenshaw.

	BORN. Mo. Day. Year.
Nathaniel Bacon	12-18-1845
Deborah Ann	5-18-1848
Margaret Elizabeth	6-22-1849
James Hoge	12-23-1851
Eliza Catharine	11-22-1853
Rachel Frances	10-20-1855
John Austin	5-16-1857
John Chapman	7-30-1858

Children of John Bacon and Judith Willets Crenshaw.

Willetts Bassett	12-16-1861
Mary Frances	11- 9-1863
Judith Isabella	7-10-1865
Edmund Bacon	5-27-1869
Walter Crew	8-17-1870
Sarah Willetts	2-17-1872

Children of Alfred and Hannah Cranstone.

Charles	4- 1-1853
Alfred Henry	3-12-1855
William	3- 4-1859

Children of James Hoge and Belle Pleasants Crenshaw.

James H., Jr.	2- 8-1880
William Pleasants	3-11-1881
Rachel	3-25-1882
Henry Pleasants	4-29-1884
Walter Crew	6-11-1887
Joseph Pleasants	11- 2-1890

Children of John and Judith Douglas.

Charles	4-29-1732
Elizabeth	12-18-1733
Thomas	9- 2-1740
Polly	6-12-1744
Judith	7-18-1746
John	8- 8-1748

	BORN. Mo. Day. Year.
Anne	2-10-1750
Achillis	2-22-1752
Dorcas	1- 9-1755

Children of David and Mary Garland.

Elizabeth	9-10-1745

Children of Daniel and Mary Harris of Hanover County.

John	1-11-1731
Edith	12-20-1733
Cornelius	11-11-1735
Moses	3-31-1738
Mary	10-20-1740
Daniel	———
Nicholas	———
Thomas	———

Children of Samuel and Martha Hargrave of Caroline County.

Jesse	7- 8-1752
Samuel	9- 9-1754
Elizabeth	12-28-1756
Mary	3- 7-1759
Martha	8-10-1761
Sarah	10-15-1763
Thomas	1-31-1766
John	8-21-1768

Children of Moses and Elizabeth Harris.

Sarah	11-11-1762

Children of Moses and Sophia Harris.

William Eley	12- 3-1768
Sally and Priscilla	4-27-1772

Children of Henry Philip and Mary Hart.

James Philips	6-20-1741
William	2-13-1743
John	3-18-1745

	BORN. Mo. Day. Year.
Joseph	12- 3-1748
Elizabeth	2- 3-1751

Children of Jeremiah and Ann Harris, Cedar Creek, Hanover.

Sally	6- 7-1767
John	8-14-1769
Lucy	3-15-1772
Cheadle	6- 9-1774
Elizabeth	11-22-1779

Children of John and Alice Hutchins of Goochland County.

Jonathan	2-28-1763
Agatha	1-21-1764
Susanna	1-15-1769
Mary	1-20-1771
Elizabeth	1-12-1772
Thomas	11-23-1774
Strangeman	9-15-1776
William	8-14-1778
Patrick	3-10-1781

Children of Joseph and Rachel Hargrave of Caroline County.

Garland	1-30-1793
Lucy	2- 3-1797

Children of Thomas and Chlotilda Harris of Hanover County.

Deborah	12-17-1787
Rebecca	9-24-1790
Benjamin	2-24-1794
Isabella	4- 2-1803
Sarah Ann	1-15-1809

Children of Samuel and Lucy Hargrave of Caroline County.

Salley	3-12-1784

Children of Benjamin and Sarah Harris of Caroline County.

Thomas	3-17-1760

Children of James and Rebecca Hunnicutt of Goochland County.

	BORN. Mo. Day. Year.
John Murdaugh	12-16-1773
Ann	9- 6-1775
Miriam Murdaugh	9-21-1777
James	2-12-1780
Thomas Pretlow	9- 5-1782

Children of Thomas and Unity Harris of Hanover County.

Benjamin	2-10-1806

Children of Benjamin and Mary Johnson.

Thomas	11-14-1749
John	1-14-1751
Andrew	4- 7-1754
William	8-12-1756

Children of Ashley and Agatha Johnson of Amelia County.

John	12-19-1747

Children of Ashley and Mary Johnson of Amelia County.

Elizabeth	5-14-1752
Mary	12-18-1753
Jane	5-29-1755
Gerard	1-26 1757
Benjamin	7-10-1758
Drusilla	4-26-1761
Anne	1-15-1763
Ashley	5- 4-1766
Edith	9-11-1769
Thomas Watkins	11-23-1771

Children of Jesse and Elizabeth Johnson of Amelia County.

Benjamin	10-21-1752
John	1-31-1754
Jesse	9-7-1755
William	5- 8-1757
Sarah	4-10-1759
Thomas	12- 1-1760

	BORN. Mo. Day. Year.
Elizabeth	9- 7-1763
Jane	4-19-1766
Agatha	10- 8-1768
Watkins	4-15-1770

Children of William and Agatha Johnson of Amelia County.

Milley	3-12-1766
Elizabeth	10-24-1768
Zachariah	1-27-1770
William	7-28-1771
Rachel	11-30-1774
Charles	3- 4-1777
Pleasants	8-12-1780
Thomas	4-14-1783
Christopher	5-24-1785
Moorman	6-26-1787

Children of John and Lydia Johnson of Amelia County.

Judith	8-13-1755
Susanna	3-28-1757
James	8-27-1758
Samuel	2-18-1761
Joseph	10- 1-1763
John	2- 5-1766
Thomas	12-29-1769
Lydia	1-29-1779

Children of Gerard and Judith Johnson.

Jane	5-30-1762
Elizabeth	12—-1763
Benjamin	10-21-1765
Judith	11-11-1767
Gerard	6- 4-1769
John Watkins	3- 5-1771
David	9-30-1772
Elizabeth	12- 3-1774
Samuel	—16-1776

Children of John and Lydia Johnson.

	BORN. Mo. Day. Year.
Jonathan	3-13-1771
Strangeman	9-28-1772
Benjamin	3-26-1774
Agatha	11-21-1776
Ashly	1-15-1780

Children of Robert and Sarah Johnson of Louisa County.

Margaret	8- 5-1752

Children of Benjamin and Agnes Johnson of Louisa County.

Sarah	1-30-1729
Christopher	11-22-1731
William	4-25-1734
Benjamin	8-24-1736
Penelope	2-27-1739
Collins	6-28-1741
Edward	2-23-1744
Agnes	12-11-1746

Children of Elijah and Betsy Johnson of Louisa County.

Thomas Garland	4-22-1794
James	1-12-1796
Sally	6-26-1797
Patsey	2-16-1801

Children of John and Dorothy Johnson of Hanover.

Benjamin	12-15-1797
Sarah	10-27-1799
Penelope	2-13-1802
Judith	5- 9-1804
James and Deborah	5-28-1807
Deborah	11- 8-1809
Unity and Mary	4-11-1811

Children of Catlett and Sarah Jones.

Ann	4- 8-1804
Benjamin	4-20-1805

Children of Thomas and Rachel Moorman of Louisa County.

	BORN. Mo. Day. Year.
Mary	12-19-1730
Zachariah	2- 2-1732
Micajah	6-28-1735
Elizabeth	2- 2-1738
Thomas	6- 6-1740
Mildred	11-25-1742
Pleasant	3-19-1745

Children of Charles and Mary Moorman of Louisa County.

Elizabeth	2- 9-1738
Lucy	2-20-1741
Aggy	2-26-1743
Charles	6-28-1746
Judith	6-26-1748
Molley	9-25-1751
Robert	11-16-1753
Thomas	11-25-1756

Children of John Wilson and Mildred Maddox of Hanover County.

Thomas	4- 2-1775
John	1-16-1777
William Griffin	3- 9-1779
Wilson	4- 9-1781

Children of William Griffin and Mary Maddox of Hanover County.

Edwin Milton	7-21-1810
William Garland	6- 1-1812
Maria Ann	5-10-1815

Children of Thomas and Jane Maddox of Caroline County.

Eliza	4- 2-1811
Wilson	7-24-1813

Children of John and Sarah Peatross of Caroline County.

Mary	1-11-1776
Amey	1-22-1778
Anna	4- 5-1780

	BORN. Mo. Day. Year.
Rhoda	6-27-1784
Elizabeth	2- 9-1790
Nelson	4-25-1792

Children of Samuel and Sarah Parsons, Bellville, Goochland County.

Samuel Pleasants	9- 5-1783
Margaret P.	11-25-1786

Children of Thomas Snowden and Elizabeth Tucker Pleasants.

Elizabeth Snowden	1-20-1792

Children of William Henry and Mary Pleasants of Goochland County.

Thomas Snowden	11-29-1796
Joseph Jordan	1-19-1799

Children of Joseph Jordan and Martha Bates Pleasants of Hanover.

Benjamin Bates	7-23-1820
Mary Snowden	8-3-1824
William Henry	5-16-1827
George Dillwyn	10- 7-1830
Ann Josephine	8-16-1833
Margaret Isabella	6-26-1836
Walter Frederick	6-16-1839
Julia and Maria	6-30-1842

Children of William Henry and Eliza J. Pleasants of Richmond.

Lydia Alice	3-26-1853
Heney Abijah	9-15-1854
Martha Isabella	2-26-1859
Asa Janney	11-27-1869

Children of William and Elizabeth Ratcliffe.

Mary	3-25-1760
Harrison	3-11-1762
William	1-14-1764
John	11-11-1766
Gideon	5-21-1769

Children of Alfred and Mary Terrell Ricks of Southampton County.

	BORN. Mo. Day. Year.
Julia W.	———
Elizabeth H.	———
Richard A.	———
Mary Winston	———
Walter A	———
Deborah	———
Samuella T.	———

Julia W married Bowling H. Winston, of Indiana. No children.

Elizabeth H. married Oswin White, of North Carolina.

Alfred R. White, son of Elizabeth H. and Oswin White.

Walter A., never married.

Deborah married John Pretlow, of Southampton County. No children.

Ella T. married John C. Winston. No children.

Children of Richard A. and Eliza Crenshaw Ricks.

*Julian W.	3-11-1882
Katharine C.	6-20-1883
Richard A., Jr.	6-10-1885
James Hoge	7-15-1886

Children of Mary W. Ricks and Samuel B. Pretlow.

Mary Terrell	———
Fannie M.	———
Julia	———
Jane D.	———

Children of Thomas Stanley by his first Wife.

Maddox	8-17-1715
Elizabeth	3-29-1718

Children by Elizabeth his second Wife.

Margery	8-1-1722
Mary	6- 5-1729
Thomas	2- 9-1731
Pleasant	4-25-1733
John	1-27-1735

* Died 6-29-1882.

	BORN. Mo. Day. Year.
Zachariah	10- 6-1737
Sarah	1- 6-1739
Anne	6- 7-1741
Nathan	1- 7-1743
Joseph	10-21-1747

Children of James and Catharine Stanley of Hanover County.

William	6- 4-1729
James	3-26-1731
Mary	6-27-1733
Martha	3-21-1736
Micajah	4-28-1739
Agnes	6-20-1743
Strangeman	11- 7-1745
Elijah	10- 7-1750

Children of Huldah and Maddox Stanley of Hanover County.

John	1-23-1747
Elizabeth	5-15-1749
William	7-22-1750
Obediah	4-27-1751
Mary	10- 7-1753
Rachel	6- 6-1757
Huldah	9- 2-1759
Maddox	3-15-1761

Children of James and Elizabeth Stanley.

Caleb	8- 6-1758

Children of William and Elizabeth Stanley.

Samuel	9-21-1759
Hannah	1- 2-1762

Children of Achillis and Elizabeth Stanley.

Agnes	6-24-1768
Jesse	10-24-1770

Children of Zachariah and Sarah Stanley.

	BORN. Mo. Day. Year.
Susannah	12- 8-1775
Abraham	8- 7-1777
Abigal	2- 5-1780
Zachariah	19-15-1782

Children of Thomas and Unity Stanley.

Moses	11-15-1781
John	11- 2-1783
Temperance	2-22-1786
James	3-10-1787
Joseph	2- 9-1789
Benjamin	2-10-1791
Judith	9-28-1793
Abigal	10-19-1796
Unity	8-19-1799

Children of Littlebury and Agness Stanley.

Solomon	12-26-1787
Martha	11- 8-1789

Children of Thomas and Edith Stanley.

Milley	9- 7-1791
Edmund	2-10-1793
John	9-19-1795
Elijah	9- 8-1796
Frances	10- 1-1798

Children of Thomas and Priscilla Stanley.

Isaac	3-24-1803
Thomas Binford	9- 5-1805

Children of Waddy and Rebekah Stanley.

Samuel	4- 1-1796
Priscilla	7-15-1798
Lucy	4- 9-1801
Anne	6-23-1803
Joel	11-18-1805

Children of Henry and Anne Terrell of Caroline County.

	BORN. Mo. Day. Year.
Henry	1-29-1735
Thomas	8-20-1736
Betty	9- 7-1738
Anne	9-15-1740

Children of Henry and Sarah Terrell of Caroline County.

Ursula	3-11-1746
Charles	8- 3-1748
Judith	2- 6-1750
Abigal	10- 6-1751
George	6-28-1753
Tarlton	11-19-1754

Children of David and Sarah Terrell of Caroline County.

Agga	12-17-1749
Benjamin	11- 7-1750
Edward	2-12-1753
Sarah	1-10-1755
Winifred	10-14-1760
Mary	4- 6-1757
David	3-11-1763
Henry	8-13-1767
Samuel	12-12-1769

Children of Pleasant and Catharine Terrell.

Lucy	9-17-1763
Jesse	5-10-1765
Robert	1-24-1768
Samuel	1- 8-1770
Rachel	5- 3-1772
Nancy	2-17-1775
Pleasant	11-26-1778
Lemuel	7- 2-1781
Mary	2- 3-1784

Children of Samuel and Elizabeth Harris Terrell.

	BORN. Mo. Day. Year.
Mary Ann	11- 3-1801
Samuel	12-29-1802
Walter	4-14-1805
James O.	12- 2-1808
Henry O.	3- 2-1815
George Fox	10-16-1817

Children of Lemuel and Rebecca Terrell.

Catharine Pleasant ("Kitty")	3-28-1805
Robert S.	——1807
Nancy Ann	——1809
Nicey Lynch	——1812
Lindsy L.	——1814
Rhoda W.	——1816
Mary	——1818
Sarah Rebecca	——1822
Thomas Henry	——1825

Children of Catherine Pleasant (Terrell) Bell.

James Pinkney	11-18-1830
William Lemuel	3——1833
Robert Henry	4-19-1836
Mary Margaret	——1838
Rhoda Ann	————
Richard Thomas	——1846

Children of Thomas and Rebecca Terrell.

Mathew Peatross	11- 8-1762
Amy	11- 8-1766
Rhoda	4- 8-1770
Thomas	2-17-1772
Timothy	3-23-1774
Joannah	3-31-1776
Joseph	9-29-1777
Rebecca	12-22-1780

Children of Jonathan and Margaret Terrell.

	BORN. Mo. Day. Year.
Elizabeth	3-28-1778
Chiles	2-26-1780
Nanny	6-17-1782
John	5-24-1784
Miriam	11- 2-1786
Matilda	3-18-1789
Caleb	5-17-1791
Thomas	2-24-1794

Children of Jesse and Mary Terrell.

Sarah	6-10-1788
Parmelia	10-27-1790

Children of Jesse by Mary his second Wife.

Rhoda	10-15-1796
George	1- 1-1799
Mahlon	8-17-1802
Samuel	8-24-1804
Eliza Ann	4- 3-1807

Children of Matthew Peatross and Sally Terrell.

Mahala	4-27-1790
Rachel	11- 2-1795
Thomas	2-15-1798
Clark	11-29-1799
Joannah	4- 3-1802
Mathew	3-28-1804

Children of Timothy and Miriam M. Terrell.

Maria	4-25-1799

Children of Timothy by Mary his second Wife.

Caty	7-11-1804

Children of Joseph and Sarah Terrell.

Anna Lynch	1- 2-1807
Lucy	8-23-1810
Joseph Walker	9- 5-1812
William Penn	2-25-1815

Deaths taken from the family Bible of Mary A. Terrell Ricks.

	DIED. Mo. Day. Year.
Pleasant Terrell	1-11-1803
Caty, his wife	4-24-1813
Samuel, son of Pleasant and Caty	8-14-1844
Elizabeth, wife of Samuel	1- 5-1853

Robert, son of Pleasant and Caty Terrell, married Nancy Nelson 1-4-1817, who died 5-27-1825, and he married Sarah T. Burruss. Robert died 2-9-1845, without issue.

Children of Samuel and Elizabeth H. Terrell.

Mary A. T. Ricks	10-18-1870
Samuel	10-19-1826
*Walter	1-30-1887
James P.	10-14-1867
Henry O., supposed to have been killed by the Indians	———
George Fox	5-28-1855

Children of Benjamin and Margaret Vaughan of Hanover County.

	BORN. Mo. Day. Year.
Matilda	1-29-1796
Lemuel	8-12-1797
Bowling	8-30-1799
Joseph	8-22-1801
John Ladd	11-21-1803
Benjamin	11-30-1805
Anna Ladd	3-22-1808
Lucy Dabney	3-24-1810
Margaretta B.	7- 2-1813
Mary	7- 2-1813

Children of Nathaniel and Jemimah Winston of Caroline County.

Mary	7-28-1750
Samuel	9-19-1752
Rebecca	2-28-1755
Anthony	4- 1-1757
George	12- 7-1759

* Walter Terrell married M. Talitha Crew 10-3-1850, who died 10-13-1853, leaving one daughter, Mary Terrell, now Mrs. Euclid Saunders, of Iowa City, Iowa.

RECORD OF DEATHS TAKEN FROM THE OLD RECORD BOOK OF CEDAR CREEK MEETING OF HANOVER COUNTY.*

DIED.
Mo. Day. Year.

Byrom, son of Byrom and Eleanor Ballard...........12-14-1769
Byrom, son of Byrom and Eleanor Ballard............11- 9-1774
Bates, Fleming, son of Benjamin and Tace Bates...... 9- 8-1809
Bates, Tace, daughter of Benjamin and Tace Bates.... 9-19-1892
Bates, Margaret, daughter of Fleming and Unity Bates. 3-22-1806
Crew, Margaret, daughter of Micajah and Margaret Crew 12- 3-1863
Crew, John, son of Littlebury and Huldah...........10-26-1801
Crenshaw, Rachel, wife of John Bacon Crenshaw......11-20-1858
Crenshaw, Rachel, daughter of J. B. and R. H. .... 9—-1857
Crenshaw, John A., son of J. B. and R. H. .... 9—-1857
Crenshaw, John C., son of J. B. and R. H. 11-14-1863
Crenshaw, Willetts, son of J. B. and Judith.......... 9-17-1863
Crenshaw, Mary F., daughter of J. B. and Judith..... 9-13-1864
Crenshaw, Edmund B., son of J. B and Judith........ 3-18-1870
Crenshaw, Walter C., son of J. B and Judith......... 3-10-1871
Crenshaw, Nathaniel C., son of John and Elizabeth... 5-22-1866
Crenshaw, John Bacon, son of Nathaniel and Deborah.. 5-10-1889
Hargrave, Salley, daughter of Samuel and Lucy Hargrave, of Caroline County 10-27-1786
Johnson, Sarah, daughter of Jesse and Elizabeth Johnson 9- 4-1794
Jones, Ann, daughter of Catlett and Sarah Jones...... 5- 2-1805
Johnson, Deborah, daughter of John and Dorothy 7-13-1810
Pleasants, Elizabeth, daughter of Thomas S. and Elizabeth T. 8-31-1796
Pleasants, Martha E., daughter of Joseph J and Martha 9-14-1842
Pleasants, Lydia A., daughter of William H. and Eliza J. 6-27-1853
Pleasants, Henry A., son of William H. and Eliza J. .. 3- 2-1883

*This Record Book has been very poorly kept, as can be seen.

RECORD OF BIRTHS AND DEATHS AMONGST FRIENDS IN CAMPBELL AND BEDFORD COUNTIES, TAKEN FROM THE OLD SOUTHRIVER MEETING BOOK.

Children of Christopher and Judith Anthony.

	BORN. Mo. Day. Year.
Mary	9-2 1766
Joseph	12- 8-1767
Elizabeth	10- 9-1769
Charles	10-21-1773

Children of Christopher and Mary Anthony.

Christopher	12- 6-1776
Samuel	1-26-1779
Hannah	10-27-1781
Sarah	2-21-1784
Penelope	4-15-1786
Jordan	8-10-1788
Rachel	6-25-1791
Charlotte	10-19-1793

Children of Joseph and Rhoda Anthony.

Samuel Parsons	2-12-1792

Children of John and Rachel Anderson.

Richard P	4- 9-1780
Rachel	1-20-1783
Orpah	6-24-1785
Elizabeth	7-16-1788
Wm. Pauling	4- 4-1792

Children of Byrum and Eleanor Ballard.

Mary	6-16-1764
Betty	11- 1-1765
William	7-20-1767
Byrum	5-14-1769
Amos	11-15-1770

Children of Barclay and Judith Ballard.

	BORN. Mo. Day. Year.
Byrum	6- 9-1773
Johnson	11- 3-1776
James	10-23-1777
Lydia	12- 7-1778
William	1-15-1780
Susanna	2- 9-1781
Samuel	6-26-1783
Thomas	3-21-1785

Children of William and Elizabeth Ballard.

Anthony	2-22-1789
Eleanor	6- 5-1790
Mary	1-23-1792
Asa	8-19-1793

Children of William and Nancy Ballard.

Granderson B.	4-27-1808

Children of Byrum and Sarah Ballard.

Philip	6-18-1793

Children of Richard and Ann Bloxom.

Charles	10-27-1784

Children of William and Nancy Bloxom.

James	8-11-1795
Ann Smith	5- 8-1797
Elizabeth T.	12-23-1799
Mariah	12-11-1802

Children of Benjamin and Rachel Butterworth.

Nancy	5-21-1791
Moorman	3- 5-1793
Benjamin	10-24-1794
Isaac	5- 7-1796
Samuel	6-30-1798
Rachel M.	7-11-1800

	BORN. Mo. Day. Year.
William	9-27-1802
Henry Thomas	6- 4-1809

Children of James S. and Deborah Butler.

Mary	8-11-1812
Ann Johnson	11-13-1814
Martha	8-27-1816
William	9-19-1818
James Edward	9-17-1820
Alfred	5-29-1822
Joseph	5- 5-1824

Children of Stephen and Mary Butler.

Deborah	2- 4-1797
Joseph	2-24-1800

Children of Stephen and Matilda Butler.

Anselm	10-24-1811
Edna	3-16-1813
Mary E.	5-28-1815
Matilda	7- 9-1817

Children of Josiah and Susannah Bailey.

Almeda	5- 7-1805
Robert Barclay	8-31-1806
Judith	2-24-1808
Daniel	6-11-1809
James Edwin	8- 9-1800
Mary Byrum	12- 6-1811
Susannah	5- 6-1813

Children of Stephen and Louisa Butler.

Matilda Ann	10-13-1822
William Exom	10-27-1824

Children of Thomas and Elizabeth Bailey.

Mary	4- 9-1806
John	1-21-1807

Children of Thomas and Patty Burgess.

	BORN. Mo. Day. Year.
Elizabeth	9-22-1801
Joseph	10- 9-1803
Jesse	11- 9-1805
Moses	4-28-1807
Mary	2- 1-1809
Tace and Martha	9- 5-1811

Children of James and Agatha Candler.

Lucy	2- 3-1787
Daniel	4-17-1788
Johnson	6-14-1789
Elizabeth	6- 6-1792
James	1- 4-1794
John	7- 7-1795
Henry	4-27-1797

Children of Mahlon and Elizabeth Cadwalader.

William	3-21-1810
Jane Daniel	9- 6-1812
Deborah Douglas	8-18-1815
Judith Johnson	12-26-1818

Children of John and Rachel Coffee.

William	5- 5-1786
John	9- 2-1787
Joseph	8-6-1789
Rachel	9-10-1791
Mary	2-18-1793

Children of Thomas and Jane Cadwallader.

Elizabeth	1-31-1786
Mahlon	9-26-1787
Jonah	8-11-1789
Israel	7-28-1792

Children of Nicholas and Druscilla Crew.

Micajah	6-26-1783
John	9- 3-1785

Children of Joseph and Rebecca Curle.

	BORN. Mo. Day. Year.
Sarah	12-15-1791

Children of John Candler.

John	2- 9-1766
Henry	1-22-1769

Children of Samuel and Annie Davis.

William	7- 3-1770
John	9-24-1774
Thomas	2-18-1777
Micajah	6-30-1779

Children of William and Mary Davis.

John	10-21-1775
Henry	1-21-1777
Susannah	4-29-1780
Elizabeth	12- 5-1782
Benjamin	6- 8-1785
Isaac	5-10-1788
Polly	3-25-1790
Nancy	10-26-1792
Louisa	3- 4-1794
Deborah	4-25-1797

Children of Micajah and Mary Davis.

Susanna	5-18-1776
Nancy	5- 9-1778
Martha and Mary	3- 6-1780
Samuel	3-22-1782
David	3- 7-1784
Richard	12-19-1785
Micajah	10-25-1787
Annis	7- 1-1789
Robert Pleasants	9-26-1792

Children of Elizabeth and Achillis Douglass.

Robert Terrell	8- 1-1780
Sarah	6-19-1781

	BORN. Mo. Day. Year.
Judith	6-27-1783
Milley	8-18-1785
Deborah	11-23-1787
Elizabeth	1- 9-1790
Mary	1-24-1792
Agatha	1-12-1794
Charles Terrell	9-12-1795
John Lynch	11-26-1797
Achillis Moorman	12-17-1800

Children of James and Hannah Daniel.

Mary	12- 4-1791

Children of Daniel and Edith Easley.

Sarah	2-13-1793
Mary Ann	10-17-1794
Ruth	8-20-1796
John	9- 9-1798
Daniel	6- 2-1800
Rachel	6-14-1802
Richard	9-22-1804
Isaac	8- 2-1806

Children of Moses and Mary Embree.

Rachel	10——1775
Moses	11- 8-1779
John	3-19-1784

Children of John and Ann Fowler.

Mary	10-22-1775
William	2-17-1778
John	5-22-1780
Christopher	4-25-1782
Nancy	12-10-1784
David and Judith	5-10-1787
Thomas	3-77-1790

Children of John and Rachel Fisher.

Robert	10- 2-1800

Children of Joseph and Hannah Fisher.

	BORN. Mo. Day. Year.
Sylvanus	10- 8-1797
Rachel	5-14-1799
William	11-24-1800

Children of Robert and Catharine Hanna.

Thomas	5- 2-1777
Benjamin	6-14-1779
Esther	9- 6-1781
David	1- 9-1784
Caleb	8- 4-1786
Robert	5-28-1789

Children of Isaac and Rachel Hatcher.

James	7-16-1789
William	5-22-1791
Lydia	12-17-1792

Children of Robert and Catharine Hatcher.

Esther	4-10-1792
Catharine	11-25-1794
Ann	7-30-1797

Children of Moses and Ruth Hendrick.

Amos	8-16-1759
Cloe	4- 5-1763
Sarah	11-20-1764
Judith	9- 7-1766
Obadiah	10-26-1767
Betty	11- 2-1769
Jeremiah	10-20-1772
Moses, Jr.,	2-12-1778

Children of Amos and Hepzibah Holloway.

Phebe	1- 3-1787
Job	5-10-1793
Aaron	4-16-1795
Stephen	6-13-1789

	BORN. Mo. Day. Year.
Rhoda	3-25-1793
Hulda	8-30-1798
Jason	1-14-1801

Children of Asa and Mary Holloway.

Stanton	2-26-1787
Mary	2-20-1789
Sarah	8-19-1791
Isaac	6-15-1793
Hannah	10-15-1796
Eli	9-18-1798
James	12-12-1800

Children of William and Sarah Holloway.

John	5- 7-1791
Isaac	5-19-1792
Betsy	9-17-1793
Pleasant	4-23-1795
Samuel	9-12-1797
George	6- 3-1800

Children of Ashley and Milley Johnson.

Jeptha	6- 9-1783
Jonathan	3- 8-1785
Daniel	7-29-1787
William	1- 1-1790
Nancy	4-24-1792
Abner	9- 1-1794
Agatha	1-17-1797
Martha	7- 7-1799

Children of Joseph and Agatha Johnson.

Simeon	6-20-1786
Joseph	2-10-1788
Betsy	1-22-1790
John	7-24-1793
Polly	12-16-1795
Kitty Winston	3-15-1798
Elvy	8-29-1800

	BORN. Mo. Day. Year.
Watkins	1-23-1803
Caroline Agnes	9- 9-1805

Children of Samuel and Susanna Johnson.

Thomas	3-21-1790
Samuel	12-28-1791
Moorman	1-27-1794
James	1-23-1796
Sarah	3-28-1798
John	4-19-1800

Children of Moorman and Elizabeth Johnson.

Susanna	10- 3-1780
James	12-19-1782
Milley	1- 7-1785
Micajah Moorman	1-15-1788
Christopher	11- 2-1791
Thomas Chiles	12- 8-1794
Charles M.	9-20-1797
Achillis Clark	3-11-1800

Children of William and Agatha Johnson.

Nancy	6-23-1791

Children of William and Sarah Johnson.

Unity	6-17-1793
Richard	9-11-1794
Jerusha	12-24-1796
Obadiah	5-26-1798
Gideon	4-26-1800

Children of John Jr. and Rhoda Johnson.

Joseph	4- 7-1791
Micajah	12-28-1792
John	1- 3-1795
Charles	1-14-1797
Polly	1-14-1799
Lewis	3- 7-1801

Children of Christopher and Milley Johnson.

	BORN. Mo. Day. Year.
Susanna	7- 3-1785
Micajah	1-11-1788
Penelope	2-24-1790
James	9-26-1792
Elizabeth	5-18-1795

Children of Charles and Susanna Johnson.

David Terrell	3-10-1797
Anna	10-18-1798
Susanna	7-17-1800

Children of David and Rachel Johnson.

Collins	1- 3-1799
William	10-30-1800

Children of Christopher and Sarah Johnson.

Samuel Hargrave	11-21-1785
Caleb	12- 1-1787
Patsy	7-19-1791
Lilliburn	8-20-1793
Zalinda	12- 8-1796
Adeliza	10-24-1799

Children of William and Susanna Johnson.

Ashley	7-17-1756
Agnes	1-31-1758
Martha	3-19-1760
Jeptha	3-19-1761
Ruth	6-12-1763
Robert	5-18-1765
Newby	2-12-1767
Sarah	9-29-1769
William	1- 6-1772
Johnathan	12-22-1774
Elijah	7-11-1777
Ann	1-11-1780

Children of Benjamin and Mary Johnson.

	BORN. Mo. Day. Year.
William	12-22-1757
James	12-20-1759
Rachel	3-26-1762
Elizabeth	5-15-1764
Mildred	7- 4-1766
Christopher	3- 4-1769
Lemuel	8-27-1782
Anselm	3-25-1786
Matilda	1-28-1792
Polly	2-13-1797
Gerard and Lucinda	3-21-1799

Children of Christopher and Betty Johnson.

Charles	9-27-1753
Ann	8-13-1755
Mary	5-27-1757
Benjamin	2-21-1759
Agnes	1-18-1761
Christopher	1- 4-1763
Nicholas	———
Betty	8- 3-1767
Thomas	1- 4-1770
Timothy	3-30-1772
David	10- 6-1776
Collins	10- 6-1776
Mourning	1-31-1779
Samuel	7-30-1782

Children of Charles and Molley Johnson.

Moorman	2-21-1780
Betty	10-22-1781

Children of James and Rachel Johnson.

John	7-24-1782
Micajah	5-24-1784
Edmond	5-24-1786
Rhoda	5-27-1788

	BORN. Mo. Day. Year.
Chiles	11-28-1790
Barclay	11-18-1792
Achillis	2- 6-1795
Lydia	5-11-1797
Susanna	3-18-1800

Children of Nicholas and Patsy Johnson.

Nancy	2- 3-1789
Garland	10-26-1790
Pleasant	10- 4-1795
Jessie	6-26-1798
Johanna	3-26-1800
Salley	10-23-1804
Minor	5-29-1806
Martha	11-23-1809

Children of Newby and Sarah Johnson.

Achillis Douglas	6-18-1802
Edward Lynch	1- 9-1806

Children of Jonathan and Judith Johnson.

Wm. Douglas	11-14-1805
Micajah T.	11-23-1807
Robert	2-19-1810
Elizabeth	7-14-1812
Susannah	9-29-1814
Achillis Douglas	2- 8-1817
Sarah Ann	10-28-1819
Mildred Tyree	1-12-1822

Children of Simeon and Delilah Johnson.

Alfred Carroll	8-18-1806

Children of Anselm and Deborah Johnson.

Anselm Douglas	3-18-1811

Children of Nicholas and Caty Johnson.

Griffin	1- 5-1812
Mary Ann	12-30-1830

Children of Isaac and Sarah Johnson.

	BORN. Mo. Day. Year.
John	9-30-1787
Elizabeth	4-18-1789
Joseph	3-30-1791
Mary	2-29-1793
Catharine	3- 5-1795
Sarah	12- 1-1798
Isaac	4 -3-1801

Children of John and Martha James.

Benjamin	10-13-1799
Elizabeth	4-16-1801

Children of Henry and Mary Kerby.

Esther	11- 5-1762
Obadiah	2-13-1765
Jeremiah	10- 5-1767
Archibald	11- 6-1769
Ezekiel	6-23-1771
Sarah	9-11-1773
Hendrick	12-17-1774
Orpah	10-28-1775
Mary	1- 6-1778
Richard	6-30-1780

Children of John and Mary Lynch.

Matilda	1-19-1769
Zalinda	2- 6-1772
Edward	6 24-1774
Sarah	3-31-1777
John	8-20-1779
Christopher	5-19-1782
Mary	12- 6-1784
Charles Clark	4——1787
William	4- 9-1789
Anselm	11-25-1793
Hannah B.	11-26-1796

Children of Joel and Sarah Lewis.

	BORN. Mo. Day. Year.
John	7-13-1791

Children of Edward and Mary Lynch.

Sarah	10- 8-1796
Zalinda	7- 6-1798
Micajah Terrell	10- 1-1800
John	8-15-1802
Charles Edward	10-30-1804
Christopher	3-29-1807
Mary	9-15-1808
Matilda	9-16-1811
Elizabeth Ann	8-24-1813

Children of Jocabad and Sarah Lodge.

Wm. Johnson	3-21-1794
Laban	7-16-1796
Nelson	2- 1-1799
Selina	6-17-1801

Children of Zachariah and Betty Moorman.

Anna	10-18-1756
Molly	5-10-1758
Milley	10- 2-1760
Henry	12-11-1762
Rachel	1-26-1765
Agatha	5-13-1767
Thomas	10-22-1769
Samuel	———

Children of Micajah and Sarah Macy.

John	7- 1-1795
Sarah	11-25-1796
Samuel	4- 1-1802

Children of Micajah and Susannah Moorman.

Chiles	6-16-1758
Thomas	12-11-1755
Betty	10-30-1760

	BORN. Mo. Day. Year.
Rachel	3-11-1763
Milley	3-15-1765
Charles	1- 8-1767
Rhoda	8-15-1769
Susannah	———
Dosha	———
Nancy	3-18-1775
Sarah	6-1 1778
Micajah	9-20-1779
Molly	4-15-1782

Children of John and Ann Martin.

Samuel	7-29-1768
James	9-14-1770
Sarah	3-28-1773

Children of Stephen and Mary Morelan.

Aden	7-20-1774
Abigal	11-14-1776
Jonah	3-16-1779
William	12-11-1781
Isaac	4-18-1785
Huldah	3-28-1788
Richard	2-18-1791
Mordica	5-14-1793

Children of Thomas and Affrica Moorman.

Reuben	3-29-1777
Nancy	1- 7-1779
Micajah	3-10-1781
John Hoye	11-13-1783
Chiles	8-15-1786
Thomas	1- 5-1789
James	2-10-1791
Charles Terrell	6-25-1795

Children of Charles and Elizabeth Moorman.

William	3- 8-1792
Nancy Paxon	7-20-1796

	BORN. Mo. Day. Year.
Fanny Herndon	4-10-1798
Robert Alexander	2-15-1801

Children of Daniel and Elizabeth McPherson.

Mary	10-20-1783
Anna	6-27-1786
Sarah	7-29-1789
Elizabeth	3-10-1792
Martha	4-22-1794

Children of Beverly and Ann Milner.

Dudley	7-15-1779
Ruth	4-27-1783
Moses	7- 4-1785
Beverly	1- 1-1788
Sarah	4-7 1790
Amos	11-29-1792
Joseph	10-16-1795
John	8-25-1800

Children of Reuben and Lydia Moorman.

Pauline	3-12-1800

Children of Andrew and Sarah Millbourne.

Zenas	9- 8-1783
Samuel	12-12-1786
Johnathan	1-20-1789
William	6-17-1791
Jacob	5-10-1792
Lot	7-31-1795
Annie	8-24-1797
David	3-15-1800

Children of Isaac and Elizabeth Pidgeon.

John	1-10-1794
William	3-5- 1796
Isaac	3-10-1798
Rachel	2-25-1801

Children of John Paxon.

	BORN. Mo. Day. Year.
Dosha	5-12-1794

Children of Asa and Grace Plummer.

Eli	2-11-1797
Deborah	10-20-1798
Anna	4-10-1802
Jesse	7-12-1803
Ezra	11-21-11805

Children of Minter Pim and Jemima Perdue.

Gresham	12-28-1790
Rebecca	6-23-1793

Children of Zenas and Elizabeth Preston.

Albert	4-17-1813
Vickers	9-29-1815
Urban	10- 9-1817

Children of Enoch and Matilda Roberts.

John Lynch	11-12-1789
John Lynch	5-10-1791
Samuel	10- 2-1793
William	2-28-1798
Mary Ann	11-28-1799
Zalinda	——-1806

Children of Joseph and Martha Rhodes.

Amy	10-12-1791
Moses	4-28-1794

Children of William and Phebe Stanton.

Aaron	8-10-1784

Children of James and Mary Stanton.

Hannah	12-19-1794
John	12- 7-1798

Children of William and Catharine Stanton.

Elizabeth	10-18-1789
Phebe	12-31-1791

	BORN. Mo. Day. Year.
Ann	9-28-1794
Mahlon	3-28-1797
Samuel	10- 1-1799

Children of Latham and Huldah Stanton.

Hepzibah	10-14-1798
Elizabeth Hunnicutt	12-16-1800
Gulielma	4- 8-1803
Daniel	4- 6-1805
William	9- 7-1807
Stephen Butler	9- 8-1809

Children of Joseph and Dosha Stratton.

David	11-23-1793
Susanna	11- 2-1795
Nancy	11-16-1797
Joseph	2- 2-1800
Micajah	1-22-1802
Esther	2- 4-1804

Children of Daniel and Mary Stratton.

David	6- 6-1782
John	12-16-1784
Margaret	8-11-1787
Mary	2- 6-1793
Daniel	3- 9-1797

Children of Benjamin and Anna Stratton.

Rebecca	12-24-1796
Naomi	7-28-1798
Levi	8-23-1800

Children of Mahlon and Salley Stratton.

Levi	5- 8-1799

Children of Micajah and Sarah Terrell.

Robert	5-23-1755
Elizabeth	8- 6-1757
Agatha	9-28-1759
Charles L.	10-30-1761

	BORN. Mo. Day. Year.
Sarah	11- 3-1763
Samuel	4- 7-1766
Ann	10-26-1768
Mary	4-28-1773

Children of Edward and Mary Terrell.

Lucy	4-25-1773
Sarah	10-15-1775
Edward	2-18-1778
Elizabeth	9- 8-1781
Mary	7- 2-1784
Johnson	10-21-1786

Children of David and Mary Terrell.

Christopher	5- 5-1793
David	11-26-1795
Judith	1-23-1798
Pleasant	2- 2-1791

Children of Edward and Jane Terrell.

Judith	8-28-1796
Christopher	7-18-1798
Gerard	11- 3-1800
Jean	12-25-1802

Children of Richard and Jane Tullas.

John	9-26-1762
Elizabeth	2- 3-1765
Richard	8-24-1768
Martha	2- 9-1771

Children of John Tullas.

Nancy	1-11-1801

Children of John and Mary Timberlake.

Elizabeth	2- 9-1783
Mary	8-26-1784

	BORN. Mo. Day. Year.
Richard	9- 6-1786
Agnes	7-16-1788
Christopher	9- 6-1790
John	9- 4-1792
Mourning	10- 8-1794
Sally	8-26-1797

Children of Joseph and Elizabeth Wright.

Thomas	9- 7-1779
Nancy	2- 1-1783
Mary	10- 6-1784
John	10-27-1786
Elizabeth	10-27-1788
Benjamin	9-21-1791

Children of Samuel and Chloe Welch.

Ruth	7- 7-1784
John	12-19-1785
Moses	2-10-1788
Turner	2-16-1790

Children of Abraham and Lettia Wildman.

Jonah	7- 8-1779
Elizabeth	7-11-1781
Amey	3-25-1783
Deborah	8-21-1785
Mahlon	1-19-1788
Mary	2-20-1790
Sarah	2-26-1792
Nancy	7- 6-1794
Jesse	10- 1-1796
William	7-19-1800

RECORD OF DEATHS AMONGST FRIENDS OF CAMPBELL AND BEDFORD COUNTIES, TAKEN FROM THE OLD SOUTHRIVER MEETING BOOK.

	DIED. Mo. Day. Year.
Anthony, Judith, wife of Christopher Anthony.......	1- 9-1774
Ballard, Byrum, son of Byrum and Eleanor Ballard...	12--20-1769
Bloxom, Obadiah, ...	4- 8-1790
Ballard, Rachel, (82 years of age)	6-10-1792
Butterworth, Isaac, son of Benjamin and Rachel......	12- 2-1801
Butler, James, Jr.	11- 8-1801
Butler, Joseph, ...	9-24-1802
Ballard, James, ...	5- 7-1810
Ballard, William	— 8-1816
Ballard, Barclay, ...	5- 4-1814
Butler, Stephen, ...	12- 2-1815
Bailey, Exom, ...	5-10-1818
Butler, Matilda, daughter of Stephen and Matilda Butler	9-20-1817
Butler, Matilda, wife of Stephen Butler.............	11-10-1817
Bailey, Anna, wife of Exom..........................	8-11-1818
Bond, Isaac, ...	12- 7-1823
Butler, Mary, daughter of James L. and Deborah Butler	8- 8-1825
Ballard, Judith, wife of Barclay Ballard.............	7-17-1824
Butler, James, ...	6-26-1828
Curle, Sarah, daughter of Joseph and Rebecca Curle...	2- 6-1792
Curle, Rebecca, (40 years of age)	7-17-1793
Candler, Agatha, wife of James Candler.............	12-31-1817
Candler, James,, ...	1- 3-1826
Douglas, Robert Terrell, son of Achillis and Elizabeth Douglas	9- 7-1780
Douglas, Agatha, ...	10- 5-1794
Douglas, Achillis, (aged 57)	11- 5-1810
Douglas, Charles Terrell, ...	8- 5-1818
Douglas, Mary Terrell, (aged 29)	10-13-1820
Douglas, Elizabeth, widow of Achillis...............	2- 8-1826
Davis, Samuel, son of William and Zalinda Davis.....	9- 4-1818
Davis, John, son of William and Zalinda Davis.......	3-16-1824
Davis, Sarah, wife of Henry Davis...................	3- 9-1824
Davis, William, ...	9- 1-1829

	DIED. Mo. Day. Year.
Davis, Mary, widow of William, (aged 85)	2-29-1839
Davis, Zalinda, widow of William Davis, Jr. (aged 67)	5- 9-1839
Davis, Annis, widow of Samuel Davis, (aged 91)	12-14-1831
Eccols, William,	4—1771
Eccols, Sarah,	2—1778
Eccols, William,	2-16-1794
Embree, Rachel, daughter of Moses and Mary Embree	4- 9-1788
Embree, Mary, wife of Moses Embree	2- 1-1793
Farmer, Henry,	5- 9-1787
Farmer, Agnes,	11-10-1797
Fisher, Robert,	8-27-1797
Fowler, John,	3-12-1810
Fowler, Ann, (aged 77)	4- 7-1819
Hanna, Caleb, son of Robert and Catharine Hanna	7-15-1790
Hanna, David, son of Robert and Catharine Hanna	10-25-1791
Hanna, Esther, daughter of Robert and Catharine Hanna	11- 5-1791
Hendrick, Moses,	9-11-1794
Hargrave, Elizabeth D. J.,	6-14-1847
Johnson, Martha, daughter of William and Susannah Johnson	5-14-1760
Johnson, Agnes, daughter of William and Susannah Johnson	11- 8-1773
Johnson, Jeptha, son of William and Susannah Johnson	3-8-1775
Johnson, Benjamin,	8-18-1769
Johnson, Edmund, son of James and Rachel Johnson	7-18-1790
Johnson, Achillis, son of James and Rachel Johnson	11-11-1796
Johnson, Chiles, son of James and Rachel Johnson	5-29-1794
Johnson, Timothy,	12- 5-1801
Johnson, Sarah, wife of William Johnson, Jr. (of Seneca) (aged 40)	5-21-1804
Johnson, Rachel, wife of David,	12- 5-1805
Johnson, Agatha, wife of Joseph Johnson (aged 42)	7-26-1805
Johnson, Betty, wife of Christopher, Sr.,	3-16-1809
Johnson Martha, wife of Nicholas Johnson	11-23-1809
Johnson, John, Sr. (Ivy Creek) (aged 84)	8-31-1816
Johnson, David, (aged 63)	4-15-1816

	DIED. Mo. Day. Year.
Johnson, Sarah Ann, daughter of Johnathan and Judith Johnson	3- 7-1821
Johnson, Deborah, wife of Lilliburn,	5-13-1820
Johnson, Mildred Tyree, daughter of Johnathan and Judith Johnson	1-12-1822
Johnson, Sarah, wife of Newby,	9-26-1826
Johnson, Mary, (aged 93)	7-25-1849
Johnson, Gerard,	6-16-1857
Johnson, Judith, wife of Johnathan Johnson,	3-26-1848
Jones, Martha, widow of Thomas Jones, (aged 82)	2-26-1825
Kerby, Elizabeth, (in her 80th year)	11- 6-1778
Kerby, Richard, Jr.,	10—-1781
Lynch, Salley, daughter of John and Mary	2-25-1794
Lynch, Anna, widow of Charles Lynch	2-14-1804
Lynch, Hannah B., wife of Stephen Lynch	11-10-1817
Lynch, Anselm, son of John Lynch, Sr.	11-12-1814
Lynch, John,	10-31-1820
Lynch, Mary, (aged 77)	8- 5-1829
Moorman, Thomas,	11-10-1767
Moorman, Chiles, son of Micajah and Susannah	9-22-1768
Moorman, Betty, wife of Zachariah	7-14-1773
Moorman, Reuben, (aged 36)	9- 7-1813
Macy, Sarah, daughter of Micajah and Sarah Macy	8-12-1797
Macy, Sarah, wife of Micajah Macy	1-25-1797
Moorland, William, son of Stephen and Mary Moorland.	6-3 -1786
Plummer, Deborah,	10-11-1802
Plummer, Anna,	8-23-1804
Pidgeon, Elizabeth, wife of Isaac Pidgeon	8-15-1806
Pidgeon, Sarah, wife of Isaac Pidgeon	5- 1-1810
Russell, Elizabeth,	11-18-1763
Roberts, John Lynch,	7-21-1790
Roberts, John Lynch, (two sons of the same name)	11-16-1813
Roberts, Enoch,	4- 7-1819
Roberts, Zalinda, daughter of Enoch	11-21-1814
Roberts, Matilda,	12-22-1830
Stanton, Phebe, wife of William Stanton, (aged 63)	5-22-1802
Stabler, Mary Annis, wife of Robinson Stabler	8- 5-1838

	DIED. Mo. Day. Year.
Terrell, Samuel, son of Micajah and Sarah Terrell	11——1776
Terrell, David, (aged 76)	2-14-1805
Tellas, Jane, (aged 79)	1-22-1813
Terrell, Jane,	6- 2-1815
Welch, Moses, son of Samuel and Chloe	6-26-1790
West, Jane,	12-20-1791
Ward, Sarah,	1-20-1792
Wildman, William,	3-10-1801

CEDAR CREEK MEETING-HOUSE, HANOVER COUNTY, VA.—ERECTED 1770

MARRIAGES

MARRIAGE CERTIFICATES TAKEN FROM THE OLD RECORD BOOK OF CEDAR CREEK MEETING, HANOVER COUNTY, VIRGINIA.

WHEREAS Achillis Douglas, son of John Douglas, of Orange county, and Elizabeth Terrell, daughter of Micajah Terrell, of Caroline county, having published their intentions of taking each other in marriage before several Monthly Meetings of the people called Quakers, according to good order used amongst them, whose proceedings therein after deliberate consideration thereof, with regard to the righteous law of God, and example of his people recorded in the Scriptures of truth, in that case was approved of by the said Meeting, they appearing clear of all others and having consent of parents and friends concerned.

Now these are, therefore, to certify to all whom it may concern, that for the full accomplishment of their intention this 10th day of the 10th Month, 1779, they, the said Achillis Douglas and Elizabeth Terrell, appearing in a public assembly of the said people and others, met together at their public Meeting House in Caroline county, and in a solemn manner he, the said Achillis Douglas, did take the said Elizabeth Terrell by the hand and openly declared as followeth: Friends, you are my witnesses that I do this day take this, my friend, Elizabeth Terrell, to be my wife, promising, with the Lord's assistance, to be a good and faithful Husband to her till death separates us (or words to that effect), then and there Elizabeth Terrell did in like manner declare as followeth: Friends, you are my witnesses that I do this day take this, my friend, Achillis Douglas, to be my husband, promising, with divine assistance, to be to him a good and faithful wife until death should separate us (or words to that effect). And the said Accillis Douglas and Elizabeth (now his wife) as a further confirmation, did then and there to these present set their hands, she assuming his name. And we whose names are hereunto subscribed being present at the solemnization of their said marriage and subscription as witnesses, have hereunto set our hands, the day and date first written.

ACHILLIS DOUGLAS,
ELIZABETH DOUGLAS.

WITNESSES:—Micajah Terrell, Elizabeth Eastin, Pleasant Terrell, Sarah Terrell, John Douglas, Ann Barksdale, Ursula Cheadle, Salley Hargrave, Elijah Johnson, Milley Douglas, Mary Hargrave, Catlet Jones, Rachel Moorman, Rebecca Terrell, Agatha Terrell, Thomas Terrell, Elizabeth Cheadle, Judith Cheadle, Martha Hargrave, Salley Chiles, Lucy Cheadle.

Whereas Pleasant Cobb, son of Robert Cobb, of Caroline county, and Amy Terrell, daughter of Thomas Terrell, of said county, having published their intention of taking each other in marriage, before several Monthly Meetings of the people called Quakers, according to the good order used among them, whose proceedings therein, after deliberate consideration, was approved by the said Meetings, they appearing clear of all others, and having consent of parents, and other Friends concerned. Now these are to certify all whom it may concern, that for the further accomplishment of their intentions, this 15th day of the 6th Month, 1785, they the said Pleasant Cobb and Amey Terrell, appearing in a public assembly of the said people, met together at their public Meeting House in Caroline county, and in a solemn manner he, the said Pleasant Cobb, did take the said Amey Terrell by the hand and did openly declare as followeth: Friends, you are my witnesses that I do this day take this, my Friend, Amey Terrell, to be my wife, promising, with divine assistance, to be unto her a true and faithful Husband until death should separate us (or words to the like effect); then and there Amey Terrell declared as followeth: Friends, you are my witnesses, that I do this day take my friend, Pleasant Cobb, to be my husband, promising, with divine assistance, to be unto him a true and faithful wife until death should separate us (or words to that purpose). And the said Pleasant Cobb and Amey, his wife, as a further confirmation, did then and there to these presents set their hands, she assuming his name as Cobb, and we whose names are hereunto subscribed, being present at the solemnization of their said marriage and subscription, and as witnesses have hereunto set our hands the day and date above written.

PLEASANT COBB,
AMEY COBB.

WITNESSES:—Nancy Hunnicutt, Eliza Cheadle, Rebecca Terrell, Milicent McGhee, Rhoda Terrell, Mary Terrell, Agatha Cobb, Rachel Moorman, Pleasant Terrell, James Bates, Ursula Cheadle, Rebecca Winston, Clark T. Moorman, Samuel Winston, Nancy Macgey, Mathew P. Terrell, Nathan Winston, Nancy Bates, Thomas Terrell, Samuel Cobb, Jos. Hunnicutt, Martha Winston, Jonathan Terrell, Lewis Cobb.

Whereas Mathew P. Terrell, son of Thomas Terrell, of Caroline county, and Salley Moorman, daughter of Clarke T. Moorman, of said county, having published their intentions of taking each other in marriage, before several Monthly Meetings of the people called Quakers, according to the good order used among them, and after deliberate consideration, was approved by the said Meeting, they appearing clear of all others, and having consent of parents and other concerned Friends. Now these are to certify to all whom it may concern that for the further accomplishment of their intentions this 11th day of the 5th Month, 1788, they the said Mathew P. Terrell and Salley Moorman, appearing in a public Assembly of the said People in the county of Caroline, and in a solemn manner, he the said Mathew P. Terrell taking the said Salley Moorman by the hand did then and there openly declare as followeth: In the presence of this assembly, I take Salley Moorman to be my wife, promising, with Divine assistance, to be unto her a faithful Husband until death doth separate us (or words to that effect). Likewise the said Salley Moorman declared as followeth: In the presence of this assembly, I take Mathew P. Terrell to be my Husband, promising, with divine assistance, to be unto him a faithful wife until death doth separate us (or words to that effect). And the said Mathew P. Terrell and Salley Moorman (now his wife) as a further confirmation, did then and there to these presents set their hands (she assuming her name to be Terrell) and we whose names are hereunto subscribed, being present at the solemnizing of their said marriage, and subscription, and as witnesses, have hereunto set our hands the day and date above written.

MATHEW P. TERRELL,
SALLEY TERRELL.

WITNESSES:—Thomas Terrell, James Peatross, Clarke T. Moorman, Rachel Moorman, Jonathan Terrell, Rebecca Terrell, Elizabeth Cheadle, John Peatross, Rhoda Terrell, Ursula F. Cheadle, William Peatross, Rhoda Moorman, Margaret Terrell, Pleasant Cobb, Martha Hargrave, Mary Hargrave, Thomas Terrell, Jr., Sarah Peatross, Polley Hewlett, Salley Chiles, Pleasant Terrell, Amey Cobb, Jemmina Nelson, Fanny Temple, Archillis Moorman, Frances Moorman, Ann McGhee, Mary Peatross.

Whereas Samuel Hargrave, son of Samuel Hargrave, deceased, of the county of Caroline, and Lucy Terrell, daughter of Pleasant Terrell, of said county, having declared their intentions of marriage with each other before several Monthly Meetings of the people called Quakers in Virginia, according to the good order used among them; and having consent of parents, and relations concerned, their said proposal of marriage was allowed by the said Meeting. Now these are to certify whom it may concern that for the full accomplishing their said intentions this the Tenth Day of the First Month in the year of our Lord, One Thousand, Seven Hundred and Seventy Nine, they, the said Samuel Hargrave, and Lucy Terrell, appearing in a public meeting of the said people and others in Caroline county, and the said Samuel Hargrave, taking the said Lucy Terrell by the hand, did in a solemn manner openly declare that he took her, the said Lucy Terrell, to be his wife, promising, with Divine assistance, to be unto her a faithful and loving Husband until death shall separate them (or words to that effect), and then and there in the said assembly the said Lucy Terrell did in like manner declare that she took the said Samuel Hargrave to be her Husband, promising, as aforesaid, to be unto him a faithful and loving wife until death should separate them (or words to the same purport). And, moreover, they, the said Samuel Hargrave and Lucy Terrell (she, according to the custom of marriage, assumed the name of her Husband), as a further confirmation thereof, did then and there to these presents set their hands, and we whose names are hereunto subscribed, being present at the solemnization of the said marriage have as witnesses hereunto set our hands, the day and year first above written.

SAMUEL HARGRAVE,

Witnesses:—Pleasant Terrell, Mary Hargrave, David Terrell, Elizabeth Hargrave, Micajah Terrell, Mary Harris, Thomas Terrell, Salley Chiles, Thomas Chiles, Elizabeth Terrell, Jesse Hargrave, Rachel Burruss, Judith Cheadle, Anthony Winston, Ann McGhee, Lucy Cheadle, George Winston, Rachel Moorman, Deborah Terrell, Robt. Farish, Molley Chiles, Steven Farish, Rebecca Winston.

Whereas, Joseph Hargrave, son of Samuel Hargrave, deceased, of Caroline County, and Rachel Terrell, daughter of Pleasant Terrell, of the said County, having publickly declared their intentions of taking each other in marriage, before several Monthly Meetings of the people called Quakers in said County of Hanover, according to the good order used amongst them whose proceedings therein was approved by the Meeting, they appearing clear of all other engagements, and having consent of parents and Friends.

Now these are to certify all whom it may concern, that for the accomplishment of their said intentions, this 14th day of the 3rd month 1790, they, the said Joseph Hargrave and Rachel Terrell, appearing in a publick assembly at our Meeting House in Caroline County, and in a solemn manner he, the said Joseph Hargrave, taking the said Rachel Terrell by the hand, did openly declare as followeth: "Friends, you are my witnesses that I take Rachel Terrell to be my wife, promising, with Divine assistance, to be unto her a faithful husband until death," or words to that effect, and then and there, in the said assembly, she, the said Rachel Terrell, did declare in substance as followeth: "Friends, ye are my witnesses that I take Joseph Hargrave to be my husband, promising, with Divine assistance, to be unto him a faithful wife until death," and the said Jos. Hargrave and Rachel, his now wife, as a further confirmation thereof, did then and there to these presents set their hands, and we whose names are hereunto subscribed, being present at the solemnizing of the above said marriage and subscription, as witnesses have hereunto set our hands, the day and date as above.

Joseph Hargrave,
Rachel Hargrave.

Witnesses:—Pleasant Terrell, Jesse Hargrave, Samuel Hargrave, Thomas Hargrave, Samuel Terrell, John Hargrave, Robert Terrell, Obadiah Crew, Christopher Terrell, William Burrus, Polley Hewlett, Henry Burruss, Mathew P. Terrell, Pleasant Cobbs.

Jonathan Terrell, John Peatross, Clark T. Moorman, Thomas Terrell, Samuel Chiles, Millicent Hargrave, Nancy Terrell, Amey Cobbs, Rebecca Terrell, Rachel Moorman, Margaret Terrell, Salley Terrell, Rhoda Terrell, Rhoda Moorman, Judith Harris, Elizabeth Cheadle, Lucy Hargrave, Ursula Cheadle, Lucy Temple, Catharine Ellis, Susana Hargrave, Molley Terrell, Sarah Terrell, Lealy Cobbs, Millicent Hewlett.

Whereas, David Terrell, of Campbell County, and Patty Johnson (daughter Ashley and Martha Johnson), of Louisa County, having declared their intentions of marriage with each other before several Monthly Meetings of the people called Quakers at Cedar Creek, in the County of Hanover, according to the good order used among them, they appearing clear of all other marriage engagements, were approved by said meeting.

These are to certify all whom it may concern, that for the accomplishment of their said intention, they, the said David Terrell and Patty Johnson, appearing in a Publick Meeting of the aforesaid people, at Cedar Creek Meeting House in Hanover County aforesaid, this twenty-fifth day of the Second month, in the year of our Lord One Thousand Seven Hundred and Ninety-three; and in a solemn manner he, the said David Terrell, taking the said Patty Johnson by the hand, did openly declare as followeth: "In the presence of the Lord and this assembly, I take Patty Johnson to be my wife, promising, with Divine assistance, to be unto her a true and faithful husband until death shall separate us," or words to the same effect, and then and there in the said assembly the said Patty Johnson did in like manner declare as followeth: "In the presence of the Lord and this assembly, I take David Terrell to be my husband, promising, with Divine assistance, to be unto him a true and faithful wife until death shall separate us," or words to that effect. And the said David Terrell and Patty, now his wife, as a further confirmation of their said marriage did then and there to these presents set their names, and we whose names are hereunto subscribed, being present at the solemnization of the above said marriage and subscription in the manner aforesaid as witnesses thereto, have also to these presents subscribed our names the day and year above written.

David Terrell,
Patty Terrell.

Witnesses:—Henry Terrell, Samuel Parsons, Micajah Crew, Clark T. Moorman, William Johnson, Benjamin Bates, Jr., Thomas Harris, John Harris, Jonathan Terrell, Mathew Terrell, Thomas Ladd, William Stabler, Nathan Bell, Joshua Stanley, Waddy Stanley, Gerard Johnson, Ann Jones, Sarah Bell, Mary Brooks, Nancy Hunnicutt, Thomas Hatton, Samuel Terrell, John Crew, Jr., Rachel Harris, Mary Ladd, Rachel Ladd, Betsy Watkins, Thomas Doswell, Lemuel Crew, Judith Crew, Edith Harris, Tace Crew, Sarah Harris, Salley Watkins, Cattlet Jones, Robert H. Crew, Rachel Moorman, Margaret Crew, Mary Hatton, Susannah Harris, Salley Ladd.

Whereas, Robert Crew, son of Benjamin Crew, deceased, of Charles City County, and Nancy Terrell, daughter of Pleasant and Caty Terrell, of Caroline County, having declared their intentions of taking each other in marriage, before several Publick Meetings of Friends in Virginia (according to the good order used amongst them), and having consent of parents and Friends concerned.

Now, these are to certify all whom it may concern that for the full accomplishment of their said marriage this 14th day of 9th month 1794, they, the said Robert Crew and Nancy Terrell, appearing in a Publick Meeting of Friends and others at their Meeting House in the above said County of Caroline, and the said Robert Crew, taking the said Nancy Terrell by the hand, did solemnly declare as followeth: In the presence of this assembly I take Nancy Terrell to be my wife, promising, with Divine assistance, to be unto her a true and faithful husband until death. And then and there, in like manner, the said Nancy Terrell did declare as followeth: In the presence of this assembly I take Robert Crew to be my husband, promising, with Divine assistance, to be unto him a true and loving wife until death. And we, whose names are hereunder written, being present at their said solemnization, have as witnesses of their said marriage and subscription hereunto set our hands, the day and year above written.

Robert Crew,
Nancy Crew.

Witnesses:—Rachel Hargrave, Amy Cobb, Salley Terrell, Pleasant Cobb, John Peatross, Samuel Terrell, Robert Terrell,

Margaret Crew, Margaret Terrell, Lucy Hargrave, James D. Ladd, John Johnson, Mathew Terrell, Joseph Hargrave, Ann Jones, Salley Chiles, Jonathan Terrell, Jesse Hargrave, Pleasant Terrell, Catlett Jones, Samuel Hargrave.

Whereas, Timothy Terrell, son of Thomas Terrell, of Caroline County, and Miriam Murdauh Hunnicutt, daughter of James Hunnicutt, deceased, late of the County of Goochland, having published their intentions of taking each other in marriage before several Monthly Meetings of the people called Quakers in Hanover County, agreeable to the good order used among them (they appearing clear of all others), and having the consent of parents and Friends concerned.

Now, these are to certify all whom it may concern, that for the full accomplishment of their marriage, they, the said Timothy Terrell and Miriam Murdaugh Hunnicutt, appearing in a Publick Meeting of the aforesaid people and others, at their Meeting House at Geneto in Goochland County, the 10th day of the Sixth month in the year of our Lord One Thousand Seven Hundred and Ninety-eight, the said Timothy taking the said Miriam by the hand and openly declaring as followeth: "In the presence of this assembly, I take Miriam Murdauh Hunnicutt to be my wife, promising, with Divine assistance, to be unto her a true and faithful husband until death." And there in the said assembly the said Miriam Murdauh Hunnicutt did in like manner declare as followeth: "In the presence of this assembly I take Timothy Terrell to be my husband, promising, with Divine assistance, to be unto him a true and faithful wife until death," or to that effect. And as a further confirmation of their marriage, they, the said Timothy Terrell and Miriam Murdauh, now his wife, did then and there to these presents set their hands, and we whose names are hereunto subscribed being present at the solemnization of their said marriage and subscription, have as witnesses thereof, hereunto set our hands, the day and year above written.

TIMOTHY TERRELL,
MIRIAM M. TERRELL,

WITNESSES:—John Hunnicutt, Joseph Terrell, James Hunnicutt, Joseph Hunnicutt, William H. Pleasants, Obadiah Crew, Samuel Couch, Thomas Harris, Samuel Parsons, Jesse Crew, Benjamin

Russel, Samuel P. Parsons, Thomas Hunnicutt, Ann Hunnicutt, Mary Peatross, Elizabeth Winston, Elizabeth Peatross, Mary Pleasants, Elizabeth Pleasants, Henrietta M. Pleasants, Elizabeth Stanley, Susannah Hatton, Mary P. Younghusband, Amey Peatross, Margaret P. Parsons, Mary Hatton, Sarah Parson, Mary Brooks.

Whereas, John Bell, son of Nathan Bell, of the County of Hanover, and Joanna Terrell, daughter of Thomas Terrell, of the County of Caroline, having declared their intentions of taking each other in marriage before two Monthly Meetings of the people called Quakers, according to the good order used among them, and having permission of parents and Friends concerned.

These are to certify all whom it may concern, that for the full accomplishment of their said marriage that they, the said John Bell and Joanna Terrell, appearing at a Publick Meeting of the aforesaid people and others at their Meeting House in Caroline County the twelfth day of the Fifth month One Thousand and Eight Hundred, and the said John Bell taking the said Joanna Terrell by the hand, did in a solemn manner declare as followeth: "In the presence of the Lord and before this assembly I take this my friend Joanna Terrell to be my wife, promising, with Divine assistance, to be unto her a true and loving husband until death." And then and there in the same assembly the said Joanna Terrell did in like manner declare as followeth: "In the presence of the Lord and before this assembly I take this my friend John Bell to be my husband, promising, with Divine assistance, to be unto him a true and loving wife until death" (or words to that purport), and as a further confirmation of their said marriage the said John Bell and Joanna, his now wife (she assuming the name of her husband), have hereunto set their hands, and we whose names are hereunto subscribed being present at the solemnization and subscription, have as witnesses set out hands, the day and year above written.

JOHN BELL,
JOANNA BELL.

WITNESSES:—Thomas Terrell, Joseph Terrell, Rebecca Bell, Margaret Terrell, Pleasant Cobb, Jonathan Terrell, Ann Peatross, Jesse Terrell, Lemuel Crew, Rebecca Terrell, Mathew Terrell, Timothy Terrell, Nancy Chiles, Caty Terrell, Mary B. Terrell, Sally Terrell, Pleasant Terrell, Lewis Cobb, Amey Cobb, Mary Bell.

Whereas, Timothy Terrell, son of Thomas Terrell, of Caroline County, and Mary Terrell, daughter of Pleasant Terrell, of said County, having published their intention of taking each other in marriage before several Monthly Meetings of Friends, according to the good order used among them, which, after deliberate consideration, was approved by the said meetings, they appearing clear of all other marriage engagements, and having consent of parents and other concerned Friends.

Now, this is to certify all whom it may concern, that for the further accomplishment of their intention, this 10th day of the Third month 1803, they, the said Timothy Terrell and Mary Terrell appearing in a Publick Assembly of Friends in the County of Hanover, he, the said Timothy Terrell, in a solemn manner, taking the said Mary Terrell by the hand, did openly declare as followeth: In the presence of this assembly I take Mary Terrell to be my wife, promising, with Divine assistance, to be to her a faithful husband until death shall separate us (or words to that effect), and the said Mary Terrell did in like manner declare as follows: In the presence of this assembly I take Timothy Terrell to be my husband, promising, with Divine assistance, to be unto him a faithful wife until death shall separate us (or words to that effect). And the said Timothy Terrell and Mary (now his wife) did as a further confirmation, then and there to these presents set their hands. And we whose names are hereunto subscribed, being present at the solemnization of the said marriage and subscription as witnesses, have hereunto set our hands, the day and year above written.

TIMOTHY TERRELL,
MARY TERRELL.

WITNESSES:—Lucy Hargrave, Salley Terrell, Sarah Jones, Rachel Moorman, Salley Terrell, Jr., Susanna Hatton, Pleasant Terrell, Jr., Lemuel Terrell, Catlett Jones, Thomas Harris, Benjamin Bates, Jr., Rebecca Terrell, Margaret Crew, Sarah Hatton, Jane Ladd, Unity Crew, Mathew Terrell, Joseph Terrell, Pleasant Cobb, Micajah Crew, Lemuel Crew, Thomas Stanley, Walter Crew, Thomas Hatton, Waddy Stanley, Isaac Ratcliff, Joshua Crew, Wm. H. Pleasants, Joseph Wilkins, Thomas Hatton, Jr., Philip Brooks, John Maddox.

Whereas, Joseph Terrell, son of Thomas Terrell, of Caroline County, and Sarah Terrell, daughter of Jesse Terrell, of said county, having published their intention of taking each other in marriage, before several Monthly Meetings of Friends, according to the good order used amongst them, which, after deliberate consideration, was approved by said meetings, they appearing clear of all others, and having consent of parents and other concerned Friends.

Now, these are to certify to all whom it may concern, that for the accomplishment of their said intentions, this 15th day of the Fourth month 1804, they, the said Joseph Terrell and Sarah Terrell, appearing in a public assembly of Friends in Caroline County, and in a solemn manner, he, the said Joseph Terrell, taking the said Sarah Terrell by the hand, did then and there openly declare as followeth: "In the presence of this assembly, I take Sarah Terrell to be my wife, promising, with Divine assistance, to be unto her a faithful husband until death shall separate us" (or words to that effect). Likewise the said Sarah Terrell declared as followeth: "In the presence of this assembly, I take Joseph Terrell to be my husband, promising, with Divine assistance, to be unto him a faithful wife until death shall separate us" (or words to the like effect). And the said Joseph Terrell and Sarah Terrell (now his wife), as a further confirmation did then and there to these presents set their hands. And we whose names are hereunto subscribed, being present at the solemnization of the said marriage and subscription, have as witnesses thereof hereunto set our hands, the day and year above written.

JOSEPH TERRELL.
SARAH TERRELL.

WITNESSES:—Mathew Terrell, Jesse Terrell, Pleasant Cobb, Lemuel Terrell, Timothy Terrell, Pleasant Terrell, John Bell, Chiles Terrell, Joseph Hargrave, Robert Terrell, Christopher G. Broaddus, Reuben T. Clarke, Rebecca Terrell, Patsey Hargrave, Mary B. Terrell, Lucy Hargrave, Rhoda Cobb, William Fitzhugh, Ann Peatross, Caty Terrell, Mary Terrell, Rachel Hargrave, Miriam Terrell.

Whereas, Lemuel Terrell, son of Pleasant Terrell, deceased, of the County of Caroline, and Rebecca Terrell, daughter of Thomas

Terrell, of the said County, having declared their intentions of taking each other in marriage before two Monthly Meetings of Friends, according to the good order used among them, and having consent of parents and Friends concerned.

These are to certify all whom it may concern, that for the full accomplishment of their said marriage, they, the said Lemuel Terrell and Rebecca Terrell, appearing in a Publick Assembly of the aforesaid people and others in the County of Caroline, this 15th day of the Fourth month 1804, and the said Lemuel Terrell, taking the said Rebecca Terrell by the hand, did in a solemn manner declare as followeth: "In the presence of the Lord and before this assembly, I take this my friend Rebecca Terrell to be my wife, promising, with Divine assistance, to be unto her a true and loving husband until death shall separate us," and then and there in the same assembly the said Rebecca Terrell did in like manner declare as followeth: "In the presence of the Lord and before this assembly, I take this my friend Lemuel Terrell to be my husband, promising, with Divine assistance, to be unto him a true and loving wife until death shall separate us" (or words to that purport). And as a further confirmation of their said marriage, the said Lemuel Terrell and Rebecca, his wife, have hereunto set their hands. And we whose names are hereunto subscribed, being present at the solemnization and subscription, have hereunto as witnesses set our hands, the day and year above written.

LEMUEL TERRELL,
REBECCA TERRELL.

WITNESSES:—Joseph Terrell, Mathew Terrell, Pleasant Cobb, Timothy Terrell, Pleasant Terrell, John Bell, Chiles Terrell, Joseph Hargrave, Miriam Terrell, Reuben T. Clarke, William Fitzhugh, Sarah Terrell, Ann Peatross, Caty Terrell, Mary B. Terrell, Mary Terrell, Lucy Hargrave, Rhoda Cobb, Robert Terrell, Christopher G. Broaddus, Rhoda Peatross, Patsey Hargrave.

Whereas, Robert Ladd, son of William Ladd, deceased, of Charles City County, and Mary Terrell, daughter of Pleasant Terrell, deceased, of Caroline County, having declared their intention of taking each other in marriage before several Monthly Meetings of Friends held at Cedar Creek in Hanover County, according to the good order used among them, their proceedings, after due inquiry and deliberate consideration, being approved, and having consent of parents and Friends.

Now, these are to certify all whom it may concern, that for the accomplishment of their said marriage this 15th day of the Sixth month, in the year of our Lord One Thousand Eight Hundred and Seven, they, the said Robert Ladd and Mary Terrell, appeared at a Publick Assembly of Friends and others in Caroline County, and the said Robert Ladd, taking the said Mary Terrell by the hand, did openly and solemnly declare as follows: "In the presence of this assembly, I take Mary Terrell to be my wife, promising, with Divine assistance, to be unto her a faithful and loving husband until death shall separate us," and the said Mary Terrell did then and there in the said assembly, in like manner declare as as follows: "In the presence of this assembly, I take Robert Ladd to be my husband, promising, with Divine assistance, to be unto him a faithful and loving wife until death shall separate us," and the said Robert Ladd and Mary, his wife, as a further confirmation of their said marriage, did then and there to these presents set their hands, and we whose names are hereunto subscribed, being present at the solemnization of said marriage and subscription, have as witnesses thereof set our hands, the day and year above written.

ROBERT LADD,
MARY LADD.

WITNESSES:—Robert Terrell, Joseph Terrell, Jesse Crew, Benjamin Crew, Thomas Cobb, Lucy Terrell, Mary B. Terrell, Sally Terrell, Nancy Terrell, Lucy Hargrave, Jesse Ladd, Joseph Ladd, Walter Crew, Pleasant Terrell, Pleasant Cobb, Ann Johnson, Amey Cobb, Mahala Terrell, Susan W. Mills, Nancy Crew, Ann Ladd, Margaret Vaughan.

Whereas, Alfred Ricks, of Southampton County, State of Virginia, son of Richard Ricks and Julia his wife, and Mary Ann Terrell, daughter of Samuel Terrell and Elizabeth his wife, of the County of Caroline and State aforesaid, having declared their intentions of marriage with each other before a Monthly Meeting of the religious Society of Friends held at Cedar Creek, in Hanover County, according to the good order used among them, and having consent of the parties concerned, their said proposal of marriage was allowed by the said meeting.

Now, these are to certify whom it may concern, that for the full accomplishment of their said intentions, this 12th day of the Fourth month in the year of our Lord Eighteen Hundred and Twenty-two, they, the said Alfred Ricks and Mary Ann Terrell, appeared in a Publick Meeting of the said people held in Caroline, and the said Alfred Ricks, taking the said Mary Ann Terrell by the hand, did on this solemn occasion openly declare, that he took her, the said Mary Ann Terrell, to be his wife, promising, through Divine assistance, to be unto her a faithful and affectionate husband until death. And then, in the same assembly, the said Mary Ann Terrell did in like manner declare that she took him, the said Alfred Ricks, to be her husband, promising, through Divine assistance, to be unto him a faithful and affectionate wife until death, and, moreover, they, the said Alfred Ricks and Mary Ann Terrell (she, according to custom of marriage, assuming the name of her husband), did, as a further confirmation thereof, then and there to these presents set their hands. And we whose names are hereunto subscribed, being present at the solemnization of the said marriage and subscription, have as witnesses set our hands, the day and year above written.

ALFRED RICKS,
MARY ANN RICKS.

WITNESSES:—Amelia H. Winston, Deborah Pretlow, Margaret Vaughan, Nancy Terrell, Sarah Ann Harris, Bowling Vaughan, Williamson Talley, Lemuel Terrell, Thomas Terrell, Mary W. Ricks, Isabella Harris, Sally Terrell, Anna L. Vaughan, Robert Terrell, George F. Terrell, John Bell, Robert Scott, Jr., Kittie P. Terrell, Anna L. Terrell, Samuel Terrell, Benj. Jas. Harris, Thomas Harris, John L. Vaughan, George Winston, Jr., Robert Ricks, Jr.

Whereas, Oswin White, son of Thomas and Martha R. White (the former deceased), in the County of Perquimmans and State of North Carolina, and Elizabeth H. Ricks, daughter of Alfred and Mary A. Ricks (the former deceased), in the County of Caroline and State of Virginia, having in writing laid their intentions of marriage with each other before a Monthly Meeting of the Religious Society of Friends, held at Richmond, and having consent of parents, their said proposal of marriage was allowed of by the said meeting.

Now, these are to certify whom it may concern, that for the full accomplishment of their said intentions, this the 9th day of the First month in the year of our Lord One Thousand Eight Hundred and Sixty-one they, the said Oswin White and Elizabeth H. Ricks, appeared in a meeting of the said people held at Richmond, and the said Oswin White, taking the said Elizabeth H. Ricks by the hand, did openly declare that he took her, the said Elizabeth H. Ricks, to be his wife, promising, with Divine assistance, to be unto her a loving and faithful husband until death should separate them, and then, in the same assembly, the said Elizabeth H. Ricks did in like manner declare that she took him, the said Oswin White, to be her husband, promising, with Divine assistance, to be unto him a loving and faithful wife until death should separate them. And, moreover, the said Oswin White and Elizabeth H. Ricks (she, according to custom of marriage, assuming the latter name of her husband), did, as a further confirmation thereof, then and there to these presents set their hands. And we being present, subscribed our names as witnesses.

OSWIN WHITE,
ELIZABETH R. WHITE.

WITNESSES:—Ada C. Butler, Octavia A. Whitlock, Judith A. Crenshaw, Nannie J. Pleasants, Micajah Bates, Samuel Sinton, Mary J. Crenshaw, Jos. P. Elliott, Julia W. Ricks, Pattie A. Bates, Jane C. Whitlock, Eliza J. Pleasants, R. H. Whitlock, Geo. D. Harwood, Wm. L. Elliott, E. A. White, Mary W. Ricks, Richard A. Ricks, Elizabeth P. Harwood, Mollie C. Lyne, Wm. H. Pleasants, John B. Crenshaw, Nath. C. Crenshaw, Robt. H. Whitlock, Walter F. Pleasants.

Whereas, John Pretlow, of the County of Southampton, State of Virginia, son of Joseph and Mary Pretlow (deceased), and Deborah Ricks, daughter of Alfred and Mary Ann Ricks (the former deceased), of Caroline County, having in writing laid their intentions of marriage with each other before a Monthly Meeting of the

Religious Society of Friends, held at Richmond, and having consent of parents, their said proposal of marriage was allowed of by the said meeting.

Now, these are to certify whom it may concern, that for the full accomplishment of their said intentions, this the 9th day of the Second month in the year of our Lord Eighteen Hundred and Sixty-five, they, the said John Pretlow and Deborah Ricks, appeared in a meeting of the said people, held at Prospect Hill, the residence of Mary Ann Ricks in Caroline County, and the said John Pretlow, taking the said Deborah Ricks by the hand, did openly declare that he took her, the said Deborah Ricks, to be his wife, promising, with Divine assistance, to be unto her a loving and faithful husband until death should separate them. And then, in the same assembly, the said Deborah Ricks did in like manner declare that she took him, the said John Pretlow, to be her husband, promising, with Divine assistance, to be unto him a loving and faithful wife until death should separate them. And, moreover, they, the said John Pretlow and Deborah Ricks (she, according to the custom of marriage, assuming the latter name of her husband), did, as a further confirmation thereof, then and there to these presents set their hands.

JOHN PRETLOW,
DEBORAH PRETLOW.

WITNESSES:—Jane C. Whitlock, Judith A. Crenshaw, John B. Crenshaw, Joseph J. Pleasants, Mary J. D. Crenshaw, Emma Scott, M. O. McLaughlin, Deborah A. Crenshaw, H. Virginia Whitlock, Pattie A. Bates, Maria L. Scott, Henry Bates, Samuel B. Pretlow, Robt. H. Whitlock, Joel Cook, Walter F. Pleasants, Achilles D. Johnson, Thomas C. Hackett, Mary Ann Ricks, Mary W. Ricks, Ella T. Ricks, Walter A. Ricks, Julia W. Ricks.

Whereas, Bowling H. Winston, of Sugar River Monthly Meeting, in the County of Montgomery, in the State of Indiana, son of Pleasant and Elizabeth C. Winston (the latter deceased), of the State of Indiana, and Julia W. Ricks, daughter of Alfred and Mary Ann Ricks (the former deceased), of the State of Virginia, having in writing laid their intentions of marriage with each other before a Monthly Meeting of the Religious Society of Friends, held at Cedar Creek, State of Virginia, and having consent of parents, their said proposal of marriage was allowed of by the said meeting.

Now, these are to certify whom it may concern, that for the full accomplishment of their said intentions, this the 11th day of the Seventh month in the year of our Lord One Thousand Eight Hundred and Sixty-six, they, the said Bowling H. Winston and Julia W. Ricks, appeared in a meeting of the said people, held at Richmond, and the said Bowling H. Winston, taking the said Julia W. Ricks by the hand, did openly declare that he took her, the said Julia W. Ricks, to be his wife, promising, with Divine assistance, to be unto her a loving and faithful husband until death should separate them. And then, in the same assembly, the said Julia W. Ricks did in like manner declare that she took him, the said Bowling H. Winston, to be her husband, promising, with Divine assistance, to be unto him a loving and faithful wife until death should separate them. And, moreover, they, the said Bowling H. Winston and Julia W. Ricks (she, according to the custom of marriage, assuming the latter name of her husband), did, as a further confirmation thereof, then and there to these presents set their hands. And we being present, subscribed our names as witnesses.

BOWLING H. WINSTON,
JULIA W. WINSTON.

WITNESSES:—Elizabeth P. Harwood, Wm. H. Pleasants, Ellen P. Pedin, Eliza J. Pleasants, Ann Sumner, Jane C. Whitlock, John W. Turner, Deborah A. Crenshaw, John B. Crenshaw, Judith A. Crenshaw, Robt. H. Whitlock, Henry Bates, Micajah Bates, John Pretlow, Oswin White, Richard A. Ricks, Walter A. Ricks, Mary J. Whitlock, Mary W. Ricks, E. C. Winston, M. S. Whitlock, Pattie A. Bates, Lucie K. Butler, H. Virginia Whitlock, Sallie Worthington, Joel Cook.

Whereas, Richard A. Ricks, of Caroline County, State of Virginia, son of Alfred and Mary A. Ricks (both deceased), of the aforesaid County and State, and Martha S. Whitlock, daughter of Richard H. and Jane C. Whitlock (the former deceased), of the City of Richmond, State of Virginia, having in writing laid their intentions of marriage with each other before a Monthly Meeting of the Religious Society of Friends, held at Richmond, and having consent of surviving parent, their said proposal of marriage was allowed of by the said meeting.

Now these are to certify that for the full accomplishment of their said intentions, this, the eleventh day of the Sixth month in the year of our Lord One Thousand Eight Hundred and Seventy-three, they, the said Richard A. Ricks and Martha S. Whitlock, appeared in a meeting of the said people held at Richmond, and the said Richard A. Ricks, taking the said Martha S. Whitlock by the hand, did openly declare that he took her, the said Martha S. Whitlock, to be his wife, promising, with Divine assistance, to be unto her a loving and faithful husband until death should separate them. And then, in the same assembly, the said Martha S. Whitlock did in like manner declare that she took him, the said Richard A. Ricks, to be her husband, promising, with Divine assistance, to be unto him a loving and faithful wife until death should separate them. And. moreover, they, the said Richard A. Ricks and Martha S. Whitlock (she, according to the custom of marriage, assuming the latter name of her husband), did, as a further confirmation thereof, then and there to these presents set their hands. And we being present, subscribe our names as witnesses.

RICHARD A. RICKS,
MARTHA S. RICKS.

WITNESSES:—M. J. Vest, Kate Crenshaw, Sallie S. Summerell, Jane C. Whitlock, Deborah R. Pretlow, Martha A. Bates, John B. Crenshaw, I. H. Holladay, Sallie B. Leeds, A. St. C. Butler, M. J. Whitlock, Ella T. Ricks, G. W. Taylor, O. A. Whitlock, M. Bates, Emma E. Hall, R. H. Whitlock, Cora B. Butler, Judith A. Crenshaw, M. E. Crenshaw, I. J. Hawkes, M. D., Laura P. Hall, James G. Whitlock, Ellen P. Pedin, Frank T. Bates, Wm. J. Hart, Samuel Sinton, David Jordan, Maggie Bates, Henry A. Pleasants, Samuel A. Swann, H. V. Whitlock, Isaac Hawkes, James W. Pedin, W. A. Ricks, John C. Winston, Mary Willetts, Jeremiah Willetts, Eloise Carpenter, Julia W. Winston, Ellen Harwood, Deborah C. Leeds, Charles E. Whitlock, E. P. Harwood, James H. Crenshaw, S. J. Harwood, Geo. D. Harwood.

Whereas, Richard A. Ricks, of Caroline County, State of Virginia, son of Alfred and Mary A. Ricks (both deceased), of the aforesaid County and State, and Eliza C. Crenshaw, daughter of John B. and Rachel H. Crenshaw (the latter deceased), of the County of Henrico, State of Virginia, having declared their intentions of marriage with each other before a Monthly Meeting of the Religious Society of Friends held at Richmond, and having consent of surviving parent, their said proposal of marriage was allowed of by the said meeting.

Now these are to certify to whom it may concern, that for the full accomplishment of their said intentions this, the twenty-third day of the Sixth month, in the year of our Lord One Thousand Eight Hundred and Eighty-one, they, the said Richard A. Ricks and Eliza C. Crenshaw, appeared in a Public Meeting of the said people held at Richmond, and the said Richard A. Ricks, taking the said Eliza C. Crenshaw by the hand, did on this solemn occasion openly declare that he took her, the said Eliza C. Crenshaw, to be his wife, promising, with Divine assistance, to be unto her a loving and faithful husband until death should separate them; and then, in the same assembly, the said Eliza C. Crenshaw did in like manner declare that she took him, the said Richard A. Ricks, to be her husband, promising, with Divine assistance, to be unto him a loving and faithful wife until death should separate them. And, moreover, they, the said Richard A. Ricks and Eliza C. Crenshaw (she, according to the custom of marriage, assuming the name of her husband), did, as a further confirmation thereof, then and there to these presents set their hands. And we whose names are hereunto subscribed, being present at the solemnization of the said marriage and subscription, have as witnesses thereto set our hands, the day and year above written.

RICHARD A. RICKS,
ELIZA C. RICKS.

WITNESSES:—John B. Crenshaw, Judith A. Crenshaw, Nathl. B. Crenshaw, Deborah C. Leeds, Josiah W. Leeds, Margt. E. Crenshaw, James H. Crenshaw, M. Belle Crenshaw, J. Belle Crenshaw, Sara W. Crenshaw, Elizabeth H. White, Deborah R. Pretlow, Ella T. Ricks, J. D. Pretlow, Mary J. D. Pretlow, Sallie B. Leeds, W. H. Pleasants, I. J. Hawkes, Geo. D. Pleasants, Wm. F. Terrell, Mrs. J. C. Hann, Mrs. Leroy A. Crenshaw, A. L. Pleasants, A. J. Pleasants, Charles H. Corey, Mabel Burruss, O. A. Whitlock, R. H. Whitlock, Eliza J. Pleasants, Sadie B. Leeds, Chas. K. Willis, Samuel B. Lucy, Annie M. Hill, Elvira M. Hawkes, Mary Louisa Butler, Maggie A. Ferrell, M. M. Terrell, C. G. Paleske, Mrs. Thos. W. Sydnor, Jane C. Whitlock, Lucy K. Butler, D. C. Richardson, John C. Winston, John P. Bates, J. A. Terrell, E. P. Harwood, Wm. M. Coulling, Frank T. Bates, Rowland Hill, Samuel Sinton, Mrs. E. L. Crenshaw, Mary J. Whitlock, H. A. Pleasants, Austin C. Leeds, James G. Whitlock, Jos. J. Pleasants.

To Friends at Cedar Creek Monthly Meeting, Hanover County, Va.

DEAR FRIENDS:

Our Esteemed Friend, David Terrell, a member of our Meeting, being about to join in marriage with Patty Johnson, a member of yours, requests our Certificate for the purpose; this may certify on his behalf that, on enquiring, we do not find anything to hinder his proceeding therein.

Signed on behalf of South River Monthly Meeting, held this 19th day of the 1st Month, 1793. ACHILLIS DOUGLAS, Clerk.

To the Monthly Meeting at White Oak Swamp in Henrico County.

DEAR FRIENDS:

Jesse Terrell having requested our Certificate in order to join in marriage with a member of your meeting, these are to certify on his behalf that he hath a right of membership amongst us, and is clear of marriage engagements as far as we know.

Signed in, and by direction of our Monthly Meeting, held at Cedar Creek, in Hanover county, the 8th of the 3rd Month, 1794.

MICAJAH CREW, Clerk.

To Friends of Henrico Monthly Meeting.

DEAR FRIENDS:

Samuel Terrell having requested our Certificate in order to accomplish his marriage with a member of your meeting, we have to inform you that he is a member of this meeting; he has the consent of parents and friends concerned and is clear of all other marriage engagements as far as appears to us; we, therefore, recommend him in his undertaking to your Christian care and regard, and remain your friends and brethren.

Signed in and on behalf of our Monthly Meeting, held at Cedar Creek, in Hanover county, the 12th of the 4th Month, 1800.

BENJAMIN BATES, JR., Clerk.

MARRIAGE CERTIFICATES OF SOUTH RIVER MONTHLY MEETING.*

William Ballard and Rachel Moorman were married at South River Meeting-house 8-25-1768.

The following witnesses signed the marriage certificate: Zach Moorman, Micajah Moorman, Charles Moorman, Clark Moorman, Gillis Moorman, Benjamin Johnson, William Johnson, Byrum Ballard, Thomas Ballard, Bowling Clark, Micajah Terrell, Christopher Anthony, Henry Tate, Sarah Terrell, Winifred Clark, Susanna Johnson, Eleanor Ballard, Martha Ferrall, Martha Ferrall, Jr., Betty Moorman, Susanna Moorman, Lucy Johnson, Elizabeth Ferrall, Sarah Tate, Penelope Johnson, Mary Ferrall, Mary Timberlake, Judith Goode, Agnes Clark.

William Ballard and Elizabeth Anthony were married at South River Meeting-house 4-24-1788.

The following witnesses signed the marriage certificate: Mary Anthony, Molley Anthony, Mary Ballard, Anna Sea, Mary Johnson, Judith Ballard, Phebe Stanton, Penelope Johnson, Salley Johnson, Robert Hanna, Ashley Johnson, James Candler, Elizabeth Douglas, Betty Johnson, Jane Gipson, Hepzabih Holloway, Edward Lynch, Christopher Anthony, Jr., Christopher Anthony, Christopher Johnson, Achillis Douglas, William Johnson, William Ballard, John Lynch, William Stanton, John Candler, Mary Lynch, Matilda Lynch, Mary Timberlake, Rachel Ballard, Sarah Tate Anthony, Barclay Ballard, Moses Cadwalader, Jr., Charles Anthony, John Timberlake, William Clement, Robert Johnson, Timothy Johnson, Sarah H. Tate.

Byrum Ballard and Sarah Hutton were married at South River Meeting-house 9-20-1792.

The following witnesses signed the marriage certificate: Minto P. Perdue, Christopher Anthony, James Erwin, Mary Embree,

*The form of the certificate of marriage amongst Quakers is substantially the same in all cases, and the abridgement here of the form is made to save space and useless repetition.

Elizabeth Embree, Sarah Turner, Sarah Lewis, Elizabeth Turner, Newman Rugus, James Mazley, Edward Tend, William Pidgeon, Evan Lewis, Esther Richards, Elijah Richards, Dèlia Turner, Joel Lewis, Sarah Lewis, Hannah Larrew, Mary Anthony, Nathan Hale, Samuel Oliphant, Jesse Lewis, Polley Haynes, Henry Thurman, Magdalen Erwin, Susanna Perdue, Mary Erwin, Alice Bond, Rebekah Moorlan, Rachel Coffee, Thomas Cadwalader, Moses Embree, Ruth Paxon, Benjamin Paxon, Elizabeth Hamner, Joseph Evoute, Rachel Pidgeon, John Coffee, Nancy Moorlan, Moses Cadwalader, William Ballard, Jr., Amos Ballard, Jesse Cadwalader, Mourning Ballard, Elizabeth Ballard, Ruth Cadwalader.

WILLIAM BLOCKSOM and MARY BUTLER were married at South River Meeting-house 1-21-1795.

The following witnesses signed the marriage certificate: Agatha Johnson, Patty Terrell, Mary Johnson, Sarah Johnson, Nancy Davis, Susannah Terrell, Elizabeth Pidgeon, Harrison Ratcliff, William Johnson, Gideon Blocksom, Jonathan Butler, John W. Johnson, Charles Smith, Isaac Pidgeon, Thomas M. Clark, Mary Davis, Drusilla Crew, Sally Butler, Mildred Ratcliff, Nancy Butler, Mary Blocksom, Richard Bloxsom, Sr., James Butler, Nicholas Crew, David Terrell, Abner Grigg, Wm. Johnson, Richard Blocksom.

JOSEPH BRADFIELD and CYNTHIA CARY were married at South River Meeting-house 9-13-1798.

The following witnesses signed the marriage certificate: Martha Baugham, Mary Lynch, Mary Terrell, Sarah Millburn, Elizabeth Lea, Jesse Williams, Joseph Fisher, Jr., Benjamin Hanna, Thomas Maddox, John Bradfield, William Butler, Samuel Carey, Rachel Cary, Sarah Cary, John Cary, John Fisher.

THOMAS BURGESS, son of Joseph Burgess, and BETSY HENDRICK, daughter of Moses Hendrick, of the County of Halifax, were married at Banister Meeting-house, in the County of Halifax, 10-16-1791.

The following witnesses signed the marriage certificate: Robert Hanna, Ashley Johnson, Betsy Anderson, Sally Slaughter, Daniel

Terry, George Wood, Daniel Easly, Rachel Anderson, Joseph Kirby, Anna Anderson, Edith Easly, Joseph Fisher.

THOMAS BAILEY and ELIZABETH TIMBERLAKE were married at South River Meeting-house 6-16-1803.

The following witnesses signed the marriage certificate: Lydia Johnson, Susanna Ballard, Polly Timberlake, Hannah Pennock, Mary Butler, Sarah Johnson, Priscilla Butler, James Stanton, James Martin, John Timberlake, Jonathan Johnson, Josiah Bailey, John Pennock.

JOSIAH BAILEY, of Campbell County, and SUSANNA BALLARD, daughter of Barclay and Judith Ballard, of Bedford County, were married at Ivy Creek Meeting-house, in Bedford County, 7-15-1804.

The following witnesses signed the marriage certificate: Thomas Johnson, Johnson Ballard, William Butler, Amos Holloway, Nicholas Johnson, Benjamin Johnson, John Swinney, Joseph Johnson, Rhoda Johnson, Agatha Johnson, Hepsabeth Holloway, Salley Macey, Betsy Butterworth, Nancy Johnson, Susanna Stone.

WILLIAM BALLARD, son of Barclay and Judith Ballard, of Bedford County, and NANCY BUTTERWORTH, daughter of Benjamin and Rachel Butterworth, of Campbell County, Virginia, were married at South River Meeting-house 11-14-1805.

The following witnesses signed the marriage certificate: Barclay Ballard, Benjamin Butterworth, James Ballard, William Stanton, James Candler, John P. Swinney, Edward Lynch, Timothy Grewell, Isaac Pidgeon, Polly Butterworth, Betsy Butterworth, Polly Ballard, Huldah Stanton, Nancy Johnson, Deborah Douglas, Mildred Ratcliff.

DANIEL BURGESS, son of Joseph and Deborah Burgess, of the County of Campbell, and RUTH MILLINER, daughter of Beverly and Ann Milliner, of Halifax County, were married at South River Meeting-house 11-14-1805.

The following witnesses signed the marriage certificate: William Stanton, Barclay Ballard, Stephen Butler, Mary Butler, Enoch

Roberts, Isaac Pidgeon, Polly Burgess, Grace Plummer, Thomas Burgess, John Burgess, Joseph Burgess, Jr.

JAMES BALLARD, son of Barclay and Judith Ballard, of Bedford County, and BETSY BUTTERWORTH, of Campbell County, were married at South River Meeting-house 2-13-1806.

The following witnesses signed the marriage certificate: William Ballard, Benjamin Butterworth, Josiah Bailey, Jonathan Johnson, William Butler, John Lynch, James S. Butler, Thomas Burgess, Wm. Davis, Jr., Polly Butterworth, Milley Butterworth, Nancy Ballard, Susanna Bailey, Mildred Ratcliff, Anna Lynch, Matilda Roberts, Druscilla Burgess, Sally Lodge, Mildred Tyree, Judith Johnson, Betsy Douglass, Alice Grewell, Mary Butler, Zalinda Davis, William Stanton.

WILLIAM BUTLER, son of Stephen and Mary Butler, and NANCY JOHNSON, daughter of William and Susanna Johnson, both of Campbell County, were married at South River Meeting-house 4-15-1806.

The following witnesses signed the marriage certificate: Latham Stanton, Stephen Butler, Jr., Edward Butler, Jonathan Butler, Harrison Ratcliff, Deborah Butler, Jeptha Johnson, Enoch Roberts, William Johnson, Jr., Mary Butler, Susannah Johnson, Sarah Lodge, Huldah Stanton, Elizabeth Douglas, Newby Johnson, Sarah Johnson, Matilda Roberts, Mary Douglas, Zalinda Davis, Jonathan Johnson, Stephen Butler, William Johnson, Sr., Robert Johnson, Deborah Douglas, Elizabeth Douglas, Sarah Johnson, Judith Johnson.

JOSEPH C. BURGESS, son of Jonathan and Margaret Burgess, of Campbell County (Margaret deceased), and MARTHA JOHNSON, daughter of Christopher and Sarah Johnson (both deceased), of Bedford County, were married at South River Meeting-house 4-13-1808.

The following witnesses signed the marriage certificate: Stephen Butler, Josiah Bailey, Jonathan Burgess, Charles T. Arthur, Thomas Burgess, Benjamin Johnson, Nicholas Johnson, Joseph Johnson, Samuel Fisher, Daniel Burgess, John H. Moorman, Caleb Johnson,

Nancy Johnson, Matilda Johnson, Elizabeth Fisher, Mary Burgess, Betty Burgess, Rhoda Johnson, Agatha Johnson, Susanna Bailey, James Mallory.

STEVEN BUTLER, son of Stephen and Mary Butler, of the town of Lynchburg, and LOUISA BAILEY, daughter of Exom and Tabitha Bailey, were married at South River Meeting-house 12-13-1821.

The following witnesses signed the marriage certificate: Lilbourn Johnson, William Butler, William Davis, Jonathan Johnson, William Davis, Jr., James S. Butler, Achillis M. Douglas, William Butler, Jr., Daniel Johnson, John L. Douglas, John L. Davis, Micajah T. Johnson, Mary A. Davis, Deborah Butler, Ann Eliza Bailey, Delitha Butler, Sarah Johnson, Sarah L. Davis, Sarah Snead, Mary Jane Adams, Anselm D. Johnson.

TRISTRAM COGGSHALL and LUCY TERRELL, of Campbell County, were married at South River Meeting-house 3-21-1790.

The following witnesses signed the marriage certificate: Sarah Terrell, William Johnson, Byrum Ballard, Mary Davis, Samuel Davis, Betty Hendrake, Susanna Johnson, Dosha Moorman, Nancy Moorman, Achillis Douglas, Mary Betts, Ann Fowler, Elizabeth Douglas, Betty Johnson, John Paxon, Thomas Bedford, John Candler, Jr., William Bloxom, Rachel Paxon, Mary Baughan, Anna Terrell, Ruth Pidgeon, Sarah Tennison, Sarah Johnson, Susanna Davis, Sarah Johnson, William Stanton, William Davis, Rachel Ballard, Sarah Hutton, James Candler, Henry Terrell, Robert Hanna, Ashley Johnson, Richard Bloxom, Robert Johnson.

MOSES CADWALADER, JR., and MARY BALLARD, of Bedford County, were married at South River Meeting-house 5-23-1792.

The following witnesses signed the marriage certificate: Joseph Teazel, Abigal Moorlan, Rebecca Morland, Elizabeth Teazel, Susan Morlan, Thomas Davis, Henry Hurt, Joseph Moorland, Polly Haynes, Stephen Moorland, Christopher Anthony, Ann Moorland, Mevory Anthony, Annis Davis, Sarah Johnson, Rachel Pidgeon, Rachel Coffee, Sarah Hutton, Ruth Cadwalader, Judith Ballard,

Elizabeth Ballard, William Pidgeon, Samuel Davis, Moses Cadwalader, Mary Cadwalader, Joseph Wright, Philip Teazle, Aden Moorland, Moses Hurt, Byrum Ballard, Thomas Cadwalader, Jesse Cadwalader.

MAHLON CADWALADER, son of Thomas and Jane Cadwalader, and ELIZABETH DOUGLAS, daughter of Achillis and Elizabeth Douglas, were married at South River Meeting-house 6-10-1809.

The following witnesses signed the marriage certificate: Achillis Douglas, Thomas Cadwalader, Joseph Stratton, Jonathan Johnson, John Lynch, Sr., Richard Tyree, Benjamin Johnson, Reubin Moorman, Isaac Pidgeon, Etchison Grigsby, Jonah Cadwalader, Joel Lewis, Judith Johnson, Deborah Douglas, Mildred Tyree, Polly Lynch, Penelope Anthony, Mary, Butler, Susanna Johnson, Elizabeth Cadwalader, Sarah Johnson.

WILLIAM DAVIS, son of Samuel and Annis Davis, of Bedford County, and ZALINDA DAVIS, daughter of John and Mary Lynch, of Campbell County, were married at South River Meeting-house 5-13-1793.

The names of witnesses: William Johnson, Arch Lacy, William Stanton, George Roberts, Robert Hanna, Catharine Hanna, Gerard Johnson, Susanna Miller, Vernon Metcalf, Matilda Roberts, Mary Terrell, Ann Terrell, Sally Lynch, Elizabeth Douglas, Polly Fowler, Sarah Lodge, Agatha Dicks, Elizabeth Johnson, John Lynch, Samuel Davis, Enoch Roberts, John Davis, Sr., Achillis Douglas, Thomas Davis, Micajah, Mary Timberlake, Gideon Lea, Ashley Johnson, John Baughan, David Johnson, William Dicks, Ashley Johnson, Jr., Edward Terrell, Newberry Johnson, Dudley Cave, Penelope Johnson, Susanna Johnson, Millie Johnson, Rebecca Preston, Joseph Johnson, Sarah Terrell, Mildred Johnson, Anna Lea, Alice Taylor, Tace Nichols, Micajah Terrell, Jr., Samuel Terrell, Robert Johnson, Christopher Johnson, Robert Burton, Isaac Parrish, James Martin, Tace Baugham, Mary Terrell, Mourning Johnson.

SAMUEL ERWIN, son of James and Mary Erwin, and SARAH HOLMS, daughter of William and Mary Holms, were married at Goose Creek Meeting-house, in Bedford County, 7-4-1793.

The following witnesses signed the marriage certificate: Margaret Dobyns, Moses Embree, Joel Lewis, Sarah Lewis, Thomas Cadwalader, Jane Cadwalader, Rachel Pidgeon, Ben Paxon, John Coffee, Rachel Coffee, Will Tuggle, Moses Cadwalader, Carls Anthony, Susanna Erwin, William Pidgeon, Mary Bond, Moses Cadwalader, Jr., Samuel Oliphant, Esther Richards, Benjamin Bond, Ruth Cadwalader, Hannah Anthony, Lucy Phelps, Betsy Bobbitt, Sarah Pidgeon, Sally Gregg, Amos Harris, Elizabeth Harris, Jane Bobbitt, James Erwin, Mary Erwin, Margaret Harris, Elizabeth Sehoby, Jane Erwin, Mary Harris, Magdalen Erwin, Hanna Harris, Daniel McPherson, Mary McPherson, Mary Anthony, Mary Burns, James Burns.

ELIAS FISHER, son of Joseph and Ann Fisher, and HANNAH CURLE, daughter of Joseph and Rebecca Curle, all of Campbell County, were married at South River Meeting-house 9-24-1793.

The following witnesses signed the marriage certificate: Wm. Stanton, Wm. Johnson, Gerard Johnson, Robt. Johnson, Robt. Hanna, Robt. Wright, Catharine Hanna, Abel Lodge, Benjamin Hanna, Thomas Hanna, Jane Tillus, Elizabeth Douglas, Humphrey Baugham, Sally Lynch, Elizabeth Lea, Ann Leer, Sarah Johnson, Phebe Stanton, Martha Baugham, Sarah Lodge, Joseph Curle, Joseph Fisher, Robt. Fisher, John Baugham, Samuel Fisher, Samuel Cary, Ann Curle, Tacy Baugham, Cynthia Cary.

JOHN FISHER, son of Joseph Fisher, and RACHEL JAMES, daughter of Thomas James, of the County of Campbell, were married at South River Meeting-house 10-17-1799.

The following witnesses signed the marriage certificate: William Stanton, Stephen Butler, Phebe Stanton, Mary Butler, Hannah Fisher, Mary Holloway, Joseph Fisher, Elias Fisher, Isaac James.

NIMROD FARGUSON, son of Nimrod Farguson, and ANNA ANDERSON, daughter of John Anderson (all of Halifax), were married at Bannister Meeting-house 1-14-1801.

The following witnesses signed the marriage certificate: Daniel Easly, Dudley Milner, James Turpin, John Farguson, Richard Anderson, Obed Hendrick, Abner Gregg, Edith Kirby, Judith Anderson, Mary Parker, Betsy Parker, Isaac James, Thomas Burgess, Betsy Burgess, Mary Milner, Judith Borum, Orpha Kirby, Rachel Anderson.

SAMUEL FISHER, son of Joseph Fisher, and ELIZABETH JOHNSON, daughter of Benjamin Johnson, of Bedford County, were married at Ivey Creek Meeting-house, Bedford County, 12-22-1802.

The following witnesses signed the certificate: Benjamin Johnson, John Johnson, Amos Holloway, William Butler, Joseph Fisher, Elias Fisher, Betty Burgess, Tacy Lodge, Hannah Fisher, Hepzabah Holloway, Sarah Johnson, Ann Fisher.

AMOS HOLLOWAY and HEPZIBAH STANTON, of Campbell County, were married at South River Meeting-house 10-20-1785.

The following witnesses signed the marriage certificate: William Stanton, Wm. Johnson, Achillis Douglas, John Fowler, Ashley Johnson, Wm. Stanton, Jr., James Johnson, Wm. Ferrell, Matilda Lynch, Mary Lynch, Latitia Wileman, Rachel Ballard, Susanna Johnson, Rachel Moorman, Ann Fowler, Sarah Johnson, Ruth Johnson, Mary Anthony, Ann Lea, Elizabeth Douglas, Judith Feddell.

WILLIAM HALLOWAY and SARAH STANLEY, of Bedford County, were married at the South River Meeting-house, in Campbell County, 7-19-1790.

The following witnesses signed the marriage certificate: Micajah Davis, Wm. Stanton, William Ballard, John Lynch, Robeda Hanna, Abijah Richards, Achillis Douglas, David Terrell, Tristram Coggshall, William Snead, Mary Betts, Rachel Coffee, Ruth Pidgeon, Rachel Pidgeon, Sarah Bloxom, Susanna Johnson, Sarah Lewis, Anna Lea, Rachel Ballard, Amos Holloway, Wm. Stanton, Catharine Stanton, Hepzibah Halloway, Jane Johnson, Elizabeth Douglas, Sarah Stanley.

ABNER HOLLOWAY and BETSY STANLEY, of the County of Bedford, were married at South River Meeting-house 10-14-1797.

The following witnesses signed the marriage certificate: Elias Fisher, Jesse Williams, Aaron Stanton, Mourning Johnson, Sarah Cary, Nancy Ferrell, William Butler, Elizabeth Curle, Christopher Johnson, Robt. Hannah, Richard Bloxsom, Elizabeth Hendricks, Benj. Hanna, John Johnson, Thos. Hanna, John Lynch, Amos Halloway, Hapzibah Holloway, Wm. Stanton, Latham Stanton, Huldah Stanton, Mary Butler, Mary Halloway.

CHARLES JOHNSON and MOLLEY MOORMAN (daughter of Zacheriah Moorman), of Bedford County, were married at South River Meeting-house, in Campbell County, 8-16-1778.

The following witnesses signed the marriage certificate: Christopher Johnson, Zachariah Moorman, William Johnson, Benj. Johnson, Ashley Johnson, Benj. Johnson, Jr., Thomas Moorman, William Ballard, John Clarke, Edward Terrell, Elijah Bocock, John Lynch, Christopher, Edward Clarke, Samuel Stanley, Zedekiah Candler, Lucy Johnson, Mary Miller, Elizabeth Johnson, Molley Johnson, Mary Ferrell, Susanna Johnson, Miller Moorman, Rachel Moorman, Rachel Johnson, Anna Bocock, Agnes Johnson, Susanna Moorman, Rachel Ballard, Rachel Moorman, Sarah Goode, Mary Anthony, Priscilla Stanley, Jane Tillus, Elizabeth Terrell, Ann Candler, Mary Terrell, Elizabeth Moorman.

JAMES JOHNSON and RACHEL MOORMAN, of the County of Bedford, were married 3-18-1781.

The following witnesses signed the marriage certificate: Micajah Moorman, Rachel Ballard, James Johnson, Samuel Johnson, Barclay Ballard, Judith Ballard, William Johnson, Christopher Johnson, Ashly Johnson, Benjamin Johnson, Henry Moorman, William Ferrell, John Lynch, Micajah Davis, Charles Johnson, Mary Johnson, Milley Moorman, Penelope Johnson, Elizabeth Johnson, Christopher Anthony, David Johnson, Mary Anthony, William Davis.

JOSEPH JOHNSON and AGATHA MOORMAN, daughter of Zachariah Moorman, were married at South River Meeting-house 4-17-1785.

The following witnesses signed the marriage certificate: Christopher Johnson, John Lynch, William Stanton, Christopher Anthony, Ann Candler, Milley Johnson, Molly Johnson, James Johnson, William Davis, Elizabeth Douglas, Judith Ballard, Susanna Miller, John Candler, Samuel Davis, Mary Timberlake, Rachel Johnson, Mary Johnson, Salley Johnson, Samuel Johnson, Zachariah Moorman, Rachel Ballard, John Johnson, Rachel Moorman, Achillis Douglas, Betty Johnson, Ann Lay, Susanna Johnson.

SAMUEL JOHNSON, of the County of Campbell, and SUSANNA MOORMAN, of said County, were married at South River Meeting-house 1-20-1788.

The following witnesses signed the marriage certificate: Rachel Ballard, Judith Ballard, Rhoda Moorman, Dosha Moorman, Micajah Moorman, John Johnson, David Terrell, Eleanor Ballard, Elizabeth Douglas, Mary Johnson, Ruth Johnson, Sarah Johnson, Susanna Miller, Betsy Johnson, Charles Moorman, James Johnson, William Johnson, Christopher Anthony, Samuel Davis, Micajah Davis, Mary Anthony, William Ballard, Christopher Johnson, William Davis, Charles Brooke, Achillis Douglas, Barclay Ballard, Ashley Johnson.

JOHN JOHNSON, of Bedford County, and RHODA MOORMAN, of Campbell, were married at South River Meeting-house 10-21-1789.

The following witnesses signed the marriage certificate: Micajah Moorman, William Johnson, Joseph Johnson, Andrew Moorman, James Johnson, Samuel Johnson, Thomas Moorman, William Bloxom, Charles Moorman, Thomas Johnson, Moorman Johnson, Thomas Johnson, Joseph Stratton, Samuel Davis, Richard Bloxom, Mary Davis, Annis Davis, Agatha Johnson, Susanna Johnson, Betty Moorman, Dosha Moorman, Sarah Stratton, Milley Johnson, Susanna Johnson, Nancy Moorman, Rachel Johnson, Prudence Moorman.

WILLIAM JOHNSON, son of William Johnson, and SARAH BLOXOM, daughter of Richard Bloxom, all of Campbell County, were married at South River Meeting-house 11-30-1791.

Names of witnesses to marriage certificate: William Bloxom, Benjamin Stanton, William Johnson, Richard Bloxom, John Johnson, Micajah Moorman, Joseph Johnson, Thomas Johnson, Wm. Johnson, James Johnson, Charles Moorman, Samuel Johnson, David Johnson, Christopher Johnson, Henry Terrell, Charles Johnson, Thomas Moorman, Achillis Moorman, Barclay Ballard, Benjamin Johnson, Henry Brown, Ashley Johnson, Gerard Johnson, Jr., Mary Davis, Betty Johnson, Neoma Stratton, Agatha Johnson, Judith Johnson, Betty Moorman, Dosha Moorman, Rachel Moorman, Nancy Moorman, Africa Moorman, Jean Johnson, Milley Johnson, Salley Moorman, Mary Herndon, Salley Johnson.

CHARLES JOHNSON and SUSANNA TERRELL, of Campbell County, were married at Hill Creek Meeting-house 3-17-1796.

The following witnesses signed the marriage certificate: David Terrell, Wm. Johnson, Henry Terrell, David Terrell, Jr., Samuel Terrell, Charles Moorman, David Johnson, John Richardson, Richard Bloxom, Nancy Davis, Milly Johnson, Molly Johnson, Mathew Davis, Letitia Wildman, Mary Davis, Mildred Ratcliff, Susanna Davis, Druscilla Crew, Agatha Johnson, Rachel Johnson, Molly Richardson, Mourning Johnson, Betsy Moorman, M. Davis.

TIMOTHY JOHNSON and LYDIA BALLARD, of Bedford County, were married at Ivy Creek Meeting-house 8-14-1799.

The following witnesses signed the marriage certificate: Christopher Johnson, Barclay Ballard, Wm. Stanton, Benjamin Johnson, Micajah Macy, Amos Holloway, Jonathan Johnson, John Tellus, Mourning Timberlake, Susanna Ballard, Betsy Johnson, Ann Fowler, Rachel Johnson, Rhoda Johnson, Sarah Johnson, Martha Johnson.

NEWBY JOHNSON, son of William Johnson, and SARAH DOUGLAS, daughter of Achillis Douglas, were married at South River Meeting-house 2-13-1800.

The following witnesses signed the marriage certificate: Wm.

Johnson, Sr., Achillis Douglas, Elizabeth Douglas, Charles L. Terrell, Sarah Lodge, Nancy Johnson, John Lynch, Wm. Stanton, Harrison Ratcliff, Ann Lynch, Enoch Roberts, Ann Pidgeon, Mildred Ratcliff, Sarah James, Betsy Lea.

PLEASANT JOHNSON and NANCY MOORMAN, both of Campbell County, were married at Seneca Meeting-house, 1-14-1801.

The following witnesses signed the marriage certificate: Agatha Johnson, Polly Moorman, Lydia Moorman, Betsy Moorman, Mary Ferrall, Mildred Ratcliff, Letitia Wildman, Mary Timberlake, Wm. Johnson, Sr., Thomas Moorman, James Johnson, Daniel Stratton, Ashley Stratton, Micajah Moorman, Charles Johnson, William Johnson, Jr., Joseph Stratton, Jr.

JONATHAN JOHNSON, son of William and Susanna Johnson, and JUDITH DOUGLAS, daughter of Achillis and Elizabeth Douglas, all of Campbell County, were married at South River Meeting-house 1-17-1805.

The following witnesses signed the marriage certificate: Achillis Douglas, Wm. Johnson, Mildred Douglas, Micajah Terrell, Robert Johnson, Nancy Johnson, Matilda Roberts, Zalinda Davis, Elijah Johnson, Mary Butler, Wm. Butler, Richard Tyree, Deborah Douglas, Betsy Terrell, Polly Lynch, Wm. Davis, Jeptha Johnson, Joseph Fisher, William Stanton, Newby Johnson.

ANSELM JOHNSON, son of Benjamin and Mary Johnson, of Bedford County, and DEBORAH DOUGLAS, daughter of Achillis and Elizabeth Douglas, were married at South River Meeting-house 7-10-1810.

The following witnesses signed the marriage certificate: Achillis Douglas, Benj. Johnson, Lemuel Johnson, Samuel Johnson, Samuel Fisher, Nicholas Johnson, Mahlon Cadwalader, James S. Butler, Etchison Grigsby, James Cox, Garland Johnson, Stephen Butler, Jr., Nathan Dicks, Wm. Davis, Jr., Samuel Davis, William Davis, Harrison Ratcliff, Stephen Butler, John Lynch, Josiah Bailey, Latham Stanton, Daniel Burress, Isaac Pidgeon, Edward Lynch, Jonathan Butler, Elias Fisher, Elizabeth Fisher, Mary Lynch, Mary Butler, Zalinda Davis, Matilda Johnson, Lucy Johnson, Jonathan Johnson, Nancy Butler.

JOSEPH JOHNSON, son of James and Penelope Johnson, of Bedford County, and BETSY BALLARD, daughter of Benjamin and Rachel Butterworth, of Campbell County, were married at South River Monthly Meeting-house 2-8-1812.

The following witnesses signed the marriage certificate: Benjamin Butterworth, Milley Defer, Jonathan Johnson, Anthony Johnson, Jas. S. Butler, John L. Roberts, Jonah Cadwalader, Jonathan Butler, Judith Johnson, Moorman Butterworth, Zalinda Lynch, Matilda Roberts, Josiah Bailey, John H. Moorman, George Akers, Stephen Butler, Rachel Johnson, Thomas Ballard, Mary Butler, Susanna Bailey, Priscilla Butler, Stephen Butler, Jr., Matilda Butler, Deborah Butler, Deborah Butler, Jr.

LILBURN JOHNSON, son of Christopher and Sarah Johnson, and DEBORAH BUTLER, daughter of Stephen and Mary Butler, were married at South River Meeting-house 1-14-1819.

The following witnesses signed the marriage certificate: James S. Butler, Pleasant Johnson, Caleb Johnson, Jonathan Butler, Lemuel Johnson, John Davis, John H. Moorman, Joseph Boyce. Richard Tyree, John F. Hawkins, Micajah T. Lynch, Charles Fisher, Achillis Douglas, James Butler, Sr., Polley Lynch, Mary Johnson, Lucinda Johnson, Zalinda Lynch, Mildred Tyree, Louisa Bailey, Ann T. Lynch, Rebecca Preston, Mary Lynch, Zalinda Davis, Judith Johnson, Anna Lynch, Mary Ann Lynch, Sally Bailey, Lucy Jones, Eliza Lynch, Sarah L. Davis, Mary A. Davis.

JOHN JAMES, son of Thomas and Sarah James, and MARTHA BAUGHAM, daughter of Humphrey and Elizabeth Baugham, were married at South River Meeting-house 4-18-1799.

The following witnesses signed the marriage certificate: Thomas Reeder, Priscilla Reeder, Joseph Fisher, Thomas Hanna, Jonathan Carey, James Butler, Lucy Baugham, John Lynch, Stephen Butler, Sarah Lodge, Judith Douglas, Mary Lynch.

MARRIAGE CERTIFICATES BEDFORD MONTHLY MEETING, BEDFORD COUNTY.*

HENRY KERBY and MARY ANDERSON were married at Bedford Monthly Meeting held 12-20-1761.

The following witnesses signed the marriage certificate: Charles Lynch, Charles Neal, Bowling Clark, Micajah Moorman, William Johnson, Daniel Candler, John Candler, Christopher Johnson, Sarah Lynch, Sarah Terrell, Winfred Clarke, Susanna Johnson, Anna Lynch.

EVAN LEWIS (son of Jehu Lewis and Alice his wife), of Bedford County, and SARAH TENNISON, daughter of John and Ann Tennison, of Amherst County, were married at South River Meeting-house, in Campbell County, 4-22-1790.

The following witnesses signed the marriage certificate: William Johnson, William Ballard, Ashley Johnson, Robert Johnson, William Betts, Enoch Roberts, Christopher Gatt, Micajah Boudlas, Susanna Johnson, Betty Johnson, Sarah Johnson, Rachel Ballard, William Stanton, John Johnson, Christopher James, Robert Hanna, John Davis, Henry Tennison, Salley Johnson, Salley Martin, Rachel Paxon, Mary Baugham, Penelope Johnson, Mary Fowler, Phebe Stanton, Zalinda Lynch, Mary Betts, Jane Tullas, Jesse Lewis, Ann Lewis, Matilda Roberts, Margaret Tennison.

JOCABAD LODGE, son of Jocabad and Catharine Lodge, and SARAH JOHNSON, daughter of William and Susannah Johnson, of Campbell County, were married 11-22-1792 at South River Meeting-house.

The following witnesses signed the marriage certificate: William Johnson, William Stanton, John Davis, Alice Fisher, Gerard Johnson, Robert Johnson, Achillis Douglas, Polley Fowler, Betsy

---

*Taken from the minutes of Southriver Monthly Meeting, of which they were a part.

Fisher, Betty Johnson, Elizabeth Douglas, Jonathan Johnson, William Johnson, John Preston, John Johnson, Edward Lynch, Robert Fisher, Ashley Johnson, Mary Tenner, Matilda Roberts, Rebecca Preston, Ruth Micker, John Headon, James Martin, Joseph Fisher, Mariah Wright, John Roberson, Robert Hanna, Rachel Wright, Zalinda Lynch, Nancy Johnson, Sarah Johnson, Mourning Johnson.

JESSE LEWIS, son of Jehu and Alice Lewis, of Bedford County, and REBECCA MORELAN, daughter of Jason and Nancy Morelan, were married at South River Meeting-house 2-20-1793.

The following witnesses signed the marriage certificate: Amos Ballard, William Ballard, Nathan Hale, Sarah Ballard, Moses Hurt, William Reardson, Elizabeth Ballard, Edna Dickenson, Eliza Ballard, Rachel Feazel, Susannah Hanna, Elizabeth Wright, Mourning Ballard, Ruth Straasberry, Judith Ballard, Jonan Moorlan, Thomas Johnson, John Davis, Sr., Micajah Davis, Elizabeth Hamner, Sarah Blackley, Jason Moorlan, Joel Lewis, George Lewis, Nancy Morelan, Jos. Richardson, Abigal Moorelan, Martha Rhodes, Betty Richardson, Evan Lewis, Joseph Rhodes, Esther Richards, Ada Moorlan, Moses Embree, Mary Moorelan, Jr., Aaron Feazle, Barnet Feazle.

DANIEL MCPHERSON, son of Stephen and Mary McPherson, and MARY BOND, daughter of Edward and Mary Bond, all of Bedford County, were married at South River Meeting-house 6-20-1793.

The following witnesses signed the marriage certificate: Rebecca Lewis, Nancy Morelan, Jonah Dobins, William Pennock, Moses Cadwalader, William Pennock, Sr., John Pennock, Thomas Dobins, Chas. Pidgeon, James Cadwalader, Stephen Morlan, Philip Williams, Ruth Paxon, Hannah Lerrow, Sarah Pidgeon, Ruth Cadwalader, Joel Lewis, Sarah Lewis, Mary Anthony, Chris. Anthony, Benj. Bond, Moses Embree, Allan Bond, Mary Kutzs, Samuel Erwin, Wm. Pidgeon, Rachel Pidgeon, John Coffee, Abijah Richards, Jane Cadwalader, Rachel Coffee, Edward Bond, Mary Bond, Saml. Oliphant, Henry Newman, Hannah Harris, Elizabeth Dobins, Magdala Erwin, Alice Pennock, Jane Erwin, Mary Harris, Hannah Pidgeon, Sarah Holmes.

MICAJAH MACY, of Bedford County, and SARAH HOLLOWAY, of Campbell County, were married at South River Meeting-house 9-25-1794.

The following witnesses signed the marriage certificate: Samuel Cary, James Johnson, Mary Betts, Achillis Douglas, John Lynch, Elizabeth Douglas, Cynthy Cary, Salley Snead, Thomas Hanna, Judith Douglas, Elihu Macy, Amos Holloway, Asa Holloway, Isaac Holloway, Hepzibah Holloway, William Johnson, Hannah Fisher, Mourning Johnson, Sarah Fisher, Nancy Johnson, Tacy Baugham, Rachel Wright, Elizabeth Lea, Hannah Fisher, Jonathan Johnson, Wm. Stanton, Sr., Phebe Stanton, Wm. Stanton, Jr., John Preston, Joseph Coffin, Robert Hanna, Catharine Hanna, Rebecca Preston, James Stanton, Daniel James, Mary Stanton, Mary Holloway, Zacheus Stanton, Abner Holloway, Sarah Douglas, Mathew Baugham, Harry Major.

JOSEPH MORELAN and MOURNING BALLARD, of Bedford County, were married at Upper Goose Creek Meeting-house, in said County, 8-20-1794.

The following witnesses signed the marriage certificate: Micajah Moorman, Richard Bloxom, Ashly Johnson, Joseph Curle, Moorman Johnson, Thomas Moorman, James Johnson, Reuben Moorman, Gerard Johnson, Sr., David Johnson, Sarah Terrell, Susanna Moorman, Susanna Davis, Gerard Johnson, Mary Butler, Wm. Johnson, Eliza Johnson, Naomi Stratton, Rachel Johnson, Effie Moorman, Anna Bloxom, Elizabeth Douglas, Nancy Moorman, Jane Tullas.

JASON MORELAND, son of Jason and Ann Moreland, and MARTHA TULLIS, daughter of Richard and Jane Tullis, of Bedford County, were married at South River Meeting-house, in Campbell County, 5-14-1796.

The following witnesses signed the marriage certificate: Sarah Johnson, Lydia Johnson, Susanna Moorman, Lydia Ballard, Rhoda Johnson, Wm. Stanton, Mary Butler, Thomas Hanna, Ashley Johnson, Barclay Ballard, Benjamin Hanna, Mary Lynch, Betsy Johnson, Milly Johnson, Matilda Roberts, William Davis, Christopher Johnson, Achillas Douglas, Zacheus Stanton, John Lynch, Elijah

Johnson, Richard Tullis, Wm. Fowler, Joseph Bradfield, Jonathan Johnson, Samuel Cary, Hannah Fisher, Mary Holloway, Rebecca Preston, Jallis Tullis, John Tullis, Ann Tullis, Betty Hendrick, Sarah Hendrick, Mary Anderson, Hepzibah Holloway, Robert Hanna, Mildred Johnson, Mary Betts, Mourning Johnson.

REUBEN MOORMAN, of Campbell County, and LYDIA JOHNSON, of Bedford County, were married 1-13-1799.

The following witnesses signed the marriage certificate: Thomas Moorman, James Johnson, Benjamin Johnson, Thos. Johnson, Joseph Johnson, Barclay Ballard, Nicholas Johnson, Timothy Johnson, James Ballard, David Johnson, Christopher Johnson, Amos Holloway, John Wilkison, Africa Moorman, Elizabeth Johnson, Judith Ballard, Rachel Johnson, Hepzibah Holloway, Nancy Moorman, Polly Moorman, Mary Johnson, Lydia Ballard, Elizabeth Johnson, Huldah Stanton, Elizabeth Daugherty, Susan Ballard, Lettice Daugherty.

MICAJAH MACY, son of John Macy, of Bedford County, and SARAH FISHER, daughter of Joseph Fisher, of Campbell County, were married at South River Meeting-house 4-18-1799.

The following witnesses signed the marriage certificate: Hepsibah Holloway, Nancy Johnson, William Stanton, Benjamin Hanna, John Timberlake, Matilda Roberts, Joseph Fisher, Jr., Humphrey Baugham, Robert Hanna, Mary Lynch, Ann Fisher, William Johnson, Sr.

DUDLEY MILNER, son of Beverly Milner, and MARY ANDERSON, daughter of John Anderson, were married at South River Meeting-house 12-13-1800.

The following witnesses signed the marriage certificate: Daniel Easly, Nimrod Farguson, Richard Kirby, Joseph Fisher, Jr., William Davis, Jr., Edward Lynch, Robt. Hanna, William Johnson, Micajah Terrell, Jonathan Johnson, Anna Anderson, Ruth Milner, Orpha Kirby, Mary Butler, Susanna Davis.

HUGH MORGAN and JUDITH JOHNSON were married at Seneca Meeting-house, in Campbell County.

The following witnesses signed the marriage certificate: Gerard Johnson, Elias Fisher, Charles Moorman, Charles Johnson, Ashley Johnson, Wm. Johnson, Micajah Moorman, Susanna Moorman, Elizabeth Terrell, Rachel Johnson.

JOHN H. MOORMAN, of Campbell County, and BETSY JOHNSON, of Bedford County, were married 7-12-1806.

The following witnesses signed the marriage certificate: Joseph Stratton, John Lynch, Stephen Butler, Josiah Bailey, Rebecca Preston, Mary Lynch, Mildred Ratcliff, Susanna Davis, Nancy Johnson, Mary Davis, Judith Johnson, Zalinda Davis, Thomas Moorman, Reuben Moorman, Simeon Johnson, Chiles Moorman, Rhoda Johnson, Dosha Stratton.

BENJAMIN PAXON, son of Jacob and Mary Paxon, and RUTH PIDGEON, daughter of William and Rachel Pidgeon, were married at Goose Creek Meeting-house, in Bedford County, 5-24-1792.

The following witnesses signed the marriage certificate: Joel Lewis, Sarah Lewis, Samuel Anthony, Hannah Lewis, Martha Rhodes, John Pennock, Samuel Oliphant, Mentor P. Perdue, Annis Davis, Moses Cadwalader, Mary Cadwalader, Mourning Ballard, Jesse Cadwalader, William Tugg, Elisha Schooly, Thomas Davis, Amos Ballard, Patrick Hix, Mary Bond, Edward Bond, Henry Thurman, William Davis, Sarah Lewis, Ruth Curle, Isaac Hatcher, Rachel Hatcher, Mary Anthony, James Erwin, Mary Erwin, Magdala Crew, William Pidgeon, Rachel Pidgeon, Elizabeth Hanna, Ruth Cadwalader, Men. Bond, Moses Embree, Rachel Schooly, Samuel Davis, Christopher Anthony, Hannah Curle, Samuel Erwin, Benjamin Bond, Micajah Richards, Esther Richards, Moses Embree, Jane Erwin,Mary Betts, William Betts, John Coffee, Rachel Coffee, Joseph Crouch, Hannah Pidgeon, Charles Pidgeon, Isaac Pidgeon, Wm. Pidgeon.

ISAAC PIDGEON, son of William and Rachel Pidgeon, of Campbell County, and ELIZABETH HAMNER, daughter of John and Rachel Hamner, of the County of Bedford, were married at Goose Creek Meeting-house 4-5-1793.

The following witnesses signed the marriage certificate: Hannah Larrow, Moses Cadwalader, Ruth Cadwalader, Edward Bond, Mary Lenord, Mary Burruss, Evan Lewis, Jesse Lewis, Elizabeth Woodford, Rebecca W. Lewis, Sarah Holmes, Mary Harris, Aaron Betts, Stephen Moorlan, John Coffee, Wm. Pidgeon, Jr., Charles Pidgeon, Alice Lewis, Joel Lewis, Sarah Lewis, Martha Rhodes, Gulielma Perdue, Samuel Erwin, Mary Bond, Alice Pennock, Magdala Erwin, Elizabeth Harris, Mary Anthony, David Hale, Mary Richards, William Pidgeon, Sarah Pidgeon, Mary Betts, Rachel Coffee, Benjamin Bond, John Pennock, Charles Anthony, Thomas Cadwalader, Amos Harris, Christopher Anthony, Samuel Erwin, Abigal Richards, James Erwin, Mary Erwin, Rachel Schooly, Moses Cadwalader, Moses Embree, Susanna Betts, Moses Embree, Jr., John Embree.

ASA PLUMMER, son of Joseph Plummer, of Berkley County, and GRACE BURGESS, daughter of Joseph Burgess, of Campbell County, were married at Seneca Meeting-house 1-12-1796.

The following witnesses signed the marriage certificate: M. Randle, Nancy Moorman, Priscilla Butler, Rachel Hatcher, Lettia Wildman, Susanna Johnson, Ann Blocksom, Ann Blocksom, Jr., Mary Blocksom, Mary Moorman, Sarah Moorman, Mary Blocksom, Sr., Wm. Johnson, Abner Grigg, Richard Blocksom, Richard Blocksom, Jr., Benj. Stratton, Gideon Blocksom, Joseph Burgess, Thomas Burgess, Daniel Burgess, John Burgess, Druscilla Burgess, James Butler.

CHARLES PIDGEON, son of William Pidgeon, and ANN GREGG, daughter of Abner Gregg, all of Campbell County, were married at Seneca Meeting-house 5-15-1799.

The following witnesses signed the marriage certificate: Ashley Johnson, Benjamin Stratton, Daniel Burgess, Naomi Stratton, Isaac Pidgeon, Susanna Johnson, Abraham Wildman, Thomas Burgess, William Pidgeon, Elizabeth Pidgeon, Dosha Moorman, Mary Bloxom.

JOHN ROBERTS and RACHEL TAYLOR were married at Bedford Monthly Meeting 12-20-1761.

The following witnesses signed the marriage certificate: Charles Lynch, Charles Neal, Micajah Moorman, Bowling Clark, Wm. Johnson, Daniel Candler, John Candler, Chris. Johnson, Sarah Terrell, Sarah Lynch, Winnifred Clark, Susanna Johnson, Anna Lynch.

WILLIAM STABLER, of Loudoun County (son of Edward and Mary Stabler, of Petersburg, deceased), and DEBORAH PLEASANTS (daughter of Thomas and Elizabeth Pleasants, of Goochland County), were married at Cedar Creek Meeting-house, in Hanover County, 6-4-1789.

The following witnesses signed the marriage certificate: Thomas S. Pleasants, Edward Stabler, William H. Pleasants, Samuel Pleasants, Jr., Samuel Parsons, James Hunnicutt, Thomas W. Pleasants, B. Watkins, Cary Pleasants, Joel Royster, Thomas E. Pleasants, Joseph Woodson, Sarah Parsons, Mary Younghusband, Elizabeth Pleasants, Polly Younghusband, Elizabeth Pleasants, Jr., Elizabeth T. Pleasants, Rebecca Hunnicutt, Elizabeth Watkins, Frances Royster, Polly Pleasants, Sarah Pleasants.

THOMAS SNOWDEN PLEASANTS, of Goochland County, son of Thomas and Elizabeth Pleasants, of said County, and ELIZABETH TUCKER PLEASANTS, daughter of Jacob and Sarah Pleasants, of Henrico County, were married 12-16-1790.

The following witnesses signed the marriage certificate: Samuel Parsons, John S. Pleasants, Thomas W. Pleasants, Philip Pleasants, Thomas E. Pleasants, Cary Pleasants, Thomas Harris, Obediah Crew, B. Watkin, John Harris, Achillis Barksdale, Sarah Parsons, Elizabeth Pleasants, Polly Pleasants, Mary Younghusband, Eliza Pleasants, Mary Brooks, Angey Royster.

EDWARD STABLER, of Alexandria, son of Edward and Mary Stabler (deceased), of the town of Petersburg, and MARY PLEASANTS, daughter of Thomas and Elizabeth Pleasants (the latter deceased), of Goochland County, were married at Cedar Creek, in Hanover County, 2-27-1794.

The following witnesses signed the marriage certificate: Thomas Pleasants, Reuben Pleasants, James B. Pleasants, Robert Pleasants, William H. Pleasants, John Pleasants, John P. Watson, J. W. Pleasants, Samuel P. Parsons, Thomas Hunnicutt, Philip Pleasants, Gerard Hopkins, Samuel Parsons, Micajah Crew, Benjamin Russell, James Vaughan, R. Turner, Sarah Pleasants, Deborah Pleasants, Mary Younghusband, Elizabeth T. Pleasants, Jane Pleasants, Sarah Parsons, Mary P. Younghusband, Rebecca Hunnicutt, Elizabeth Stanley, Polly Watkins, Milley M. Hunnicutt.

TARLTON WOODSON PLEASANTS, son of James Pleasants, of Goochland County, and SARAH PLEASANTS, daughter of Thomas Pleasants, of the said County, were married at Friends Meeting-house at Genito 5-17-1803.

The following witnesses signed the marriage certificate: William H. Pleasants, Archibald Pleasants, John T. Pleasants, Philip S. Pleasants, Robert Watkins, Alban Gilpan, Thomas Hatton, John Johnson, Samuel Hough, Thomas B. Watkins, Obadiah Crew, Daniel Couch, James Hunnicutt, Joseph Woodson, Jr., Byars Crawford, Matilda Pleasants, Dorothea R. Pleasants, Susanna R. Pleasants, Ann Maria Smith, Sally Watkins, Eliza Hunnicutt, Eliza Pleasants, Mary Trevillian.

TARLTON WOODSON PLEASANTS, son of James Pleasants, of Goochland County, and TALITHA CREW, daughter of Micajah and Margaret Crew, of Hanover County, were married at Cedar Creek 6-13-1812.

The following witnesses signed the marriage certificate: Micajah Crew, Benjamin Bates, Lemuel Crew, Walter Crew, William H. Pleasants, Margaret Crew (Ann Taylor and Elizabeth Wood from Ohio), Margaret M. Crew, Martha Pleasants, Thomas Hatton, Daniel Couch, James Hunnicutt, Thomas Hunnicutt, Philip Brooks, Isaac Parker, Isham Burch, Abner Brooks, Ben W. Ladd, Susanna Pleasants, Margaret Vaughan, Deborah Harris, Lucy Bates, Sarah D. Ladd, Susanna Brooks, Eliza M. Gordon, Emily Pleasants.

JOSEPH J. PLEASANTS, son of William H. and Mary Pleasants, of Goochland County, and MARTHA BATES, daughter of Benjamin and Tace Bates, of Hanover County, were married at Cedar Creek 10-9-1819.

The following witnesses signed the marriage certificate: Micajah Crew, Wm. H. Pleasants, Lemuel Crew, Fleming Bates, Walter Crew, Thomas S. Pleasants, Micajah Bates, Oliver Ladd, Thomas Hatton, Josiah Ratcliff, Joshua Bates, Nathaniel C. Crenshaw, Thomas Hunnicutt, James Hunnicutt, Wm. S. Bates, Isaac Leadbetter, Benj. S. Bates, William John Clarke, Wm. R. Irby, Lemuel Hargrave, Samuel S. Gilpin, Samuel B. Rice, John Crew, Edmund B. Crenshaw, William Ellett, Margaret Crew, Lucy Bates, Tace Bates, Margaret M. Crew, Unity Bates, Elizabeth A. Pleasants, Margaret A. Webster, Margt. Vaughan, Jane Dabney, Martha Hargrave, Unity S. Harris, Sarah Stanley, Deborah Bates, Isabella Harris, Elizabeth Hunnicutt.

BENJAMIN BATES, of Hanover County, son of Benjamin Bates (deceased), of York, and HENRIETTA MARIA PLEASANTS, daughter of Thomas and Elizabeth Pleasants, of Goochland County, were married at Genito Meeting-house 8-13-1812.

The following witnesses signed the marriage certificate: Micajah Crew, William H. Pleasants, Walter Crew, Joseph Pollard, Isaac Webster, N. M. Vaughan, Isaac Pleasants, Ben. W. Ladd, Micajah Bates, Joseph Pleasants, James Hunnicutt, Henry Clarke, Thomas S. Pleasants, Philip S. Pleasants, Granville Smith, Margaret Crew, Paulina Pleasants, Lucy Bates, Martha Pleasants, Damaris Pleasants, Susanna W. Pleasants, Abby Clarke, Deborah Harris, Margaret W. Pleasants, Eliza P. Pleasants, Chlotilda Harris, Phebe Mills, Ann Pleasants, Rebekah Harris, Eliza Hunnicutt, Emily Pleasants, Rebecca M. Russell, Betsy Watkins, Lucy C. Downer, M. L. Pleasants.

EDWARD S. PLEASANTS, of the City of Richmond, in the County of Henrico, son of Tarlton and Talitha Pleasants, of Goochland County, and TACY E. BATES, daughter of Micajah and Mary Bates, of the City of Richmond (the latter deceased), were married at Friends' Meeting-house, in the aforesaid city, 3-18-1846.

The following witnesses signed the marriage certificate: Henry Clarke, Thos. M. Alfriend, Wm. John Clarke, A. Pleasants, Thos. S. Pleasants, Charles J. Sinton, David H. Read, John D. Graff, Wm. Tyree, B. Slade, W. M. Gaskins, John H. Riddick, Elizabeth R. Whitlock, Theodore Carrington, Henry B. Read, Sarah I. Sinton, Mary Ann Spencer, Jane C. Whitlock, Mary B. Ladd, Susan S. Gaskins, Marcella Tyree, Eliza H. Lee, Martha B. Nicholls, Elizabeth Waddel, Frances Andrews, Mary C. Pleasants, Rebecca Spencer, Mary M. Clarke, Micajah Bates, Martha Ann Bates, Henry Bates, Martha Ann Bates, Catharine Bates, Wm. S. Bates, Mary S. Pleasants, Mary Bates, Nathaniel C. Crenshaw, Fleming Bates, George F. Terrell, Mary Pleasants.

ENOCH ROBARDS, of Campbell County (late of Philadelphia), and MATILDA LYNCH, were married at South River Meeting-house 1-29-1789.

The following witnesses signed the marriage certificate: Elizabeth Douglas, Susanna Johnson, Betty Johnson, Elizabeth Caffery, Anna Lea, Sarah Johnson, Salley Johnson, Rachel Paxson, Lucy Terrell, Sarah Martin, Robt. Hanna, Robert Johnson, John Paxson, William Betts, Mary Betts, Robert Wright, Wm. Stanton, Catharine Stanton, James Martin, Edward Lynch, Catharine Hanna, Ashley Johnson, John Lynch, Wm. Johnson, Chris. Johnson, Zalinda Lynch, Benj. Johnson, Anselm Lynch, Wm. Stanton, Achillis Douglas, Henry Terrell, John Hargrove.

JOSEPH STRATTON, son of Joseph and Naomi Stratton, and DOSHA MOORMAN, daughter of Micajah and Susannah Moorman, all of Campbell County, were married at Seneca Meeting-house 12-19-1792.

The following witnesses signed the marriage certificate: Joseph Stratton, Micajah Moorman, Wm. Johnson, Joseph Johnson, Thomas Johnson, James Johnson, Richard Bloxsom, John W. Johnson, Thomas Moorman, Abner Gregg, Moorman Johnson, Ben Schofield, Lemuel Johnson, Charles Moorman, Wm. Johnson, Wm. Bloxsom, Naomi Stratton, Agatha Johnson, Rachel Johnson, Ann Bloxsom, Sally Moorman, Mary Betts, Jane Johnson, Judith Johnson, Nancy Moorman, Susanna Johnson, Elizabeth Johnson, Polly Moorman, Rachel Johnson.

BENJAMIN STRATTON, son of Joseph Stratton, and AMY CURLE, daughter of Jos. Curle, were married at South River Meeting-house 1-20-1796.

The following witnesses signed the marriage certificate: Letitia Wildman, Betty Moorman, Agatha Johnson, Nancy Moorman, Susannah Johnson, Rebecca Preston, Joseph Stratton, Sarah Curle, Joseph Curle, Hannah Stratton.

LATHAM STANTON, son of Wm. Stanton, and HULDAH BUTLER, daughter of Stephen Butler, all of Campbell County, were married at South River Meeting-house 9-14-1797.

The following witnesses signed the marriage certificate: Ann Lay, Rachel Cary, Nancy Johnson, Susannah Johnson, Mary Lynch, Lydia Johnson, Hannah Fisher, Sarah Lodge, Tacy Nicols, Cyntha Cary, Elizabeth Johnson, Betty Johnson, Sarah Johnson, Benjamin Johnson, Humphrey Baugham, Timothy Johnson, Robert Hanna, Jonathan Johnson, Enoch Robards, Robert Johnson, Benjamin Hanna, Jacob Nicols, Joseph Bradfield, William Fowler, Christopher Johnson, Harry Majors, Wm. Stanton, Sr., Pheby Stanton, Sally Butler, Stephen Butler, Sally Butler, Hepzibah Holloway, Aaron Stanton, James Stanton, Zacheus Stanton, Jonathan Butler, Wm. Butler, James Butler, James Staunton Butler, Asa Holloway.

MAHLON STRATTON and SARAH MOORMAN, of Campbell County, were married at Seneca Meeting-house 10-17-1798.

The following witnesses signed the marriage certificate: Micajah Moorman, Reuben Moorman, James Hunnicutt, James Stanton, William Johnson, Joseph Stratton, James Johnson, Abner Gregg,

Ashly Johnson, Druscilla Burgess, Hannah Stratton, Mary Via, Polly Moorman, Rhoda Johnson, Anna Stratton, Agatha Johnson, Milley Johnson, Sarah Gregg, Sarah Curl, Letitia Wildman.

ZACHEUS STANTON, son of William Stanton, and SALLY BUTLER, daughter of James Butler, all of Campbell County, were married at Hills Creek Meeting-house 10-16-1800.

The following witnesses signed the marriage certificate: Mary Bloxom, Sr., Nancy Butler, Sarah Curle, Elizabeth Pidgeon, Martha Terrell, Susannah Fox, Druscilla Crew, James Butler, Sr., Jonathan Butler, Wm. Bloxom, Latham Stanton, David Terrell, Richard Bloxom, Butterworth Benjamin.

JACOB STRATTON, son of Joseph Stratton, and REBECCA CURLE, daughter of Joseph Curle, all of Campbell County, were married at Senaca Meeting-house 11-12-1800.

The following witnesses signed the marriage certificate: Sarah Curle, Mary Via, Hannah Stratton, Amy Stratton, Dosha Stratton, Betty Wildman, Betty Moorman, Chisy Hubank, Nancy Moorman, Africa Moorman, Ruth Gregg, Agatha Johnson, Letitia Wildman, Shady Stratton, Joel Stratton, Joseph Curle, Daniel Stratton, Abraham Wildman, Richard Bloxom, James Johnson, Benjamin Stratton, Jonah Wildman, Reuben Moorman.

ROBINSON STABLER, of the town of Alexandria, of the District of Columbia, son of Edward and Mary Stabler (the latter deceased), and MARY A. DAVIS, daughter of William Davis, Jr., of the town of Lynchburg, Va., were married at South River Meeting-house 10-16-1828.

The following witnesses signed the marriage certificate: William Davis, Jr., Annis Davis, Edward Lynch, Susannah Davis, Jonathan Johnson, Rebecca Preston, Nancy Dudley, Mary A. Anthony, William Davis, Margaret Anthony, Edward L. Johnson, Samuel B. Anthony, Achillis D. Tyree, George E. Roberts, Sarah L. Davis, Mary M. Johns, Louisa Davis, Catharine L. Hunter, Sarah Ann Davis, Zalinda L. Winston, Matilda Lynch, Mary Ann Mays, Elizabeth H. Roberts, Mary C. Powell, James E. Royall, S.

H. Davis, Charles H. Davis, A. F. Bigger, Peter C. Nelson, Richard C. Perkins, Micajah T. Johnson, George Whitlocke, Gerard E. Johnson, Henry I. Brown, Lucy E. Ward, J. T. Patton, R. M. Johnson, Micajah T. Lynch, John W. Bagwell, Catharine F. Smithson, Robert Johnson, Deborah D. Davis, Moses Preston, Elizabeth D. Davis, Anna Stabler, Joseph Janney, Jr., George D. Davis, James Beal, Judith Johnson, Elizabeth D. Johnson, John Davis, Jr., Henry Latham, Mary Lynch, William Cadwalader, R. R. Phelps.

WILLIAM FERRELL, JR., and JUDITH GOODE, both of Bedford County, were married 1-27-1780.

The following witnesses signed the marriage certificate: John Lynch, William Ballard, Ashley Johnson, William Johnson, Christopher Johnson, Barkley Ballard, Edward Terrell, Benj. Johnson, William Martin, Glover Baker, Mary Lynch, Molley Johnson, Jacob Straley, David Johnson, Richard Timberlake, John Timberlake, Mary Baker, Lucy Johnson, Molley Johnson, Ruth Johnson, Sarah Macey, Rachel Ballard, Jane Ferrell, Rebecca Ferrell, Hannah Ferrell, Sarah Goode, Ann Fowler, Eliza Johnson, Jane Tillus, Agnes Johnson.

JOHN TILLAS and SARAH MOORLAN, of Bedford County, were married 5-14-1788.

The following witnesses signed the marriage certificate: Joseph Wright, William Ballard, Amos Harris, Mary Ballard, Elizabeth Harris, Mary Ballard, Elizabeth Ballard, Esther Richards, Eleanor Ballard, Mourning Ballard, Mary Haynes, Jason Moorlan, Abigal Moorlan, Mary Moorlan, Nathan Dabny, John Stratton, Philip Teazle, Byrum Ballard, Ann Moorlan, Stephen Morlan, Rebecca Morlan, Eliza Tillas, William Morlan, Dosha Morlan, Eliza Morlan. Mary Morlan, Hannah Morlan.

DAVID TERRELL and MOLLY ANTHONY, daughter of Christopher Anthony, were married at South River Meeting-house 9-25-1788.

Christopher Johnson, William Johnson, Ann Fowler, Matilda Lynch, John Lynch, Wm. Stanton, Joseph Anthony, Wm. Ballard,

Jr., Achillis Douglas, Saml. Terrell, Robert Hanna, Wm. Davis, David Johnson, Wm. Davis, Jr., Betty Johnson, Jane Tillas, Elizabeth Johnson, Rebecca Morlan, Elizabeth Tillas, William Betts, Ashley Johnson, Charles Anthony, Elizabeth Ballard, Betty Johnson, Rachel Ballard, Elizabeth Douglas, Sally Johnson, Ruth Johnson, Rachel Paxon, Mary Betts, Sarah Johnson, Susanna Johnson, Mary Terrell, Lucy Terrell.

EDWARD TERRELL, son of David Terrell, of Bedford County, and JANE JOHNSON, daughter of Gerard and Judith Johnson, of Campbell County, were married at Seneca Meeting-house 10-19-1794.

The following witnesses signed the marriage certificate: Micajah Moorman, Richard Blocksom, Ashley Johnson, Joseph Curl, Moorman Johnson, Thomas Moorman, James Johnson, Reuben Moorman, Gerard Johnson, Sr., David Johnson, Sarah Terrell, Susanna Moorman, Susanna Davis, Mary Butler, Gerard Johnson, William Johnson, Eliza Johnson, Naomi Stratton, Rachel Johnson, Effey Moorman, Anna Blocksom, Elizabeth B. Douglas, Nancy Moorman, Jane Tillas.

THOMAS TERRY and SARAH HENDRICK, of Bedford County, were married 1-17-1797.

The following witnesses signed the marriage certificate: Christopher Johnson, Wm. Johnson, Matilda Roberts, Elizabeth Johnson. Other names omitted for want of space.

SAMUEL WELCH, of Campbell County, and CHLOE HENDRICK, daughter of Moses and Ruth Hendrick, of Halifax County, were married 9-21-1783.

Witnesses' names: Amos Hendrick, Judith Hendrick, Mary Welch, Sarah Terrell, Sarah Ward, Mary Anthony, Mary Davis, Annis Davis, Tirzah Davis, Betsy Anthony, Patty Cavil, Lettus Gosney, Christopher Anthony, Micajah Davis, David Terrell, Wm. Davis, Sr., Richard Davis, William Davis, Patrick Cartey, Isham Welch, Samuel Terrell, Charles Anthony.

NATHANIEL WINSTON, of the city of Richmond, son of George and Judith Winston, and ZALINDA LYNCH, daughter of Edward and Mary Lynch, of Lynchburg, were married at South River Meeting-house 5-6-1819.

The following witnesses signed the marriage certificate: John Lynch, Edward Lynch, Eliza H. Clark, Sarah L. Davis, Henry Clark, Sarah L. Terrell, Pleasant Winston, A. T. Lynch, Micajah Lynch, John Davis, Charles Johnson, D. D. Davis, Mary Lynch, Zalinda Davis, Ann Lynch, Mildred Tyree, Matilda Roberts, Judith Johnson, Sarah Johnson, Mary Davis, Rebecca Preston, Mary A. Davis, Betsy Moorman, Mary Ann Mays, Wm. Davis, Lucy Moorman, Richard Tyree, Mahlon Cadwalader, Jonathan Johnson, Wm. Davis Jr., Charles Fisher, Achillis Douglas, A. Liggett, James Benaugh, Wm. Gray, Joseph Boyce, Ammon Hancock, Thomas Moore, Jr., Richard Adams, Matilda Roberts, Jr., M. Davis, Jr.

JOSEPH ANTHONY, of Campbell County, and RHODA MOORMAN, of Caroline County, were married at Golansville 5-15-1791.

The following witnesses signed the marriage certificate: Clarke T. Moorman, Mathew P. Terrell, Thomas Terrell, John Payne, Catlett Jones, Jonathan Terrell, Ursula Cheadle, Salley Terrell, Ann Stevens, Pleasants Cobbs, John Peatross, Anthony New, Isaac Winston, Joanna Terrell, Lucy Winston, Salley Chiles, Judith Cheadle, Rachel Moorman, Salley Terrell, Rebecca Terrell, Rhoda Terrell.

BENJAMIN BATES, son of Benj. and Hanna Bates, of York County, and TACE CREW (daughter of Micajah and Margaret Crew), were married at Cedar Creek Meeting-house, in Hanover County, 12-16-1793.

The following witnesses signed the marriage certificate: Deborah Darbey and Rebecca Young, ministers from Old England, and David Cummings, from Pennsylvania, Margaret Crew, Chlotilda Harris, Mary Pleasants, Sarah Pleasants, Mary P. Younghusband, Unity Stanley, Edward Stabler, Thomas Hatton, Fleming Bates, Lemuel Crew, Wm. H. Pleasants, Thomas Ladd, Wm. Jackson, Micajah Crew, Clark T. Moorman, Thomas Stanley, Joshua Stanley, Thomas Harris, Jr.

FLEMING BATES, of Prince William County, son of Benjamin and Hannah Bates, of York County, and UNITY CREW, daughter of Micajah and Margaret Crew, of Hanover County, were married at Cedar Creek 11-16-1803.

The following witnesses signed the marriage certificate: Micajah Crew, Benj. Crew, Lemuel Crew, Walter Crew, Nicholas Crew, Micajah Crew, Jr., Daniel Couch Samuel Johnson, Joshua Crew, David Evans, Thomas Hatton, Littleberry Crew, Thomas Stanley, Sr., Joshua Stanley, Isaac Ratcliff, Thomas Stanley, Thomas Hatton, Jr., Catlett Jones, Clarke Moorman, Waddy Stanley, Thomas Stanley, Jr., James Cowgill, Thomas Harris, Margaret Crew, Talitha Crew, Unity Ladd, Deborah Harris, Eliza R. Pleasants, Mary Hatton, Rachel Moorman, Margaret Ratcliff, Susannah Hatton, Sarah Jones, Sarah Richardson, Martha Richardson, Margaret Crew, Louisa Storrs, Jane Brooks, Charlotte Cowgill, Marianna L. Pleasants.

BARCLAY BALLARD, son of William Ballard, of Bedford County, and Judith Johnson, daughter of John Johnson, of Amelia County, were married 2-27-1776.

The following witnesses signed the marriage certificate: Ashley Johnson, Jesse Johnson, Gerard Johnson, William Johnson, Ben. Johnson, Mary Johnson, Elizabeth Johnson, Judith Johnson, Agatha Johnson, Jane Johnson, Susannah Johnson, John Johnson, Sr., Lydia Johnson.

ASHLEY JOHNSON, of Campbell County, and Milley Johnson, of Amelia County, were married 3-13-1782.

The following witnesses signed the marriage certificate: William Johnson, Ashley Johnson, Sr., Jesse Johnson, Gerard Johnson, John Johnson, Joseph Johnson, Thomas Johnson, Elizabeth Johnson, Elizabeth Johnson, Jr., Mary Johnson, Lydia Johnson, Jane Johnson, Sarah Johnson, Druscilla Johnson, Samuel Johnson.

CHRISTOPHER JOHNSON, son of Christopher Johnson, of Campbell County, and SARAH HARGRAVE, daughter of Samuel Hargrave (deceased), of Caroline County, were married at Golansville Friends' Meeting-house, Caroline County.

The following witnesses signed the marriage certificate: Samuel Hargrave, Thomas Hargrave, Pleasant Terrell, Thomas Terrell, John Burch, John Russell, Pleasant Cobbs, Mathew Terrell, Jesse Terrell, Rebecca Terrell, Martha Hargrave, Elizabeth McGeehee, Amey Terrell.

ELISHA JOHNSON, son of Robert Johnson, of the County of Surrey, in North Carolina, and JANE JOHNSON, daughter of Ashley Johnson, of Amelia County, Va., were married 3-16-1783.

The following witnesses signed the marriage certificate: Agatha Johnson, Judith Johnson, Elizabeth Johnson, Jane Johnson, Susan Johnson, Drusilla Johnson, Anne Johnson, Lydia Johnson, Elizabeth Johnson, Elizabeth Piller, Jesse Johnson, Jr., Ben. Johnson, Thomas Johnson, Samuel Johnson, Wm. Johnson, Wm. Johnson, Jr., Andrew Johnson, Andrew Moorman, Gerard Johnson, Johns Johnson, Wm. Johnson, Gerard Johnson, Sr., Ashley Johnson, Sr., Jesse Johnson, Milley Piller, Judith Johnson, Lucy Winston, Christian Winston, Sarah Johnson.

JAMES CANDLER, son of John Candler, of Campbell County, and AGNESS JOHNSON, daughter of James Johnson, of Louisa County, were married 1-16-1786.

The following witnesses signed the marriage certificate: James Johnson, Catlett Jones, George Bell, Sr., Elijah Johnson, Lewis Johnson, Peter Crawford, George Bell, Nehemiah Bloomer, Martha Johnson, Patty Johnson, Mary Johnson, Massey Johnson, Cisley Bell, Betsy Johnson, Lucy Johnson, Ashley Johnson.

NICHOLAS JOHNSON, son of Christopher Johnson, of Campbell County, and MARTHA HARGRAVE, daughter of Samuel Hargrave (deceased), of Caroline County, were married at Golansville Meeting-house 4-16-1788.

The following witnesses signed the marriage certificate: Jesse Hargrave, Thomas Hargrave, Joseph Hargrave, Pleasant Terrell,

Jonathan Terrell, Clarke T. Moorman, Pleasant Cobbs, Mathew P. Terrell, Henry Chiles, Ben. Burch, Robert Terrell, Joseph McGeehee, Samuel Winston, Ann McGeehee, Margaret Terrell, Salley Chiles, Ursula F. Cheadle, Caty Terrell, Rhoda Moorman, Rachel Moorman, Sarah Pettrus, Rebecca Terrell, Salley Moorman, Salley Rogers, Polley Hewlett, Rhoda Terrell, Elizabeth Redd.

JOHN JOHNSON, son of Jesse Johnson, of Amelia County, and NANCY HUNNICUTT, of Powhatan County, were married at Genito Meeting-house, in Goochland County, 12-12-1790.

The following witnesses signed the marriage certificate: Joseph Hunnicutt, Jesse Johnson, Ashley Johnson, Jr., Ben. Watkins, Joseph Watkins, Watkins Johnson, Thomas Watkins, Thomas Stanley, Samuel Parsons, John S. Pleasants, Cary Pleasants, Reuben Pleasants, Daniel Clark, Robert H. Ross, James Pleasants, Jr., John Hunnicutt, Mary Watkins, Elizabeth Watkins, Salley Watkins, Polly Pleasants, Elizabeth T. Pleasants, Mary Brooks, Mary Watkins, Nancy Jude.

ELIJAH JOHNSON, son of Ashley and Martha Johnson, of Louisa County, and BETSY WATKINS, daughter of Benjamin and Prissilla Watkins, of Goochland County, were married at Cedar Creek Meeting-house, in Hanover County, 4-13-1793.

The following witnesses signed the marriage certificate: Polly Watkins, Sarah Harris, Betsy Johnson, Ann Jones, Janey Redole, Rachel Moorman, Margaret Crew, Unity Stanley, Mary Pleasants, Rachel Harris, Sarah Parsons, Sarah Hatton, Sarah Pleasants, Judith Crew, Mary Hatton, Tace Crew, Edith Harris, Thomas Stanley, Catlett Jones, William Jackson, Samuel Terrell, Samuel Parsons, Thomas Harris, Thomas Hatton, John Harris, Joshua Stanley, Benjamin Russell, Clark T. Moorman, Micajah Crew, Thomas Harris, Pleasant Cobbs.

JOHN JOHNSON, son of James Johnson, of Bedford County, and DOROTHY CREW, daughter of James Crew (deceased), of Hanover County, were married at Cedar Creek Meeting-house 11-16-1796.

The following witnesses signed the marriage certificate: Judith

Crew, Elizabeth Johnson, Unity Stanley, Chlotilda Harris, Rachel Moorman, Judith Hart, Mary Crew, Tace Bates, Margaret Vaughan, Unity Crew, Susannah Hatton, Susannah Davis, Micajah Crew, Thomas Harris, Jesse Crew, Littleberry Crew, Obadiah Crew, Catlett Jones, Joshua Stanley, Thomas Stanley, Waddy Stanley, Edmund James, Malcolm Hart, Benj. Bates, Jr.

THOMAS T. COBBS, son of Pleasant Cobbs, of Caroline County, and ELIZABETH JOHNSON, daughter of Benjamin Johnson (deceased), of Hanover County, were married at Golansville Meeting-house, in Caroline County, 4-16-1806.

The following witnesses signed the marriage certificate: Pleasant Cobbs, Joseph Terrell, Jonathan Terrell, Lewis Cobbs, Samuel Terrell, Pleasant Terrell, Matilda Terrell, Rebecca Terrell, Mary Terrell, Salley Terrell, Rebecca Terrell, Salley Terrell, Rhoda Cobbs, Ann Cobbs.

CATLETT JONES and ANN BARKSDALE, of Orange County, were married at Cedar Creek, in Hanover County, 3-2-1789.

The following witnesses signed the marriage certificate: Achillis Douglas, Christopher Johnson, Clark T. Moorman, Robert Pleasants, James Hunnicutt, Benjamin Johnson, John Harris, Micajah Crew, Benjamin Crew, Thomas Terrell, Pleasant Terrell, Nathan Bell, Thomas Harris, Elijah Johnson, Thomas Pleasants, Samuel Parsons, Thomas Hatton, Robert Watkins, Rachel Moorman, Rebecca Terrell, Rachel Harris, Chlotilda Harris, Edith Harris, Sarah Parsons, Judith Crew, Susan Watts, Deborah Pleasants, Margaret Crew, Sarah Hatton, Rhoda Moorman, Judith Harris, Salley Terrell, Mary Baughan, Mary Johnson, Ann Ladd, Sarah Crew, Mary Pleasants, Priscilla Ladd.

JOSEPH JORDAN, of the County of Southampton, and REBECCA HARRIS, daughter of Thomas and Chlotilda Harris, were married 11-17-1819, at Cedar Creek Meeting-house, in Hanover County.

The following witnesses signed the marriage certificate: Thomas Harris, Micajah Crew, Benjamin Harris, Ruth Jordan, Thomas Hunnicutt, Samuel Terrell, Thos. S. Pleasants, P. Winston, Lemuel

Crew, Olivia Ladd, Joshua Bates, Micajah Bates, Samuel B. Rice, Lemuel Vaughan, James Holman, Thomas Terrell, Bolling Vaughan, Joseph Maule, Jos. D. Bates, Walter Crew, Joseph Vaughan, Elizabeth Terrell, Eliza M. Gordon, Isabella Harris, Margaret Vaughan, Unity S. Harris, Mary Ann Terrell, Margaret M. Crew, Mary M. Pope, Elizabeth Hunnicutt, Elizabeth Maule, Unity Bates, Anna Crew, Catharine M. Dabney, Martha M. Dabney, Anna L. Vaughan, Jane Dabney.

OBEDIAH CREW, son of James Crew (deceased), of Goochland County, and MARY PEATROSS, daughter of John and Sarah Peatross, of Caroline County, were married at Golansville Meeting-house 3-10-1799.

The following witnesses signed the marriage certificate: John Peatross, Thomas Terrell, John Johnson, Jesse Crew, Timothy Terrell, Thomas Peatross, William Peatross, Malcolm Hart, Richard Peatross, Anthony New, Pleasant Terrell, Pleasant Cobb, Mathew Terrell, Dorothy Johnson, Joanna Terrell, Sally Terrell, Caty Terrell, Rhoda Anthony, Amey Cobbs, Anna Peatross, Nancy New, Elizabeth Peatross, Rebecca Terrell.

GILBERT CONGDON, son of Jonathan and Elizabeth Congdon, of Providence, R. I., and ELIZABETH A. CRENSHAW, daughter of Nathaniel C. and Ann C. Crenshaw (the latter deceased), of Hanover County, were married at Cedar Creek Meeting-house 2-14-1856.

The following witnesses signed the marriage certificate: Wm. J. Carpenter, J. Alonza Smith, J. Walker Carpenter, J. D. G. Brown, William R. Winn, Edward W. Kimloys, Chas. H. Vaughan, Thos. L. Jones, Benjamin Vaughan, John Ellett, Robert W. Biglow, J. Clifton Carpenter, Jesse Stanley, Thos. F. Waldrop, Jos. P. Terrell, H. L. Tiller, John I. Jones, Abram Stanley, Mary I. Vaughan, Lavinia A. Brown, Unity W. Fulcher, Indianna H. Crenshaw, Endora I. Lowry, Francis I. Stanley, Nathaniel C. Crenshaw, Eliza H. Crenshaw, Samuel H. Congdon, Mary J. Crenshaw, John B. Crenshaw, Rachel H. Crenshaw, F. Edmonia Crenshaw, Nathaniel B. Crenshaw, Margaret M. Crew, Edmund Taber, Mary H. Pretlow,

Julia C. Pretlow, Joshua Pretlow, Jordan D. Pretlow, Tace C. Bates, Samuel Janney, Gerard Hopkins, Abram V. Trimble, Richard A. Ricks, Martha A. Bates, Micajah Bates, Hannah Bates.

JOEL COOK, son of Josiah and Lydia Cook, of Isle of Wight County, and DEBORAH HARRIS, daughter of Thomas and Chlotilda Harris, of Hanover County, were married at Cedar Creek 1-17-1817.

The following witnesses signed the marriage certificate: P. Winston, Micajah Bates, Bowling Vaughan, Lemuel Vaughan, Joseph Pretlow, Nathaniel C. Crenshaw, Lemuel Crew, Philip Brooks, Thomas Hunnicutt, John Crew, Thomas Harris, Benjamin Harris, Elijah Cook, Joseph Poster, Wm. H. Pleasants, John Pretlow, George I. Knight, Thomas S. Pleasants, Thomas Hargrave, James Crew, Rebecca Harris, Elizabeth Cook, Isabella Harris, Eliza M. Gordan, Margaret Vaughan, Elizabeth Bates, Elizabeth Maule, Margaret M. Crew, Jane Brooks, Eliza Hunnicutt, Martha Hargrave, Lucy Bates.

THOMAS STANLEY, son of John Stanley, and UNITY CREW, daughter of James Crew, were married at Cedar Creek Meeting-house, in Hanover County, 12-20-1780.

The following witnesses signed the marriage certificate: John Stanley, James Crew, Micajah Crew, Joshua Stanley, Littlebury Stanley, Shadrack Stanley, Moses Harris, John Harris, John Shelton, Nicholas Stanley, Hutchins, John Anderson, Agnes Stanley, Ursula Stanley, Mary Payne, Elizabeth Strong, Sarah Strong, Rebecca Stanley, Sarah Stanley, Huldah Stanley, Mary Strong, Margaret Stanley, Nancy Shelton, Dolley Payne, Elizabeth Harris, Susannah Stanley.

LITTLEBERRY STANLEY, son of Thomas Stanley, and AGGATHA STANLEY, daughter of John Stanley, were married at Cedar Creek Meeting-house, in Hanover County, 3-2-1787.

The following witnesses signed the marriage certificate: Ursley Stanley, Elizabeth Strong, Rebecca Stanley, Judith Crew, Peggy

Stanley, Lucy Camron, Edith Harris, Rachel Harris, Nancy Stanley, Mary Alvis, Susannah Stanley, Jane Callihan, Dorothy Austin, Sarah Harris, Mildred Maddox, Susannah Harris, Elizabeth Camron, Catharine Camron, Edith Stanley, Rachel Callihan, Fanney Stanley, Fanney James, Huldah Stanley, Martha Stanley, Waddy Stanley, Joshua Stanley, James Crew, Thomas Stanley, Micajah Crew, John Harris, John W. Maddox, John Harris, Samuel Harris, James Stanley, John Strong, George Strong, Fort. Sydnor.

LITTLEBERRY CREW, son of James and Judith Crew, and HULDAH STANLEY, daughter of John and Milley Stanley, were married at Cedar Creek Meeting-house 7-11-1797.

The following witnesses signed the marriage certificate: John Stanley, Jesse Crew, Obadiah Crew, Jonathan Stanley, Joshua Stanley, Thomas Stanley, Waddy Stanley, Benj. Bates, Jr., Thomas Hatton, Catlitt Jones, Lemuel Jones, Fleming Bates, Micajah Crew, Edwin James, John Thompson, Thomas Mallory, Judith Crew, Huldah Stanley, Unity Stanley, Edith Stanley, Rebecca Stanley, Mary Crew, Agness Stanley, Chlotilda Harris, Rachel Moorman.

JOSHUA STANLEY, son of John Stanley, and RACHEL HARRIS, daughter of John Harris (deceased), were married at Cedar Creek Meeting-house, in Hanover County, 12-12-1798.

The following witnesses signed the marriage certificate: John Stanley, Thomas Stanley, Thomas Harris, Jonathan Stanley, Joshua Stanley, Thomas Harris, Littleberry Crew, Catlett Jones, Clark Moorman, Thomas Stanley, Jr., Waddy Stanley, Thomas Hatton, Jesse Crew, Fleming Bates, Lemuel Crew, Obadiah Crew, John Johnson, Rachel Harris, Edith Harris, Sarah Harris, Rebecca Stanley, Unity Stanley, Mary Hatton, Rachel Moorman, Margaret Vaughan, Judith Crew, Chlotilda Harris, Unity Crew, Susanna Hatton.

JONATHAN STANLEY, son of John Stanley, and MARY CREW, daughter of James Crew (deceased), were married at Cedar Creek Meeting-house 12-19-1798.

The following witnesses signed the marriage certificate: John Stanley, Littleberry Crew, Jesse Crew, Joshua Stanley, Sr., Joshua Stanley, Jr., John Johnson, Thomas Stanley, Sr., Obadiah Crew, Thomas Stanley, Jr., Waddy Stanley, Catlitt Jones, Clark Moorman, Micajah Crew, Thomas Harris, Thomas Maddox, Lemuel Crew, Moses Stanley, Fleming Bates Judith Crew, Dorothy Johnson, Judith Hart, Unity Stanley, Rachel Moorman, Margaret Vaughan, Sarah Harris, Rachel Stanley, Unity Crew, Jane Hart, Margaret Crew, Ann Jones.

THOMAS T. COBB, son of Pleasant Cobb, of Caroline County, and MARTHA STANLEY, daughter of Littleberry Stanley, of Hanover County, were married at Cedar Creek Meeting-house 12-4-1808.

The following witnesses signed the marriage ceremony: Littleberry Stanley, Pleasant Cobb, Thomas Maddox, Solomon Stanley, John Maddox, Thomas Stanley, Joshua Crew, Thomas Stanley, Walter Crew, Benjamin Bates, Lemuel Crew, James Winston, Edward N. Clough, Samuel Higgason, Benjamin Vaughan, Jr., Tace Bates, Susanna Maddox, Elizabeth Harris, Elizabeth Blackburn, Abigal Cobb, Rebecca Cobb, Nancy Stanley, Margaret Vaughan, Agness Stanley, Deborah Harris, Rachel Moorman, Susanna Hatton, Amy Stanley, Sarah Blackburn, Milly Stanley, Sally Pleasants, Margaret Crew, Guli E. M. Stanley, Sarah Ladd, Elizabeth Clough, Nancy Stanley.

CERTIFICATES OF REMOVAL

CERTIFICATES OF REMOVAL.

To the Monthly Meeting of Friends at Cedar Creek, Hanover County.

DEAR FRIENDS:

Mary Terrell having lately removed from these parts (by marriage) and now resides within your limits: these are therefore to inform you that she is of an orderly life and conversation, a frequenter of our religious meetings, and a friend in Unity. We, therefore, recommend her to your Christian regard, and are your affectionate Friends. Signed by order and on behalf of our Monthly Meeting, held at the White Oak Swamp in Henrico County, the 1st day of the 12th month, 1789. JAMES LADD, Clerk.

UNITY LADD, Clerk This Time.

To Friends of Cedar Creek Monthly Meeting.

DEAR FRIENDS:

Mary Bailey Terrell, being removed by marriage to reside within your limits, requests a few lines by way of certificate. These do, therefore, certify on her behalf that she is a member in unity with us, and of orderly life, as such we recommend her to your Christian care and notice. We remain your loving friends and brethren.

Signed in and on behalf of our Monthly Meeting held at White Oak Swamp, the 7th day of the 2nd month, 1795.

THOMAS LADD,
ISABETH LADD.

To the Monthly Meeting of Friends held at Southriver, in Campbell County.

DEAR FRIENDS:

Pattey Terrell (wife of David), having removed from us and settled within the limits of your meeting, we certify that she is a member of our religious society and orderly in her life and conversation whilst among us, and as such we recommend her to your care, and remain your friends.

Signed in and on behalf of a Monthly Meeting of Friends, held at Cedar Creek, in Hanover County, the 13th of the 6th month, 1795.

MICAJAH CREW,
CHLOTILDA HARRIS,
Clerks.

To the Monthly Meeting of Friends held in Henrico County at White Oak Swamp.

DEAR FRIENDS:

Our Friend Nancy Crew, having (by marriage) removed within the limits of your Monthly Meetings, requests our certificate to join her thereto. These may certify on her behalf that she was a diligent attender of our religious meetings, and as far as appears, of an orderly life whilst amongst us; and as such we recommend her to your Christian care, and are your friends.

Signed in and on behalf of our Monthly Meeting, held at Cedar Creek, in Hanover County, the 28th of the 2nd month, 1795.

MICAJAH CREW,
CHLOTILDA HARRIS,
Clerks.

Littleberry Crew was granted a certificate of removal from Wrightsborough Monthly Meeting, held the 5th day of the 3rd month, 1796, at Wrightsborough in Georgia, to Cedar Creek Monthly Meeting, held in Hanover County in Virginia.

CAMM THOMAS, Clerk.

Margaret Crew was granted a certificate of removal from White Oak Swamp Monthly Meeting in Henrico County to Cedar Creek Monthly Meeting in Hanover County.

Signed in and on behalf of our Monthly Meeting held at White Oak Swamp the 2nd day of the 1st month, 1802.

ROBERT CREW,
JANE LADD,
Clerks.

Jesse Crew was granted a certificate of removal from Cedar Creek Monthly Meeting held the 13th of the 3rd month, 1802, to the Southland Monthly held in Culpeper County.

BENJAMIN BATES, JR., Clerk.

Joshua Crew was granted a certificate of removal from a Monthly Meeting held at White Oak Swamp, Henrico County, the 6th of 3rd month, 1802, to Cedar Creek Monthly Meeting, Hanover County.

ROBERT CREW, Clerk.

To Cedar Creek Monthly Meeting.

DEAR FRIENDS:

Jesse Crew having made application to us for a certificate in order to be joined to your meeting, he sometime ago produced one to this meeting, was received, and as he has not been much among us since, therefore we cannot say much more about him, than as a member of our Society we recommend him to your care and are your friends.

Signed in and by order of Southland Monthly Meeting, held the 2nd of the 11th month, 1803. LEVI LUKENS, Clerk at This Time.

To Cedar Creek Monthly Meeting in Hanover County.

DEAR FRIENDS:

Nicholas Crew, with his wife Druscilla, and their two sons, Micajah and John, having removed and settled within the limits of your meeting, hath requested our certificate to join them thereto. On enquiring we do not find but that their outward affairs are settled, and they being members of our Society, we recommend them to your care, and are your friends.

Signed in and on behalf of our Monthly Meeting at South River, in Campbell County, the 10th day of the 9th month, 1803.

JOSEPH FISHER, Clerk.

REBECCAH PRESTON, Clerk This Time.

A certificate of removal to White Oak Swamp Monthly Meeting was granted to Joshua Crew by Cedar Creek Monthly Meeting the 11th of the 2nd month, 1804. BENJAMIN BATES, Clerk.

To Salem Monthly Meeting in Ohio State.

DEAR FRIENDS:

Obadiah Crew and his wife Mary with their children, John, Sara, Judith and Eliza Ann, having removed within your limits, we hereby inform you that they are members of our religious Society, of conduct in a good degree orderly, and that his affairs are settled to satisfaction, as far as we find. As such we recommend them to your Christian care and oversight and remain your friends.

Signed in and on behalf of a Monthly Meeting held at Cedar Creek, in Hanover County, the 11 of the 4th month, 1807.

To the Monthly Meeting of Friends at Salem in the State of Ohio.

DEAR FRIENDS:

Lemuel Terrell, a member of our Meeting, requests our certificate to join himself, his wife Rebecca and daughter Kitty, to your Meeting. These are to certify that they have been frequent attenders of our Meetings and have settled their affairs to satisfaction and as such we recommend them to your Christian care and oversight and remain your friends and brethren.

Signed in and on behalf of our meeting, held at Cedar Creek, in Hanover County, Virginia, this 13th day of the 9th month, 1806.

BENJAMIN BATES,
CHLOTILDA HARRIS,
Clerks.

To the Monthly Meeting at Wayne Oak, in Charles City County.

DEAR FRIENDS:

Thomas Scattergood Terrell having removed within the limits of your meeting these are to certify that he hath a right of membership among us and inquiry being made we find his affairs settled as far as we know, we therefore recommend him to your Christian care and oversight and are your friends.

Signed in and on behalf of Cedar Creek Monthly Meeting, the 12th day of the 9th month, 1812. BENJAMIN BATES, Clerk.

To Cedar Creek Monthly Meeting in Hanover County, Virginia.

DEAR FRIENDS:

Rebecca Terrell having removed with her husband within the

verge of your Meeting, requests our certificate thereto. On enquiring, nothing appears to obstruct our recommending her with their four minor children, namely, Kitty Pleasant, Nancy Thomas, Robert Samuel and Nicy Lynch, to your Christian care and notice, and remain your friends.

Signed in and on behalf of Salem Monthly Meeting, held the 17th of the 11th month, 1812.

JOHN STREET,
ESTHER FRENCH,
Clerks.

To the Monthly Meeting of Friends, held at Short Creek, in the State of Ohio.

DEAR FRIENDS:

Sally Terrell, with her children, Mahala, Rachel, Thomas, Clarke, Joanna and Mathew, having removed within the limits of your Meeting, requests our certificate. We may inform you that she is a member of our religious society, in good esteem among us, she being diligent in the attendance of meetings, exemplary in her deportment, and, as far as appears, has settled her affairs to satisfaction. Desiring her growth in the truth, and the preservation of her infant charge, we recommend them to your Christian care and are your friends.

Signed in and on behalf of Cedar Creek Monthly Meeting the 9th of the 10th month, 1813.

LEMUEL CREW, Clerk.
DEBORAH HARRIS, Clerk This Time.

To Cedar Creek Monthly Meeting of Hanover County, Virginia.

DEAR FRIENDS:

Thomas Terrell having removed and settled within the limits of your meeting, requests our certificate to join him thereto. This may certify that on enquiry we find nothing to obstruct. We therefore recommend him as a member of our Society to your friendly care and notice and are your friends.

Signed in and by order of Short Creek Monthly Meeting of Ohio, held the 18th day of the 4th month, 1820. LEWIS WALKER, Clerk.

To Wayanoak Monthly Meeting in Henrico, Charles City County.

DEAR FRIENDS:

A certificate for Caty Terrell being requested to join her to your meeting, these are to certify that she is a member of our religious Society. As such we recommend her to your Christian care and are your friends.

Signed by direction of Cedar Creek Monthly Meeting, held the 9th day of the 4th month, 1831.

To Smithfield Monthly Meeting, Ohio.

DEAR FRIENDS:

William J. Lewis having removed within the verge of your Meeting with his wife, Ann L. T., and their infant child, Sarah E., and requested our certificate, we do therefore certify that they are members of our religious Society and that their affairs appear to be settled to satisfaction. We recommend them to your Christian care and oversight and are your friends.

Signed by direction and on behalf of our Monthly Meeting of Friends, held at Cedar Creek, in Hanover County, Virginia, the 14th of the 9th month, 1833.

NATHANIEL C. CRENSHAW, Clerk This Time.
ANN CREW, Clerk This Time.

To South River Monthly Meeting in Campbell County, Virginia.

DEAR FRIENDS:

Lucy T. Johnson having removed within the verge of your Meeting, these are to certify that she is a member of our religious Society. As such we recommend her to your Christian care and oversight and remain your friends.

Signed by direction and on behalf of Cedar Creek Monthly Meeting, held the 14th of the 9th month, 1833.

NATHANIEL C. CRENSHAW,
ANN CREW,
Clerks at This Time.

To Pleasant Plains Monthly Meeting of Friends, Jefferson County, Iowa.

DEAR FRIENDS:

Edwin Terrell, a member with us, having removed within your limits, has requested our certificate to join him to you, and finding nothing to prevent, we hereby recommend him to your Christian care and oversight.

Signed by direction and on behalf of Cedar Creek Monthly Meeting, held the 19th of the 7th month, 1847.

WALTER CREW, Clerk.

Edwin Terrell asked for a certificate to Spring Creek Monthly Meeting in the State of Iowa, which was granted by Cedar Creek Mo. Meeting, held in Richmond, Virginia, the 11th day of the 1st month, 1854.

JOHN B. CRENSHAW, Clerk.
NATHANIEL C. CRENSHAW, Correspondent.

A certificate of removal to Salem Monthly Meeting in Ohio was granted to Littleberry Crew and Huldah, his wife, with their minor children, James, Benjamin, Mildred, Judith and Sarah, by Cedar Creek Monthly Meeting Hanover County, Va., held the 14th day of the 11th month, 1807.

BENJAMIN BATES, Clerk.

A certificate of removal to Salem Monthly Meeting in Ohio was granted to Judith Crew by Cedar Creek Monthly Meeting, the 12th day of the 12th month, 1807.

BENJAMIN BATES,
CHLOTILDA HARRIS,
Clerks.

A certificate of removal to Cedar Creek Monthly Meeting in Hanover County, Va., was granted to Peggy Crew (late Ladd) by Waynoke Monthly Meeting, held the 2nd day of the 1st month, 1808.

ROBERT CREW, Clerk.
MARY LADD, Clerk at This Time.

A certificate of removal to Waynoke Monthly Meeting was granted to Joshua Crew by Cedar Creek Monthly Meeting the 14th day of the 1st month, 1809.

BENJAMIN BATES, Clerk.

A certificate of removal to Waynoke Monthly Meeting was granted to Jesse and Margaret Crew, with their infant children, Lancelot, Elizabeth Ladd, Judith, Owen Milton, and Obediah, by Cedar Creek Monthly Meeting, held the 11th of the 2nd month, 1813.

LEMUEL CREW,
DEBORAH HARRIS,
Clerks.

A certificate of removal to Cedar Creek Monthly Meeting was granted to Ann Crew (lately Hargrave) by Waynoke Monthly Meeting, held the 6th day of the 4th month, 1816.

ROBERT CREW, Clerk.
DEBORAH HARRIS, Clerk This Time.

A certificate of removal to Baltimore Monthly Meeting was granted to Micajah Crew (minor son of Lemuel Crew) by Cedar Creek Monthly Meeting, held the 13th day of the 5th month, 1837.

JOSEPH J. PLEASANTS, Clerk.

A certificate of removal to Cincinnati, Ohio, was granted to Thomas F. Crew by Cedar Creek Monthly Meeting, held the 14th day of the 9th month, 1839.

JOSEPH J. PLEASANTS, Clerk.

A certificate of removal to Short Creek Monthly Meeting, Ohio, was granted to Lemuel Crew, his wife Anna, with their children, Margaret E., Samuel H., Walter, Tarlton, Deborah D., Henriette, and Anna, by Cedar Creek Monthly Meeting, held the 11th day of the 2nd month 1843.

JOSEPH J. PLEASANTS, Clerk.

Extracts from the Certificates Granted by South River Monthly Meeting to Other Monthly Meetings.

John Stanley, Sarah, his wife, and their children, Sussanna, Abraham, Abigal and Zachariah, removed to Westfield Monthly Meeting, Surry County, 2-18-1792.

ACHILLIS DOUGLAS, Clerk.
MATILDA ROBERTS, Clerk.

William Davis, his wife, Zalinda, and daughter, Sarah, removed to Goose Creek Monthly Meeting in Bedford County, 4-11-1795.

ACHILLIS DOUGLAS,
MATILDA ROBERTS,
Clerks.

James Johnson, Penelope, his wife, and their children, Elizabeth, Sarah, Joseph, Jesse, Judith, Mary, Penelope, Anthony, Agnes and Rachel, removed to Goose Creek in Bedford County, 5-9-1795.

ACHILLIS DOUGLAS,
MATILDA ROBERTS,
Clerks.

John Johnson, son of James, removed to Cedar Creek Monthly Meeting in Hanover County, 1-18-1794.

SAMUEL DAVIS, Clerk This Time.

Abraham Runker removed to New Garden Meeting in North Carolina, 1-18-1794. SAMUEL DAVIS, Clerk This Time.

Richard Tullis, Jr., removed to Goose Creek Monthly Meeting in Bedford County, 2-13-1796. ACHILLAS DOUGLAS, Clerk.

Robert Wright and Rachel, his wife, removed to Fairfax Monthly Meeting, 4-9-1796.

JOSEPH FISHER, Clerk at This Time.
MATILDA ROBERTS, Clerk.

Joseph Anthony and Rhoda, his wife, and Samuel Parsons, their son, removed to Henrico Monthly Meeting, 9-10-1796.

ACHILLIS DOUGLAS,
MATILDA ROBERTS,
Clerks.

Thomas Burgess removed to Deer Creek Monthly Meeting in Harford County, Md., 4-18-1797. JOSEPH FISHER, JR., Clerk.

Naomi Davis removed to White Oak Swamp Monthly Meeting, 8-11-1798.

JOSEPH FISHER, JR., AND MATILDA ROBERTS, Clerks.

Jesse Williams, Sarah, his wife, and their children, Micajah Terrell, Anna and Achillis, removed to New Garden Monthly Meeting in North Carolina, 4-13-1799.

JOSEPH FISHER, JR., AND MATILDA ROBERTS, Clerks.

Agatha Dicks with her four minor children, namely, Nathan, Sarah, Micajah, Achillis, removed to New Garden Monthly Meeting in North Carolina, 2-8-1800.

JOSEPH FISHER, JR., AND REBECCA PRESTON, Clerks.

Micajah Davis, his wife Mary, and their children, Susanna, Martha, Mary, Samuel, David, Richard, Micajah, Annis and Robert Pleasants, removed to White Oak Monthly Meeting in Henrico County, 12-14-1799.

JOSEPH FISHER, JR., AND MATILDA ROBERTS, Clerks.

Samuel Carey, Rachel, his wife, and their children (to-wit), Jonathan, Sarah, John, Samuel, Rachel, Thomas and Elias, removed to Westfield Monthly Meeting, North Carolina, 8-11-1800.

JOSEPH FISHER, JR., AND MATILDA ROBERTS, Clerks.

Cynthia Bradfield and infant son, John, removed to Westfield Monthly Meeting, 11-8-1800.

JOSEPH FISHER, JR., AND MATILDA ROBERTS, Clerks.

James Stanton with Mary, his wife, and their children, Hannah and John, removed to Centre Monthly Meeting, North Carolina, 5-9-1801.

JOSEPH FISHER, JR., AND MATILDA ROBERTS, Clerks.

John James, with Martha, his wife, and their children, Benjamin and Elizabeth, removed to Westland Monthly Meeting in Pennsylvania, 7-11-1801.

JOSEPH FISHER, JR., AND REBECCA PRESTON, Clerks.

Robert Hanna, with Catharine, his wife, and their children, Robert, Esther, Catharine and Ann, removed to Westland Monthly Meeting in Pennsylvania, 9-12-1801. This same Monthly Meeting granted Certificates of removal to Thomas and Benjamin Hanna on the same date. JOSEPH FISHER, JR., Clerk.

Jonas Harris removed to Westland Monthly Meeting, 9-12-1801.

Asa Holloway, with Mary, his wife, and their children, Stanton, Mary, Sarah, Isaac, Hannah, Eli, and James, removed to Westland Meeting, 9-12-1801.

Benjamin Stratton, with Amy his wife, and their children, Rebecca, Naomi and Levi, removed to Westland Monthly Meeting, 9-10-1801.

James Ferrell (being in his minority) removed with his father to Westland Meeting in Pennsylvania, 10-10-1801.

Daniel Stratton, with Shady, his wife, and their children, John, Margaret, Mary, Daniel, and Elias, removed to Westland Monthly Meeting in Pennsylvania 10-10-1801.

JOSEPH FISHER, JR., AND REBEKAH, Clerks.

Mary Via removed to Westland Monthly Meeting in Pennsylvania, 9-11-1802.

JOSEPH FISHER, JR., AND MATILDA ROBERTS, Clerks.

Jacob Stratton, with Rebecah, his wife, removed to Westland Meeting, 9-11-1802.

John Tellus, with Sarah, his wife, and their children, Rebeccah, Richard, Jane and Mary, removed to Westland Meeting, 9-11-1802.

Joseph Stratton, with Naomi, his wife, and their children, Hannah and Joe, moved to Westland Meeting, 9-11-1802.

JOSEPH FISHER AND MATILDA ROBERTS, Clerks.

Nicholas Crew, with Drucilla, his wife, and their sons, Micajah H. and John, moved to Cedar Creek Meeting in Hanover County, 9-10-1803.

JOSEPH FISHER, Clerk, and REBEKAH PRESTON, Clerk at This Time.

James Stanton and Agnes, his wife, moved to Gravelly Run Meeting in Dinwiddie County, 11-12-1803.

JOSEPH FISHER AND MATILDA ROBERTS, Clerks.

Extracts from the Certificates of Removal Granted by South River Monthly Meeting of Friends in Campbell County, Virginia, to Various Monthly Meetings in the State of Ohio.

Gideon Bloxom removed to Concord Monthly Meeting, 10-13-1804.

William Bloxom, his wife Mary, and their children, James, Nancy, Elizabeth and Mariah, removed to Concord, 8-10-1805.

Mourning Timberlake removed to Concord, 11-9-1805.

Abraham Wildman, with Lettia, his wife, and their children, Jonah, Elizabeth, Amy, Deborah, Mahlon, Mary, Sarah, Nancy and Jesse, removed to Concord, 9-14-1805.

JOSEPH FISHER AND MATILDA ROBERTS, Clerks.

Certificates to Middleton Meeting, Ohio.

William Reader removed 4-10-1805.

Amos Holloway with his wife, Hepsibah, and their children, Phoebe, Stephen, Rhoda, Job, Aaron, Hulda, Jason, Anna and Elizabeth, removed 8-10-1805.

John Fisher, with Rachel, his wife, and their children, Robert and Joseph, removed 8-10-1805.

Thomas Reader, with Priscilla, his wife, and their children, Elizabeth and Priscilla, removed 10-9-1805.

Nancy Terrell removed with her father 4-12-1806.

Joseph Reader removed 4-14-1804.

JOSEPH FISHER AND MATILDA ROBERTS, Clerks.

Dudley Milner, with Mary, his wife, and their children, Anna and Caty, removed to Plainfield Meeting 8-10-1805.

Daniel Easley, with Edith, his wife, and their children, Sarah, Mariam, Ruth, John, Daniel, Rachel, Isaac and Stephen, moved to Plainfield Meeting, 4-8-1809.

JOSIAH BAILEY AND JUDITH JOHNSON, Clerks at This Time.

To Salem Meeting, in Ohio.

Aaron Stanton removed 11-9-1805.

WILLIAM DAVIS, JR., Clerk at This Time.

Zacheus Stanton, with Salley, his wife, and their infant daughter, Hannah, removed 4-12-1806.

William Stanton and his daughter, Deborah, removed 4-12-1806.

Joseph Curle removed 2-8-1806.

Micajah Macy, with Sarah, his wife, and their sons, John and Samuel, removed 5-9-1807.

Timothy Grewell, with Alice, his wife, and their daughters, Sarah and Mary, removed 5-9-1807.

Joseph Fisher, Jr., with Hannah, his wife, and their children, Sylvanious, Rachel, William, Isaac, Amasa and Anne Knight, removed 5-9-1807.

WILLIAM DAVIS, JR., AND MATILDA ROBERT, Clerks.

To Miami Meeting.

Pleasants Johnson, with Nancy, his wife, and son, Thomas, removed 2-8-1806.

Susanna Johnson, wife of John Johnson, removed 2-8-1806.

Ashley Johnson, with Milley, his wife, and their children, Jonathan, Daniel, William, Nancy, Abner, Agatha, Martha, Ashley and Thomas, 4-12-1806.

Extracts from the Certificates Granted by the Various Monthly Meetings to the Following Friends to Unite Them with South River Meeting, Held in Campbell County, Virginia.

Timothy Grenell with Alice, his wife, and daughter, Sarah, removed from Goose Creek Meeting, held in Bedford county, 4-4-1805.

JOHN DAVIS AND MARY ANTHONY, Clerks.

William Coffee removed from Plainfield Monthly Meeting, held 11-24-1810.

ISAAC WILSON, Clerk.

Deborah Butler removed from Western Branch, in Isle of Wight county, 7-25-1812.

ROBERT JORDON AND MARTHA JONES, Clerks.

Ann Anthony (wife of Christopher Anthony), with her infant children, James and Mary Ann, removed from Cedar Creek, in Hanover county, 2-8-1812.

BENJAMIN BATES, Clerk.

Sarah Ballard removed from Goose Creek Meeting, in Bedford county, 1-7-1813.

JOHN DAVIS AND MARY ANTHONY, Clerks.

Sarah Snead removed from Clear Creek Monthly Meeting in Highland county, Ohio, 7-29-1814.

JAMES HADLEY AND RACHEL HUNT, Clerks.

Mariah Butler (late Bailey) removed from Upper Monthly Meeting, held alternately at Burleighly in Prince George County, 6-17-1815.

JOHN W. WATKINS AND DELITHA HUNNICUTT, Clerks.

Benjamin Butler (son of Joseph Butler) removed from Western Branch Meeting in Isle of Wight county, 1-28-1815.

SAMUEL COPELAND, Clerk.

Exum Bailey, his wife, Anna, and their children, Louisa, Eliza, William, Joshua, Mary and Delitha, removed from Upper Monthly Meeting held alternately at Gravelly Run, in Dinwiddie county, 5-24-1817.

MICAJAH BUTLER, Clerk for the day.
CHRISTIANNA PEEBLES, Clerk.

Sarah Ladd, removed from Cedar Creek 8-14-1817.

LEMUEL CREW AND REBECCA HARRIS, Clerks.

Asa Wood removed from Waynoak 10-3-1818.

ROBERT CREW, Clerk.

Ann Lynch removed from New Garden, N. C., 8-28-1819.

WILLIAM STANLEY AND ABIGAL LAMBERT, Clerks.

Charles Fisher removed from New Garden, N. C., 4-24-1823.

LEVI COFFIN, Clerk.

Nathaniel Winston removed from Waynoak, in Henrico county, 8-1-1829.

AMOS LADD, Clerk.

This meeting being informed that Martha Rogers, a minor daughter of Timothy and Anna Rogers, is placed within the compass of your Meeting. These may certify that she is a member of our Religious Society, as such we recommend her to your Christian care and oversight, and are your friends.

Signed in and on behalf of Yonge St. Monthly Meeting of Friends, Upper Canada, held 1-12-1832.

THOMAS LINVILLE,
Clerk and Correspondent.
MARGARET WRIGHT,
Clerk.

Certificates of Removal to Miami Meeting, Ohio.

Christopher Johnson, with Milley, his wife, and their three children, Micajah, Penelope and Elizabeth, removed 2-8-1806.

Richard Bloxom, with Ann, his wife, and their children, Ann, Molley, Elizabeth and Charles; also their grandchildren, Unity, Jerusha, Richard, Obediah and Gideon Johnson, removed 10-11-1806.

Jeptha Johnson removed to Salem, Ohio, 10-11-1806.

David Terrell, with Mary, his wife, and their children, Pleasant, Christopher, David, Judith, Sarah, Joseph and Mary, removed 10-11-1806.

William Johnson and Agatha, his wife, with their children, Christopher, Moorman and Nancy, moved 9-13-1806.

Charles Moorman and Betsy, his wife, and their children, William, Nancy, Fanny, Robert, Betsy and Agatha, moved 9-13-1806.

Charles Johnson and Susanna, his wife, and their children, David, Anna, Susanna, Polly, Sally and Nancy, moved 9-13-1806.

Benjamin Butterworth and Rachel, his wife, and their children, Moorman, Benjamin, Samuel, Rachel Moorman, William and Henry Thomas, moved 10-10-1806.

Elias Fisher and Hannah, his wife, moved 8-14-1813.

Agatha Dicks, with her son, Achillis, moved 9-10-1814.

Jocabed Lodge and Sarah, his wife, with their children, William Johnson, Laban, Nelson, Seline and Caleb, moved 9-10-1814.

William Butler and Nancy, his wife, moved 9-19-1814.

John Davis and Hannah, his wife, with their children, Anna Maria, Jourdon, Samuel, Anthony, Sarah and Charlotte, moved 11-12-1814.

John Davis also requested a certificate for Christopher Anthony Jonson, which was granted at the same time.

Josiah Bailey and Susanna, his wife, and their children, Almeda, Robert Barclay, Judith, Daniel, James Edwin, Mary Byrum and Susanna, moved 12-11-1814.

Joel Lewis and Sarah, his wife, and their son, Daniel, moved 10-20-1815.

Jane Cadwalader and children (names not given) moved 9-14-1816.

Thomas Cadwalader, Jr., moved 10-12-1816.

Nancy Ballard and her children, Granderson, Butterworth, Saml. Moorman, William Frederick and Elizabeth Ann, moved 7-12-1817.

Thomas Welch moved 10-9-1819.

Thomas Cadwalader moved 10-14-1820.

Charles Fisher moved 12-10-1825.

Removed to Fairfield Meeting, in Ohio.

Judith Borum and her children, Obed, Allen, Catharine and Sarah, moved 8-12-1809.

John Timberlake and Mary, his wife, and their children, Agness, John, Mourning, Salley and Judith, moved 11-11-1809.

Daniel Burgess and Ruth, his wife, and their children, Anna, John and Sarah, moved 8-11-1810.

John W. Johnson and Milley, his wife, and son, Gerard Moorman, moved 9-8-1810.

James Johnson and his wife, Rachel, with their children, Bartlett, Lydia, Susanna, Nancy, Polly and Milley, moved 9-8-1810.

Latham Stanton and Hulda, his wife, with their children, Hepsibah, Elizabeth, Hunnicutt, Gulielma, Daniel, William and Stephen Butler, moved 9-8-1810.

Rachel Anderson and her son, William, moved 1-12-1811.

Ruth Hendrick moved 1-12-1811.

John Burgess removed (with his wife, Drucilla), 10-12-1811.

Deborah Burgess removed 10-12-1811.

Certificates to Fairfield and Other Meetings in Ohio.

Gregory Bloxom removed from Southriver Meeting to Plainfield 10-12-1811.

William Johnson and his wife, Susannah, removed 8-8-1812.

William Holloway and Salley, his wife, with their children, John Isaac, Betsy, Pleasant, Samuel, George, Sally and William, removed 8-8-1812.

William Johnson, Jr., removed to Plainfield 10-10-1812.

Asa Plummer and Grace, his wife, with their children, Eli, Jesse, Ezra, Tacy and Lott, removed 8-14-1813.

Martha Burgess and her children, Adeliza and Sarah Hargrave, removed 8-14-1813.

Thomas Burgess and Elizabeth, with their children, Elizabeth, Joseph, Jenny, Moses, Mary, Tacy and Martha, removed 8-14-1813.

Ebeneazer Speakman and his wife, Elizabeth, with their children, Thomas, Ebeneazer, Jacob, Ann and Pheby, 2-8-1817.

Letishia Burgess removed 4-8-1820.

Margaret Fose removed 10-11-1821.

Gulielma Perdu removed 12-13-1821.

Certificates to Center Meeting, in Ohio.

Susanna Moorman and her granddaughter (under her care) removed 9-9-1809.

Molley Moorman removed 9-9-1809.

Rhoda Johnson and her children, Joseph, Micajah, John, Charles, Polly, Lewis and James, removed 11-11-1809.

Samuel Johnson, with Susanna, and their children, Thomas, Samuel, Moorman, James, John, George, Susanna, Lydia and Joseph, removed 9-8-1810.

Joseph Johnson, Jr., removed 10-12-1811.

Thomas Ballard, with Sarah, his wife, removed 9-10-1814.

Lydia Moorman with her children, Charlotte E., Nancy, John, Thomas and Reubin, removed 12-13-1817.

Certificates to New Garden Meeting, in Ohio.

Amos Preston, removed 4-14-1810.

Certificates to Gall Creek Meeting, in Ohio.

Joseph Johnson and his children, Polly, Kitty, Winston, Elvira, Watkins, Caroline, and his grandson, Alfred Carroll Johnson, removed 10-9-1813.

Certificates to Clear Creek Meeting, in Ohio.

Patty Terrell, removed 10-20-1815.

Ann Lea, removed 11-9-1816.

Elizabeth Lea, removed (with her parents) 11-9-1816.

Ruth Kirby, removed 5-1-1819.

Sarah Cox, removed 5-1-1819.

William Coffee moved to Plainfield 11-9-1811.

William Davis, Jr., Clerk.
Lucy Hargrave.

Jesse Cadwallader, with Amy, his wife, and their children, John, Isaac, Moses, Mahlon, Silas, Betsy and Jonah, removed 5-1-1819.

Certificates to Cincinnati Meeting, in Ohio.

William Stanton, with Catharine, his wife, and their children, Phebe, Anna, Samuel, Rhoda, David, Joseph and Mary, 10-11-1817.

Elizabeth Fisher, with her husband, and their children, Mary Ann, Lucinda, Elwood, Sarah, Hannah and Matilda, removed 12-13-1817.

Deborah Butler (with her husband) and her son, Anselm D. Johnson, removed 9-11-1819.

Mary Butler removed 9-10-1825.

Stephen Butler, with Louisa, his wife, and their children, Anselm, Matilda, Edna, Mary Elizabeth and William Exum; also his brother-in-law, William H. Bailey, removed ——.

VIEWS

OF THE

OLD QUAKER CHURCH

NEAR LYNCHBURG, VA.

THE RUINS AS THEY APPEARED IN 1900

THE RUINS AS THEY APPEARED IN 1888

ERECTED BY THE SOUTH RIVER MEETING OF THE SOCIETY ... OF FRIENDS ...

RESTORED AS THE QUAKER MEMORIAL CHURCH (PRESBYTERIAN)
DEDICATED OCTOBER 2, 1904

Certificates of Removal Received by Southriver Meeting.

From Our Monthly Meeting Held in Fredericksburgh Township, S. C., 2-14-1762.

TO FRIENDS IN VIRGINIA AND ELSEWHERE IN AMERICA.

Our esteemed friend, William Terrell, having requested this meeting some time ago of his intention of moving into your parts with his family in order to settle there, and requested a Certificate for that purpose, now these are to certify that he is of a sober and orderly life and conversation, a diligent attender of meetings, both for Worship and Discipline, and also a diligent laborer in the work of the ministry, having a sound testimony to bear, and is much esteemed by his friends and others, and on enquiry we do not find but he leaves this place clear of debt. His wife Martha is of a sober and orderly life and conversation, and a diligent attender of meeting. Their children are not yet grown up. So with desires for their preservation and growth in the truth, and that they may be serviceable where their lot may be cast, we remain your friends and brethren. Signed in and on behalf of our said Meeting. Samuel Wiley, John Millhouse, Henry Millhouse, Robert Millhouse, John English, William Elmore, James Millhouse, Wm. Smith, Zeb. Gauntt, Joshua English, Robert English, Joseph English, Timothy Kelly, Samuel Kelly, John Kelley, Mary Tomlinson, Sarah Russell, Mary Kelley, Rebecca Millhouse, Mary Cook, Mary English, Mary English, Jr.

A similar Certificate was granted by the same Meeting to Isaac and Sarah Pidgeon on the same date, 2-14-1762, and signed by the same members.

To the Monthly Meeting of Friends Held at Southriver, in Bedford County.

DEAR FRIENDS:

Our friend, Micajah Terrell, having removed from our Monthly meeting within the verge of yours, without our Certificate, these are to certify you that we have made inquiry into his life and conversation whilst among us and find that he was a member in unity (in most respects), and we recommend him to your Christian care and oversight and remain your friends and brethren. Signed by order and on behalf of our said Meeting held at Golansville in Caroline County 7-9-1762.

SAMUEL HARGRAVE, Clerk.

A similar Certificate was granted his wife Sarah at the Monthly Meeting held at Cedar Creek in Hanover County 8-14-1762.

SAMUEL HARGRAVE, Clerk.

To Friends at Their Next Monthly Meeting to Be Held at Southriver.

DEAR FRIENDS:

Whereas, our friend Byrum Ballard hath applied to us for a Certificate to you, these are therefore to inform you that after the necessary inquiry being made we find him clear from any engagements of marriage and in unity with us and as such we recommend him to your notice, desiring his growth in the truth. We remain your friends and brethren. Signed on behalf of the Monthly Meeting held at Cedar Creek 4-8-1763.

SAMUEL HARGRAVE, Clerk.

From the Monthly Meeting Held at Cedar Creek in Hanover County, 12-18-1763.

DEAR FRIENDS:

Mary Johnson and Betty Moorman having removed from under the care of our Meeting and settled within the verge of your Meeting, they have requested of us a few lines by way of recommendation unto you, and we hereby certify that their lives, conduct and conversation hath been such that we have good unity with them, and recommend them to your care and subscribe ourselves your friends and brethren. WILLIAM STANLEY, Clerk.

From Our Monthly Meeting Held at Cedar Creek, 2-11-1764, *to the Monthly Meeting at Southriver.*

DEAR FRIENDS:

Benjamin Johnson having removed within the limits of your Meeting and having requested of us a few lines by way of recommendation unto you, after the usual care taken, we do not find but what he has settled his outward affairs to satisfaction, and we further certify on his behalf that his manner of life and conversation hath always been such as rendered him held in unity with us and we recommend him to you.

STRANGEMAN HUTCHINS, Clerk.

From Our Monthly Meeting Held at Cedar Creek, 2-11-1764, *to the Monthly Meeting at Southriver.*

DEAR FRIENDS:

Whereas, Zachariah Moorman hath removed from under the care of our Meeting and settled within the verge of your Meeting, he hath requested of us a few lines by way of Certificate unto you. After due care taken we do not find but what he has settled his outward affairs to satisfaction. We further certify on his behalf that his manner of life and conversation hath been such as rendered him a member in unity among us and as such we recommend him to you.

STRANGEMAN HUTCHINS, Clerk.

From Our Monthly Meeting Held at Golansville, Caroline County, 3-9-1767, *to the Monthly Meeting at Southriver, in Bedford County.*

DEAR FRIENDS:

The bearers hereof, Thomas and Rachel Moorman, having removed from under our care and within the verge of your Meeting, requested us for a few lines as a recommendation to you. After due care taken we do not find but that he has settled his worldly affairs to satisfaction and has always been esteemed orderly persons and held in good unity among us and as such we recommend them to you. Signed in and on behalf of said Meeting by

SAMUEL HARGRAVE, Clerk.

From Our Monthly Meeting Held at New Garden, N. C., 2-25-1775, *to the Monthly Meeting Held at Southriver, in Bedford County, Virginia.*

DEAR FRIENDS:

The occasion of our writing to you is on account of James Johnson who requested our Certificate to join in membership with you and having left his outward affairs to satisfaction and condemned his going out in marriage, we therefore recommend him to Divine protection and your Christian care, desiring his growth in the best things. Signed by order and in behalf of said Meeting.

JOHN TALBOT, Clerk.

To the Monthly Meeting of Friends Held at Southriver, in Bedford County.

DEAR FRIENDS:

Edward Terrell and Mary, his wife, having removed from us within the verge of your Meeting, we therefore think it necessary to acquaint you that they have had their education amongst us. Their lives whilst amongst us were in a good degree orderly, and, after the necessary enquiry, we understand that their affairs are settled to satisfaction. We therefore recommend them to your Christian care and oversight. Signed in our Monthly Meeting held in Caroline, 5-13-1775.

SAMUEL HARGRAVE,
MARY PAYNE,
Clerks.

From Our Circular Monthly Meeting of Women Friends Held at Blackwater and Burley in Surry and Prince George Counties, 8-23-1776, *to the Monthly Meeting of Women Friends Held at Southriver, in Bedford County.*

DEAR FRIENDS:

Mary Anthony, being lately removed within the limits of your Meeting, requested our Certificate. These may certify on her behalf that she is a member in full unity and as such we recommend her to your care, ardently desiring her preservation in the blessed truth. Signed in and on behalf of our said meeting by

EDWARD STABLER,
MARY STABLER,
Clerks for the Day.

A Certificate of removal from Cedar Creek, Hanover County, to Southriver, in Bedford County, was granted Judith Ballard by Cedar Creek Monthly Meeting, 6-14-1777.

SAMUEL HARGRAVE,
MARY PAYNE,
Clerks.

To the Monthly Meeting Held at Southriver, Bedford County.

DEAR FRIENDS:

David Johnson removed within the verge of your Meeting and requested a few lines from us. This may certify on his behalf that he has been orderly and his affairs are settled to satisfaction. We therefore recommend him to your Christian care. Signed on behalf and by order of the Monthly Meeting held at Cedar Creek, 2-25-1780. JOHN PAYNE, Clerk.

To Southriver Monthly Meeting.

DEAR FRIENDS:

Application being made to us for a few lines by way of Certificate for Stephen Moreland and Mary, his wife, with their three children, namely, Edwin, Abigal and Jonah, we may inform you that they left our parts without acquainting the Monthly Meeting of their intention of removing, which was contrary to the advice of our Yearly Meeting, but with respect to their conduct it appears, after the needful enquiry, that their lives and conversation have been in some good degree orderly. They attended our religious meetings at times and have settled their outward affairs to satisfaction as far as we know. We therefore recommend them and their children as members of our Society to your Christian care and oversight, desiring their preservation and growth in the truth, and remain your loving friends. Signed on behalf of our Monthly Meeting at Fairfax, held 11-25-1780.

THOMAS MATTHEWS,
LYDIA HOUGH,
Clerks.

From the Monthly Meeting Held at Cedar Creek the 14th of the 4th Month 1781, To Friends of the Monthly Meeting at Southriver.

DEAR FRIENDS:

James Johnson and family removed within the verge of your Meeting and requested a few lines from us. This may certify on their behalf that they have lived orderly and his affairs settled to satisfaction. We therefore recommend them to your Christian care. Signed on behalf of the Meeting.

JOHN PAYNE, Clerk.

To the Monthly Meeting Held at Southriver.

DEAR FRIENDS:

Our writing to you at this time is on account of David Terrell, who now resides within the verge of your Meeting, and requests our Certificate for himself and children. These may certify that after the needful enquiry we have cause to believe his affairs are settled to satisfaction. His life and conversation being in a good degree orderly whilst among us, we therefore recommend him, together with his children (namely, Sarah, Winnifred, David, Henry, Samuel, Susanna, and Ann), to your Christian care, and with desires for their growth in the truth, we remain your friends and brethren. Signed on behalf of our Monthly Meeting held at Cedar Creek 8-24-1781.

JOHN PAYNE, Clerk.

From the Monthly Meeting Held at Cedar Creek, Hanover County, 3-9-1782, *to the Monthly Meeting at Southriver.*

Mary Johnson having moved within the verge of your Meeting and requested a few lines from us, this may certify on her behalf that she has lived orderly and has settled her affairs to satisfaction. We therefore recommend her to your Christian care. Signed on behalf of Meeting.

JOHN PAYNE AND MARY PAYNE, Clerks.

Micajah Davis and family were granted a Certificate of removal to the Monthly Meeting at Southriver by Cedar Creek Monthly Meeting, 4-13-1782.

JOHN PAYNE AND RACHEL HARRIS, Clerks.

To the Monthly Meeting of Friends at Southriver, in Campbell County.

DEAR FRIENDS:

Micajah Terrell and Deborah, his wife, having removed within the verge of your Meeting and requested our Certificate, we therefore certify in their behalf that they are in unity with us and that the said Micajah's affairs are settled to satisfaction as far as appears to us. We also recommend to your care and notice his children, viz., Agatha, Sarah, Ann, Mary and Micajah, as members of our Society, and remain your friends and brethren. Signed in and on behalf of our Monthly Meeting held at Cedar Creek 7-14-1782.

JOHN PAYNE, Clerk.
RACHEL HARRIS, Clerk at This Time.

These Certificates of removal were granted by Fairfax Monthly Meeting to unite the following Friends with Southriver Monthly Meeting: Richard Lewis and Hannah, his wife, 12-25-1790; Wm. Stabler and Sarah Mathews. Samuel Fisher, son of Joseph, Sr., being a minor and apprenticed to his brother, Elias Fisher, we commend him to your care and oversight. Signed on behalf of the Monthly Meeting held 5-1-1793. THOMAS MATHEWS, Clerk.

Mary Harris, 6-22-1793.

THOMAS AND SARAH MATTHEWS, Clerks.

Joseph Fisher and Ann, his wife, and their children, John, Hannah and Ann, 4-26-1794.

THOMAS MATHEWS AND HANNAH BEAL, Clerks.

Sarah Fisher, daughter of Joseph Fisher, 4-26-1794.

THOMAS MATHEWS AND HANNAH BEAL, Clerks.

Hannah Bradfield, 11-28-1795.
ASA MOORE AND HANNAH BEAL, Clerks.

Sarah Millburn, 2-25-1797.
ASA MOORE AND HANNAH BEAL, Clerks.

The Following Certificates were Granted by Various Monthly Meetings Uniting the Following Friends with Southriver Monthly Meeting.

John Preston and Rebecca, his wife, and their minor children, Zenas, John, Amos, Moses, Sarah, Peter, Ann and William, removed from Goose Creek Monthly Meeting, in Loudoun County, 7-30-1792.
JAMES MOOR AND SARAH SMITH Clerks.

James Curle, Ruth, his wife, and their son, Joseph, removed from Goose Creek Meeting, 5-30-1791.

James Daniel, Hannah, his wife, and their four minor children, Rebeckah, William, Jasper, and Hannah, 12-26-1791, removed from Goose Creek Meeting.

Thomas, John and Daniel Burgess removed from Deer Creek Meeting in Maryland, 9-27-1792. JOHN COX, Clerk.

Isaac Hatcher, Rachel, his wife, and their children, Nancy, James and William, removed from Goose Creek Meeting, 10-29-1792.
JAMES MOORE AND SARAH SMITH, Clerks.

Ashley Johnson, Sr., Mary, his wife, and their minor children, Ashley, Thomas, Walkins, Drusilla, Anna, and Edith, removed from Cedar Creek Meeting, in Hanover County, 1-12-1793.
MICAJAH CREW AND CHLOTILDA HARRIS, Clerks.

Abram Bunker removed from New Garden Monthly Meeting, Guilford County, N. C., 1-26-1793. ENOCH MACY, Clerk.

Mary Terrell was granted a Certificate on the same date.
ENOCH MACY AND DEBORAH EVINS, Clerks.

James Butler, Priscilla, his wife, and their children, Mary, Tabitha, Ann, Jonathan, Sarah, Edward and Mathew Robert, removed from Blackwater Monthly Meeting in Prince George County, 3-16-1793. WYKE AND ANN HUNNICUTT, Clerks.

Agatha Dix and her children, Nathan, Micajah and Sarah, removed from Springfield, N. C., 3-2-1793.
MATHEW AND HANNAH COFFIN, Clerks.

Fairfax Monthly Meeting, held 3-20-1791, granted Certificates of Removal to Southriver Monthly Meeting to Joseph Curle and Rebekah, his wife, and their seven children, viz., Hannah, Emma, Charles, Rebekah, Elizabeth, Susanna, and Samuel; also to Jacobad Lodge. Signed in and by order of Fairfax Monthly Meeting.
WILLIAM STABLER AND SARAH MATHEWS, Clerks.

Goose Creek Monthly Meeting, held 5-30-1791, granted Certificates to Samuel Cary and Rachel, his wife, and their children, namely, Cynthia, Sarah, Jonathan, John, Samuel, Rachel and Thomas.
JAMES MOORE AND SARAH SMITH, Clerks.

Cedar Creek Monthly Meeting, held 8-27-1791, granted a Certificate to Rhoda Anthony, to unite her to Southriver Meeting.
MICAJAH CREW AND CHLOTILDA HARRIS, Clerks.

Crooked Run Monthly Meeting, held 9-2-1791, granted a Certificate to Asa Holloway, Jr., to unite him with Southriver Meeting.
JONAH LUPTON, Clerk.

Fairfax Monthly Meeting, held 9-24-1791, granted Certificates of Removal to Robert and Betty Fisher and to Joseph Fisher, Jr.

THOMAS AND SARAH MATTHEWS, Clerks.

Crooked Run Monthly Meeting, held 9-24-1791, granted a Certificate to Mary Holloway.

JONAH LUPTON AND EUNICE ALT, Clerks.

Crooked Run Monthly Meeting, held 5-2-1789, granted Certificates to Meu Bond and Sarah, his wife.

GOLDSMITH CHANDLER AND SARAH BROWN, Clerks.

Cedar Creek Monthly Meeting, held 5-9-1789, granted Certificates to Mary Bunch and her Children, James and Ann Bunch.

MICAJAH CREW AND RACHEL MOORMAN, Clerks.

Crooked Run Monthly Meeting, held 7-4-1789. Certificates were granted to Edward and Mary Bond and their children, viz., Benjamin, Martha, Ruth and Hannah.

GOLDSMITH CHANDLER AND SARAH BROWN, Clerks.

Cedar Creek Monthly Meeting, held 5-8-1790. Certificates were granted to Gerard Johnson and Judith, his wife, and their children, Benjamin, Samuel, Jerard, Watkins, David, Elizabeth, Jane and Judith.

MICAJAH CREW AND RACHEL MOORMAN, Clerks.

Fairfax Monthly Meeting, held 5-22-1790. A Certificate was granted to Elizabeth Oliphant to unite her with Southriver Meeting.

JAMES MOORE AND SARAH MATHEWS, Clerks.

Extracts from the Certificates Granted by Various Monthly Meetings to the Following Friends to Unite Them with Southriver Meeting, Held in Campbell County, Virginia.

Asa Plummer removed from York Monthly Meeting 4-13-1793.
ELI KIRK, Clerk.

Patty Terrell from Cedar Creek Meeting, in Hanover County, 6-13-1795. Patty Jones from Cedar Creek Meeting, in Hanover County, 8-22-1795.
MICAJAH CREW AND CHLOTILDA HARRIS, Clerks.

James Butler removed from Blackwater Meeting, in Surry County, 12-20-1794.
WYKE HUNNICUTT, Clerk.

Stephen Butler and Mary, his wife, and their children, Huldah, William, James Stanton, Stephen and Jonathan, removed from Blackwater, in Surry County, 2-20-1796.
THOMAS PRETLOW, Clerk for the Day.
PATIENCE BAILY, Clerk.

Hanner Fisher removed from Goose Creek Monthly Meeting, in Bedford County, 2-3-1797.
MENTOR PIM PURDUE AND MARY ANTHONY, Clerks.

William Davis and Mary, his wife, and their minor children, Susannah, Elizabeth, Benjamin, Isaac, Polly, Nancy and Louisa, removed from Goose Creek, in Bedford County, 4-1-1797.
MENTOR PIM PURDUE AND MARY ANTHONY, Clerks.

William Hunnicutt removed from Blackwater, in Surry County, 4-15-1797.
WYKE HUNNICUTT, Clerk.

Thomas Maddox removed from Goose Creek, in Bedford County, 6-3-1797. MENTOR PIM PURDUE, Clerk.

Charles Pidgeon removed from Goose Creek, in Bedford County, 11-4-1797.

WILLIAM DAVIS, Clerk.

John Burgess and Drusilla, his wife, removed from Deer Creek, Maryland, 2-25-1798. JOHN COX AND SARAH ELY, Clerks.

Henry Davis removed from Goose Creek, in Bedford County, 4-7-1798.

WILLIAM DAVIS, Clerk.

William Davis removed from Goose Creek, in Bedford County, 6-1-1799.

JOHN DAVIS AND MARY ANTHONY, Clerks.

Sarah Davis removed from Goose Creek, in Bedford County, 10-4-1800.

JOHN DAVIS AND MARY ANTHONY, Clerks.

James Stanton removed from Blackwater, in Surry County, 9-18-1800.

WYKE HUNNICUTT, Clerk.

Thomas Bailey removed from Goose Creek, in Bedford County, 6-6-1801. JOHN DAVIS, Clerk.

Edward Terrell removed, with Jane, his wife, and their children, Elizabeth, Mary, Johnson, Judith, Christopher and Gerard, from Goose Creek, in Bedford County.

JOHN DAVIS AND MARY ANTHONY, Clerks.

Josiah Bailey removed from Upper Meeting, held at Gravelly Run, in Dinwiddie County, 5-22-1802.

JAMES HUNNICUTT, Clerk.

Hugh Morgan removed from Deer Creek, in Harford County, Maryland, 10-28-1802. ISAAC COLE, Clerk.

Micajah Terrell removed from Western Branch, Isle of Wight County, 11-26-1803. ROBERT JORDAN, Clerk.

William Stanton, his wife, Catharine, and children, Elizabeth, Phebe, Anna, Mahlon, Samuel and Rhoda, removed from Cane Creek, N. C., 2-4-1804.

SOLOMON DIXON AND DENAH HOBSON, Clerks.

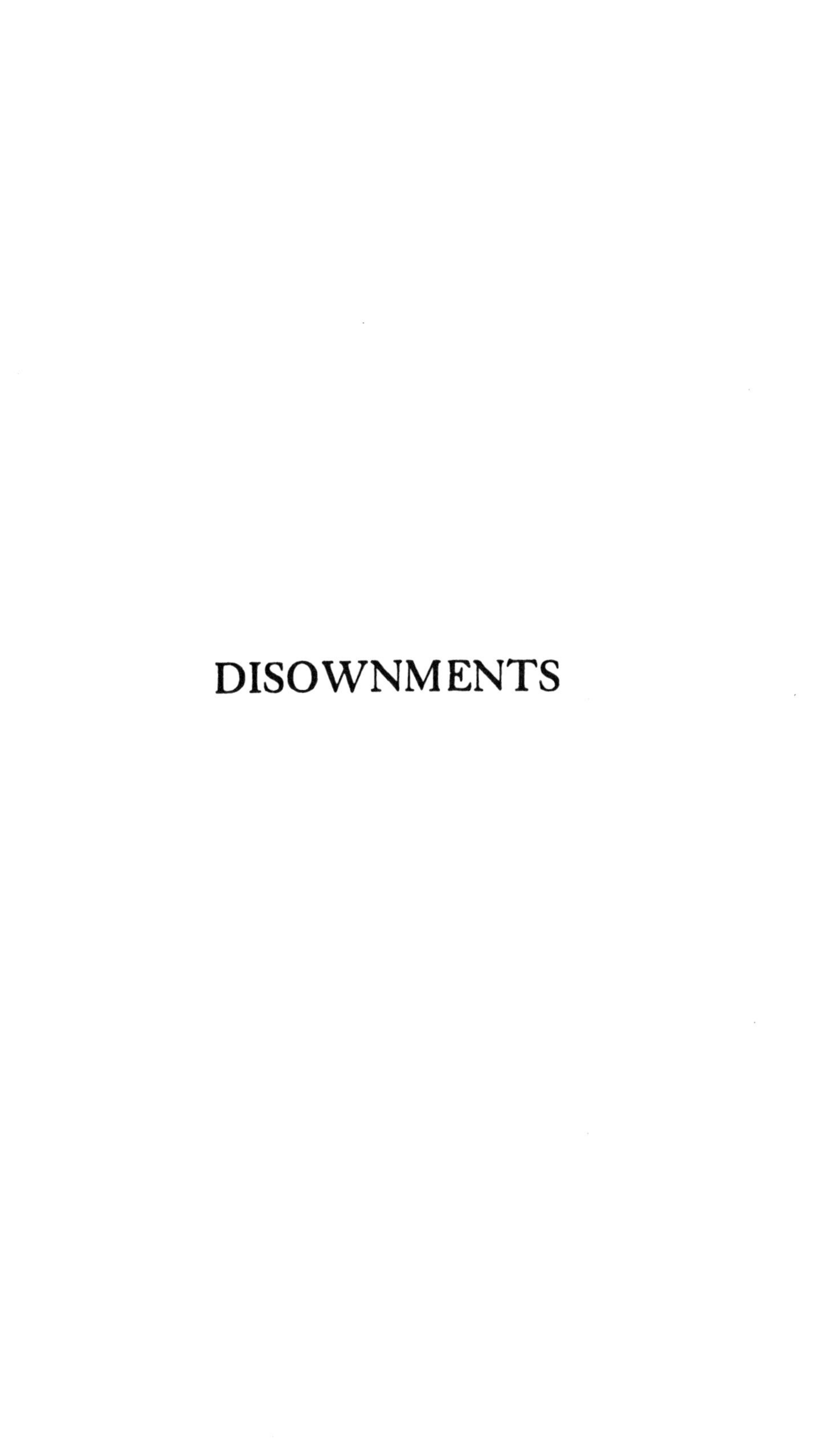

DISOWNMENTS

DISOWNMENTS.

James Crew was disowned by Cedar Creek Monthly Meeting of Friends, held Seventh month 8th, 1786, for selling one of his fellow men into bondage, and refusing to redeem him therefrom, and so far having given way unto a spirit of libertinism as to be concerned in gaming.

MICAJAH CREW, Clerk.

Sarah Crew, daughter of James Crew, was disowned the 9th day of the 5th month, 1789, for marrying one who was not a Friend, which was contrary to the Discipline.

MICAJAH CREW,
RACHEL MOORMAN,
Clerks.

Judith Crew, daughter of James Crew, was disowned the 9th of the 4th month, 1791, for marrying contrary to the Discipline.

MICAJAH CREW,
RACHEL MOORMAN,
Clerks.

Nicholas Crew was disowned for drunkenness and adultery while living in Hanover county; he removed to Campbell county, and some years later wrote a letter to Cedar Creek monthly meeting condemning his conduct and asking Friends to forgive him and to receive him into membership again. The following members of South River meeting wrote a letter to friends of Cedar Creek, testifying as to his good character since living among them, Wm. Davis, David Terrell, Micajah Davis and Richard Bloxom, and he was received again into membership Tenth month 8th, 1791.

MICAJAH CREW, Clerk.

William Crew, of Albemarle county, was disowned for using "ill words, fighting, etc.," the 10th day of 5th month, 1794.

M. CREW, Clerk

Whereas, Micajah Crew, Jr., son of Nicholas Crew, of Hanover county, has so far deviated from our known rules as to use spirituous liquors to excess, also has engaged in military services, for which conduct he has been dealt without the desired effect, and has subsequently entered into marriage contrary to the rules of our Discipline, we do, therefore, disown him from being any longer a member, until he shall make satisfaction for his conduct.

Signed in and on behalf of a monthly meeting of Friends held at Cedar Creek, in Hanover county, the 14th day of the 3rd month, 1807. BENJAMIN BATES, Clerk.

Nicholas Crew was again disowned for using spirituous liquors, and for neglecting to attend meetings for worship. Signed in and on behalf of Cedar Creek monthly meeting in Hanover county the 10th of the 4th month, 1813. LEMUEL CREW, Clerk.

Whereas, Deborah Crew, daughter of Micajah and Margaret Crew, having so far deviated from the known rules of Friends as to join in marriage with a man not of our religious society, we, therefore, disown her from being any longer a member of the same until she make satisfaction. Signed in and on behalf of a monthly meeting held at Cedar Creek the 14th of the 8th month, 1819.

LEMUEL CREW,
REBECCA HARRIS,
Clerks.

Walter Crew, son of Micajah and Margaret Crew, married contrary to the Discipline and was disowned by a monthly meeting held at Cedar Creek 4th month 8th, 1820. LEMUEL CREW, Clerk.

John Crew was disowned for using intoxicating liquors to excess at a monthly meeting held at Cedar Creek 4th month 11th, 1829.

At a monthly meeting held near Southriver the 21st of the 7th month, 1764 (Bedford county, Va.).

Whereas, John Hampton, a reputed member of our Society, the people called Quakers, has betaken himself to the vain fashions and ways of the world and entirely withdrawn himself from attending our meetings, rendering himself no ways agreeable to the rules of our Discipline, we do, therefore, testify against him and all his disorderly conduct and that we have no unity with such disorderly spirits, disowning him from being a member of our Society until it may please God to give him a place of repentance, which is our sincere desire. Signed in and on behalf of our meeting.

WILLIAM CANDLER, Clerk.

Robert Brooks disowned, 1-26-1766, for following the "corrupt ways of the world." W. C., Clerk.

John Candler disowned, 3-20-1767, for using "spirituous liquors."

Peter Holland disowned, 9-19-1767, for absenting himself from meetings for worship and Discipline and attending the Baptist church.

Charles Lynch disowned, 12-20-1767, for taking "solemn oaths."

John Caldwell disowned, 6-18-1768, for taking a wife contrary to the rule of the Discipline."

John Kerby and Joannah, his wife, disowned by request, 6-18-1768, for leaving their own meeting and worshiping with the Baptists. WILLIAM FERRELL, Clerk.

Micajah Clarke disowned, 10-21-1770, for "frequenting places of sport and gaming."

Mary Johnson disowned, 7-20-1771, for "marrying out from among Friends and by an hireling Priest."

Thomas Johnson disowned, 10-21-1771, for "following the vain fashions of the world." ZACHARIAH MOORMAN, Clerk.

Anne Moorman disowned, 4-18-1772, for "marrying out from among us and by a hireling Priest."

Zachariah Moorman disowned, 3-19-1774, for "being married by a hireling Priest."

Benjamin Terrell disowned, 5-8-1774, for "following the vain fashions and customs of the world."

Andrew and William Johnson disowned, 2-18-1775, for "joining with the vain customs of the world, such as horse racing and frequenting places of diversion." BYRUM BALLARD, Clerk.

Elizabeth Pagon (formerly Ferrell) disowned, 5-18-1776, for being married by a hireling Priest." SARAH GOODE, Clerk.

Elizabeth Johnson disowned, 5-16-1778, for marrying a near relative and being married by a hireling Priest.

JOHN LYNCH AND SARAH GOODE, Clerks.

Mary Baker (formerly Ferrell) disowned, 7-17-1779, for being married by a hireling Priest.

Milley Johnson (formerly Moorman) disowned, 920-1779, for the same cause.

Benjamin Johnson, Sr., disowned, 8-19-1780, for purchasing and receiving manumitted negroes. JOHN LYNCH, Clerk.

South River Meeting, Held in Campbell County.

Priscilla Goff (formerly Stanley) disowned, 2-15-1783, for marrying contrary to the rules of the Society.

Rachel Miller (formerly Johnson) disowned, 5-10-1785, for the same cause.

Rebeccah Ferrell disowned, 9-18-1784, for following the fashions and customs of the world.

JOHN LYNCH AND MARY ANTHONY, Clerks.

Moses Kendrick disowned, 8-18-1787, for purchasing a slave and also for retaining in bondage those that he had once liberated under his hand and seal.

Barzilla Barnard disowned, 12-20-1788, for fighting, swearing and drinking.

Charles Johnson, son of Benjamin Johnson, deceased, disowned, 7-17-1789, for fighting and using spirituous liquors.

Thomas Johnson (son of Christopher) disowned, 8-20-1791, for fighting, and spreading a report to the injury of his neighbor, also for marrying contrary to the rules of Friends.

Obediah Kerby disowned, 8-18-1792, for purchasing a slave and holding him in bondage.

Richard Tullis disowned, 12-15-1792, for retaining a negro in bondage.

Thomas Moorman, son of Zachariah, disowned, 12-15-1792, for holding a slave.

Thomas Watkins Johnson disowned, 3-21-1791, for being so far transported with passion as to utter some profane expressions.

Amos Ballard disowned, 5-10-1794, for fighting and laying a wager, etc.

Samuel Martin disowned, 12-20-1794, for the practice of gaming and for military exercises.

Samuel Jordan Harrison disowned, 8-16-1794, for joining the Free Masons and conforming to sundry practices used amongst them that are burthensome to Friends, such as marching in procession with music and weapons of war, and also in the uniform of an apron, etc.

Samuel Terrell disowned, 3-21-1795, for having allowed himself to be so transported with passion as to utter some very unbecoming speeches, and threatening expressions to the dishonor of our profession.

Samuel Moorman disowned, 3-21-1795, for holding a slave.

John Schoolfield and James Martin disowned, 8-8-1795, for enlisting in military service.

Thomas Johnson disowned, 10-6-1796, for drinking spirituous liquors.

ACHILLIS DOUGLASS, Clerk.

Gideon Lay, Jr., disowned, 4-8-1797, for enlisting himself as a soldier.

John Preston, Jr., disowned, 8-11-1798, for laying wagers and using profane language.

William Fowler disowned, 8-11-1798, for using profane language.

William Harrison disowned, 12-8-1798, for following the vain fashions of the world, making "bets" and using profane language.

Benjamin Bradford disowned, 9-14-1799, for attending and answering to his name at a military muster.

Moorman Johnson disowned, 10-13-1799, for being guilty of gaming, using profane language and attending places of diversion.

JOHN FISHER, JR.

John Bradfield disowned, 11-9-1799, for attending a meeting for military exercises and using profane language.

Betty Johnson (daughter of Charles Johnson) disowned, 12-14-1799, for dancing and attending places of diversion.

Benjamin Barnett disowned, 4-12-1800, being concerned in military services.

John Johnson, Jr., disowned, 1-9-1892, for using spirituous liquors to excess.

Samuel Johnson, son of Christopher, Jr., disowned, 4-10-1802, for using profane language and attending places of diversion.

Thomas Johnson, son of John, disowned, 12-11-1802, for taking strong drink to excess, offering to fight and hiring a slave.

Micajah Moorman, Jr., and Susanna Johnson were disowned, 3-12-1803, for marrying (they being first cousins), and for being married contrary to the rule of Friends.

John Fowler disowned, 7-9-1805, for ceasing to attend our religious meetings and for following the vain customs of the world, also using profane language.

Christopher Lynch disowned, 10-12-1805, for following the vain customs of the world and for hiring slaves.

William Johnson, Jr., disowned, 4-12-1806, for moving out of the State without endeavoring to settle with his creditors.

William Roberts disowned, 6-8-1816, for using intoxicating liquors to excess and for fighting.

Asa Wood disowned, 6-30-1821, for playing cards, taking oaths, attending places of diversion and joining the Masonic Society.

Samuel Fisher disowned, 8-12-1820, for disposing of a colored boy named James, who was entitled to his freedom, and he has since fallen into the hands of those who hold him as a slave, and said Samuel would not endeavor to restore James to his freedom, although Friends urged him to do so.

Gervas Johnson disowned, 5-8-1824, for accomplishing his marriage contrary to the rules of Friends.

Whereas, Rhoda Terrell, daughter of Thomas Terrell, of Caroline County, who had an education amongst us, hath, contrary to the good order used amongst Friends, joined in marriage to a man not of our Society; and having been repeatedly cautioned against it, we therefore disown the said Rhoda from being a member of our religious Society until she makes satisfaction. Signed in and on behalf of a Monthly Meeting of men and women Friends held at Cedar Creek in Hanover County the 8th of the 3rd month 1704.

MICAJAH CREW,
RACHEL MOORMAN,
Clerks.

Whereas, Jonathan Terrell, who had a right of membership in our religious Society, hath so far deviated from the principles we profess as to enter into marriage contrary to the rules of our Discipline, and endeavors to justify his conduct in so doing, we do therefore disown him from being a member of our Society until he make satisfaction. Signed in and on behalf of a Monthly Meeting held at Cedar Creek in Hanover County the 13th of the 6th month 1807.

BENJAMIN BATES, Clerk.

Whereas, Pleasant Terrell, son of Pleasant Terrell, deceased, late of Caroline County, who had a birthright amongst us, hath so far deviated from the known rules of our Discipline as to join himself in marriage with one not of our profession, we therefore disown him from being a member of our religious Society until he make satisfaction. Signed in and on behalf of a Monthly Meeting of Friends held at Cedar Creek in Hanover County the 8th day of the 7th month 1807. BENJAMIN BATES, Clerk.

Whereas, Robert Terrell, of Caroline County, who had a birthright with us, hath so far neglected his duty as a member of Society as to decline the attendance of our religious meetings and the observance of the rules of the Discipline of Friends generally, he having been dealt with without the desired effect, we do therefore disown him to be a member with us, until he condemns his conduct in these respects. Signed in and on behalf of a Monthly Meeting held at Cedar Creek in Hanover County the 12th of the 12th month 1807.

BENJAMIN BATES, Clerk.

Whereas, Jesse Terrell has been in the practice for some time of hiring slaves, and having been labored with, and tenderly advised with by Friends to decline a practice so contrary to the rules of our Discipline and the Divine precept which requires us to do to others as we would be done by; he hath, instead of complying therewith, further proceeded to the purchase of several. We therefore testify against such practices and hereby disown him, the said Jesse Terrell, from being a member of our religious Society until he condemn the said conduct to the satisfaction of Friends. Signed in and on behalf of a Monthly Meeting held at Cedar Creek in Hanover County the 14th day of the 4th month 1810.

BENJAMIN BATES, Clerk.

Whereas, John Terrell, of Caroline County, who had a birthright among Friends, hath so far deviated from our known rules as to join himself in marriage with a woman not of our religious profession, we do therefore disown him from being a member of our Society until he make satisfaction. Signed in and on behalf of a Monthly Meeting held at Cedar Creek in Hanover County the 10th day of the 11th month 1810.

BENJAMIN BATES, Clerk.

Whereas, Chiles Terrell, who had by birth a membership in Society with Friends, hath, contrary to our Discipline, joined in marriage with a woman not professing with us, we do therefore disown him from being a member until he make satisfaction. Signed in and on behalf of a Monthly Meeting of Friends held at Cedar Creek in Hanover County the 8th of the 12th month 1810.

BENJAMIN BATES, Clerk.

Whereas, Milley Terrell, who had a birthright among Friends, has so far deviated from the known rules as to join in marriage with a man not of our religious Society, we do therefore disown her from being a member of our society until she make satisfaction. Signed in and on behalf of a Monthly Meeting held at Cedar Creek in Hanover County the 9th day of the 3rd month 1811.

BENJAMIN BATES,
CHLOTILDA HARRIS,
Clerks.

Whereas, Caleb Terrell has, contrary to the known rules of the Society, engaged as an overseer of slaves, and been active in the performance of military services, and disregarding the advice of Friends still continues in the the practice, we do therefore disown the said Caleb Terrell from being a member of our religious Society, until he make satisfaction. Signed in and on behalf of a Monthly Meeting of Friends held at Cedar Creek in Hanover County the 10th of the 7th month 1813. LEMUEL CREW, Clerk.

Whereas, Matilda Terrell, of Caroline County, has so far deviated from the rules of our Society as to join in marriage with a person not of our profession, and having been visited and labored with in order to convince her of the error, without the desired effect, we therefore disown her from being any longer a member of our Society until she is disposed to make satisfaction. Signed in and on behalf of Cedar Creek Monthly Meeting held the 11th of the 5th month 1816.

LEMUEL CREW,
DEBORAH HARRIS,
Clerks.

Whereas, Rhoda Terrell (daughter of Jessie Terrell), who had a birthright amongst us, has so far deviated from the order and Discipline established among Friends as to become united in marriage with a man not of our religious Society, we therefore disown her from being a member of our Society until she make satisfaction. Signed in and on behalf of Cedar Creek Monthly Meeting held at Cedar Creek the 9th of the 5th month 1818.

LEMUEL CREW,
REBECCA HARRIS,
Clerks.

Whereas, George Terrell, who had a right of membership among Friends, but having so far deviated from their known rules as to marry a woman not of our Society, we do hereby disown him from being any longer a member of our Society, until he make satisfaction. Signed on behalf and by direction of a Monthly Meeting of Friends held at Cedar Creek in Hanover County the 12th day of the 7th month 1823. SAMUEL TERRELL, Clerk.

Whereas, Samuel Terrell (son of Jesse Terrell), of Caroline County, who had a right of membership amongst us, has so far deviated from the good order established by our discipline and the advice of Friends as to unite in marriage with a person not of our religious Society, we therefore disown him from being any longer a member of our Society until he shall make satisfaction. Signed by direction and on behalf of a Monthly Meeting of Friends held at Cedar Creek the 12th of the 5th month 1827.

JOSEPH J. PLEASANTS, Clerk.

Whereas, Kittie Terrell* (daughter of Lemuel and Rebecca Terrell), who had a birthright amongst us, has so far deviated from the known rules of Friends as to marry a man not professing with us, we therefore disown her from being any longer a member of our religious Society until she make satisfaction. Signed by direction and on behalf of Cedar Creek Monthly Meeting held the 11th of the 7th month 1829.

MICAJAH BATES,
TACY BATES,
Clerks.

* Catharine Pleasant Terrell (Kittie) married James Bell.

Whereas, Eliza Ann Terrell (daughter of Jesse Terrell, of Caroline County), who had a right of membership amongst us, has married contrary to the rules of our Society and the good order established among Friends, we therefore disown her from being any longer a member of our religious Society until she make satisfaction. Signed by direction and on behalf of a Monthly Meeting of Friends held at Cedar Creek in Hanover County the 12th day of the 6th month 1830.

JOSEPH J. PLEASANTS,
TACY C. BATES,
Clerks.

Whereas, Nicey L. Terrell* (daughter of Lemuel and Rebecca Terrell), who had a birthright among us, has so far deviated from the known rules of our Society as to marry a man not professing with us, we do therefore disown her from being any longer a member of our religious Society until she make satisfaction. Signed by order and on behalf of Cedar Creek Monthly Meeting held the 9th of the 4th month 1836.

WALTER CREW,
ANN CRENSHAW,
Clerks at This Time.

Whereas, Nancy Terrell,† who had a right of membership amongst us, has married contrary to the rules of our Discipline, we do therefore disown her from being any longer a member of our religious Society until she make satisfaction. Signed by direction of our Monthly Meeting of men and women Friends held at Cedar Creek in Hanover County the 14th day of the 2nd month 1835.

JOSEPH J. PLEASANTS,
TACY C. BATES,
Clerks.

Whereas, Joseph W. Terrell, who had a right of membership amongst us, has married contrary to the rules of our Discipline,

* Nicey L. Terrell married Joel Luck.
† Nancy married Liston Cobb.

we therefore disown him from being any longer a member of our religious Society until he make satisfaction. Signed by direction and on behalf of a Monthly Meeting of Friends held at Cedar Creek in Hanover County the 9th of the 5th month 1835.

WALTER CREW, Clerk at This Time.

Whereas, Robert S. Terrell,* who had a birthright amongst us, has so far deviated from the testimonies which we have deemed it our duty to bear as to engage in overseeing slaves, and having been visited by a committee of our meeting on the subject, has not only manifested no disposition to cease the practice, but has also informed the committe that he is in the habit of mustering, thereby manifesting that he has not the love and fear of God in his heart, we do therefore issue this our testimony against such practices and disown the said Robert S. Terrell from being a member of our religious Society until he makes satisfaction. And may the Lord in his mercy open his understanding to a sense of the evil of his ways and strengthen him to return to the Testimonies of Truth. Signed by direction and on behalf of the Monthly Meeting of Friends held at Cedar Creek in Hanover County the 11th day of the 7th month 1835.

JOSEPH J. PLEASANTS, Clerk.

Whereas, Edwin Terrell, who had a right of membership among us, has married contrary to the rules of our Society and the good order established among us by which he has forfeited his right, we do therefore disown him from being any longer a member of our religious Society until he shall make satisfaction. Signed by direction and on behalf of Cedar Creek Monthly Meeting held the 12th day of the 8th month 1843.

JOSEPH J. PLEASANTS, Clerk.

Whereas, Mary Ann Terrell (late Hunnicutt), who had a right of membership among us, has married contrary to the rules of our Society and the good order established among us, by which she has forfeited her right, we do therefore disown her from being any longer a member of our religious Society until she make satisfac-

* R. S. Terrell married Eliza Hargrave.

tion. Signed by direction and on behalf of Cedar Creek Monthly Meeting of Friends held the 12th day of the 8th month 1843.

JOSEPH J. PLEASANTS,
MARY BATES,
Clerks.

Whereas, Walter Terrell,* who has a right of membership with us, has married contrary to the Discipline of our Society, and having been visited by a committee of Salem Monthly Meeting of Iowa on our behalf, without manifesting any disposition to make acknowledgment for the same, we do therefore disown the said Walter Terrell from being any longer a member amongst us, until he make satisfaction. Signed by direction and on behalf of Cedar Creek Monthly Meeting of Friends held at Richmond the 14th day of the 7th month 1852. JOHN B. CRENSHAW, Clerk.

* Walter Terrell married M. Talitha Crew October, 1850. She died in 1853, and in 1854 he married her sister Jane. Talitha left one daughter, Mary T., now Mrs Euclid Saunders, of Iowa City, Iowa. Walter Terrell died January 30, 1887, and his wife Jane died in August, 1888.

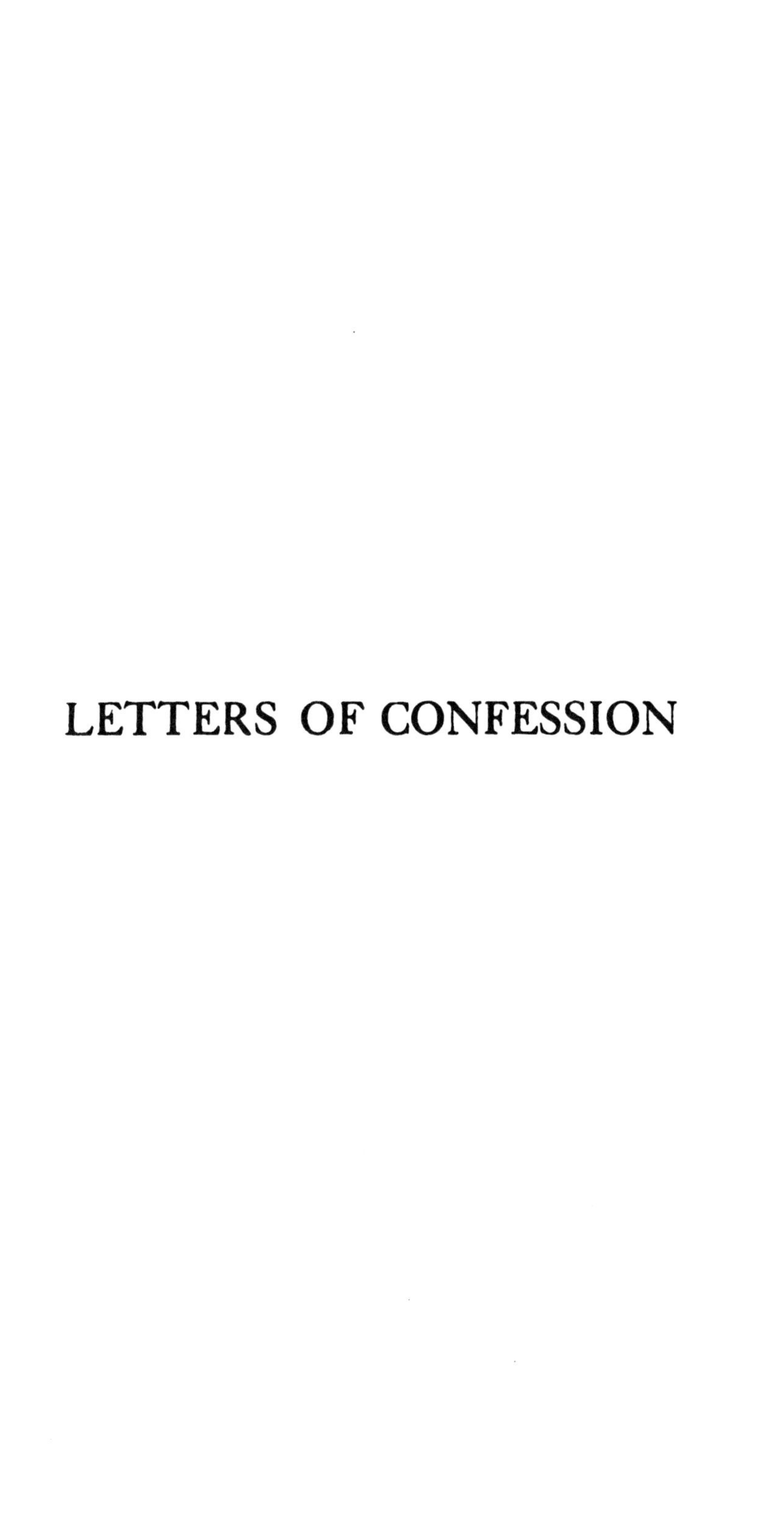

LETTERS OF CONFESSION

FRIENDS MEETING-HOUSE AT NEW GARDEN, N. C.—ERECTED IN 1701

LETTERS OF CONFESSION AND CONDEMNATION.

DEAR FRIENDS:

I having been a member of your Meeting, but going contrary to the good order and rules of Friends to be married by an hireling Priest, which practice I do fully condemn and am heartily sorry that I have been the cause of trouble and sorrow to Friends and greatly desire to be reunited to my friends, which I submit to the freedom of the meeting, 1-2-1778. RICHARD KERBY.

At a Monthly Meeting held at Cedar Creek the 14th of the 7th month, 1781, Moorman Johnson sent to this meeting condemning his outgoings in marriage, also a recommendation from some of the members of your meeting, where he has of late resided, on which he is reinstated into the Society and is recommended to the care of the Southriver Monthly Meeting. MOSES HARRIS, Clerk.

To the Monthly Meeting to be held 2-17-1787.

DEAR FRIENDS:

I have at some time past acted in a disorderly manner in fighting and thereby brought a scandal on Truth and a wound to my own mind, the practice I do utterly condemn myself in so doing, and if Friends will pass by my conduct in that respect, am in hopes through Divine assistance never to do the like again.

EDWARD TERRELL.

To the Monthly Meeting to be Held at Southriver 9-15-1787.

DEAR FRIENDS:

I have to acknowledge that being off the true watch I have given way to the spirit of resentment so far as to gratify that revengeful spirit by the putting forth mine own hand to the dishonor of Truth, which has been a matter of sorrow to me, and do sincerely condemn the same; and notwithstanding such conduct may justly deserve the censure of my friends, yet I have a hope and earnest desire remaining that I may be enabled through a watchful care and diligent attention to that principle of Light and Grace to surmount every difficulty that in future may be permitted to attend me. I therefore submit my case to the solid consideration of the Meeting, and remain your friend. JOHN LYNCH.

DEAR FRIENDS:

By birth having had a right of membership with you, I inconsiderately went out in marrying a near relative and thereby justly forfeited my right, which transgression the Father of Mercies hath been pleased to give me a sight and sense of, and it has been cause of sorrow and deep mourning to me in a particular manner that of marrying near relative, which lays with greater weight on me than any other part of my conduct, for which I was disowned; and, dear friends, I now freely and sincerely condemn all such practices as being out of the line of truth and contrary to good order, and desire to make such satisfaction that you may be easy with in receiving me again into membership, hoping, through Divine assistance, for the future to conduct myself to the satisfaction of Friends and the peace of my own mind. ELIZABETH JOHNSON.

10-8-1787.

DEAR FRIENDS:

Being suddenly overtaken with passion too unguardedly beat a man, which I am really sorry for, and do heartily condemn myself in so doing, and all such rash undue liberties, and believe if I had a little reflected I should have been preserved from such unbecoming conduct, and for your satisfaction can assure that it is my resolution to endeavor to conduct consistent with our profession for the future, and remain your very loving friend, etc. JOHN FOWLER.

6-20-1788.

DEAR FRIENDS:

Having gone out in marriage contrary to the good order amongst Friends, and having a sight and sense of my error, I do sincerely condemn the same and myself in so doing, and hope in future to conduct myself more circumspectly and agreeable to good order, and request that you may accept of this condemnation which I submit.

4-18-1789. WILLIAM TERRELL.

DEAR FRIENDS:

Having so far deviated from the peaceable principles professed by us as to suffer the spirit of anger and resentment so to prevail as to procure firearms for my safety, all which conduct I do condemn, hoping at the same time that my future conduct will evince the sincerity of this my acknowledgment. ENOCH ROBARTS.

6-20-1789.

DEAR FRIENDS:

Whereas I, the subscriber, having been so far off my watch as to be guilty of abusive conduct towards a neighbor of mine, and also using some unwary language, all which I see to be wrong and inconsistent with the peaceable principles we profess, and being sorry therefor, do condemn the same, desiring Friends to accept this my acknowledgment and continue me under their care as my future conduct shall render me worthy. Given under my hand this 16th day of the 7th month, 1789. GRIFFIN DOBBINS.

DEAR FRIENDS:

Having lately behaved myself in a very unbecoming manner to a Friend, both in words and action, which I am sorry for and do entirely condemn the same in myself and hope that in future my life and conduct will evidence the sincerity of my condemnation.

8-15-1789. WILLIAM BLOXOM.

DEAR FRIENDS:

I having married contrary to Discipline, for which I was justly disowned by you, and being lately measurably sensible of the disadvantage of such a separation, do therefore condemn my misconduct in that respect and desire to be reinstated to Friends again, and hope my future conduct will evidence the sincerity of this my acknowledgment. MILLEY JOHNSON.

9-17-1791.

DEAR FRIENDS:

I once had a right amongst you and knew not the worth of it, and by taking undue liberty and suffering myself to be married by an Hireling Minister, caused me to lose my right, which I found to be a great loss when it pleased the Lord to open my eyes and show me whereabouts I was. Therefore, like a returning prodigal, I make request to come under your care again JUDITH BROWN.

8-12-1792.

DEAR FRIENDS:

We acknowledge that we have deviated from the principles of Friends in kissing the Book, etc., which we were inadvertently drawn into not knowing the difference between an Oath and an Affirmation, which we are heartily sorry for, and if Friends can pass by this offence we hope in future to be more cautious how we commit such errors. TIMOTHY AND DAVID JOHNSON.

1-18-1794.

DEAR FRIENDS:

I acknowledge I was much to blame for fighting or seeking any revenge, which is inconsistent with what we profess, for which I have been very sorry for and blame myself for, and hope I shall endeavor to take care hereafter DAVID TERRELL, JR.

DEAR FRIENDS:

As I have been charged with beating and abusing a man, which I do confess that I suffered passion so far to prevail over me as to be guilty of the charge, for which I am sorry, and have been with the man and made him satisfaction for the same, and hope that if Friends can look over this my transgression that I may, through Divine assistance, be able for the future to govern myself in a better manner, and desire to subscribe myself. Your friend,

WM. JOHNSON, JR.

DEAR FRIENDS:

I hereby condemn my conduct in having been active in procuring a substitute to serve in the Militia, although by indirect means, also removed and left some accounts unsettled, all which has given trouble and uneasiness to Friends, which I have been made sensible of and sorry for. Hoping my future conduct may be more consistent, I desire Friends may accept this my acknowledgment and continue me under their care. WILLIAM BETTS.

1-15-1798.

DEAR FRIENDS:

Whereas I have so far deviated from the rules of good order which we profess as to be guilty of drinking strong drink to excess, I hereby give this as my humble acknowledgment that I am truly sorry for it and do condemn myself in so doing, and request my Friends to pass by this my offense, and hope my future conduct will render me more worthy. WILLIAM STANTON.

9-3-1799.

ESTEEMED FRIENDS:

Whereas I stand justly disowned for marrying contrary to Discipline, and now being sensible of my error, I do sincerely condemn the same, with desires to be reinstated. If Friends can accept this, I hope my future conduct will evidence the sincerity of the same.

8-11-1799. BETTY TIMBERLAKE.

Betsy Neelý, of Halifax County, condemned her conduct in marrying out and asked to be reinstated 4-5-1801.

Susanna Johnson made a similar confession and request 8-8-1801.

Aaron Stanton condemned his conduct in having accomplished his marriage contrary to Discipline, 5-11-1805.

DEAR FRIENDS:

I have done amiss in hiring a slave, for which I am sorry and condemn the practice, and have set her at liberty until her year is up, and if Friends will look over my misconduct I hope to be more careful for the future. MOORMAN JOHNSON.

11-9-1805.

Micajah Johnson condemns his conduct in having been married by a "hire-teacher," 8-9-1805.

William Johnson, 9-12-1812, condemns his conduct for having been married "in the ways of the world."

Garland Johnson, 2-13-1813, condemns having accomplished his marriage "contrary to the known Rules and Discipline of Friends."

Mildred Tyree, 3-14-1818, condemns "having deviated so far as to marry contrary to the Rules of Friends."

DEAR FRIENDS:

The act of fighting of which I have been guilty has often caused me to feel regret on account of its repugnance to the principles of the Society in which I have been raised and in which it is my desire to remain, and I trust that Friends will judge of my case in the spirit of forbearance. ACHILLIS D. JOHNSON.

4-7-1829.

APPENDIX

APPENDIX I.

HISTORICAL SYNOPSIS.

CHAPTER I.

THE ORIGIN OF QUAKERISM.

From volume entitled "Southern Quakers and Slavery."

The Quakers were the radicals of the Protestant Reformation, and, although they were in existence before the days of George Fox, yet to the latter is due the fact that he first put himself in the front of the movement and became its founder. Hence a history of this kind would be incomplete without some account of him.

The founder of the Society of Friends was George Fox (1624-1691). He was born at Drayton in the Clay, in Leicestershire, England, in July, 1624. His father was a Puritan weaver, and the son, originally intended for the Church, was apprenticed to a shoemaker and dealer in wool. At a very early age Fox had "a gravity and stayedness of mind and spirit not usual in children," and when he was eleven "knew pureness and righteousness." In 1643 "I left my relations, and broke off all familiarity or fellowship with young or old." For the next few years he was in spiritual darkness and groped after the light. He met with struggles, and temptations, with buffets and jeers, but the work of the Lord went forward, and many were turned from darkness to light by his labors.

He dates the beginnings of his Society from Leicestershire in 1644. The course of Quakerism was at first toward the north of England. It appeared in Warwickshire in 1645; in Nottinghamshire in 1646; in Derby, 1647; in the adjacent counties in 1648, 1649 and 1650. It reached Yorkshire in 1651; Lancaster and Westmoreland, 1652; Cumberland, Durham and Northumberland, 1653; London and most other parts of England, Scotland and Ireland in 1654. In 1655 Friends went beyond sea "where truth also sprang up," and in 1656 "it broke forth in America and many other places."

Fox was unremittent in his missionary labors, and traveled over England, Scotland, Wales and Ireland. He visited the West Indies and North America. He went twice into Holland. His first imprisonment was at Nottingham in 1649. It was a strange thing then to be in prison for religion, and some thought him mad because he "stood for purity, righteousness and perfection," but the simplicity, the earnestness, the devotion, and the practical nature of this system when contrasted with the dry husk of Episcopacy and the jangling creeds of the Dissenters soon won him adherents by the thousands. They came mostly from the lower ranks of society, but from all sects.

Quakerism is distinctively the creed of the seventeenth century. Seekers were in revolt against the established order. It gave these seekers what they were seeking for. In theology it was un-Puritan; but in cultus, forms and modes it was more than Puritan. The Quaker was the Puritan of the Puritans. He was an extremist, and this brought him into conflict with the established order. He believed that Quakerism was primitive Christianity revived. He recognized no distinction between the clergy and laity; he refused to swear, for Christ had said, swear not at all; he refused to fight, for the religion of Christ is a religion of love, not of war; he would pay no tithes, for Christ had said, ye have freely received, freely give; he called no man master, for he thought the terms rabbi, your holiness and right reverend connoted the same idea. He rejected the dogmas of water baptism and the Puritan Sabbath, and in addition to these claimed that inspiration is not limited to the writers of the Old and New Testaments, but is the gift of Jehovah to all men who will accept it, and to interpret the Scriptures men must be guided by the Spirit that guided its authors. Here was the cardinal doctrine of their creed and the point where they differed radically from other Dissenters. Add to this the doctrine of the *Inner Light,* the heavenly guide given directly to inform or illuminate the individual conscience, and we have the corner-stones of their system.

His success at first was not rapid, but sure. Even the name "Quaker," like that of "Methodist," was given in derision. The Society of Friends is their true appellation. But as our object in the publication of this book is mainly to confine ourselves to matters which touch Quakerism in Virginia and a few adjacent states, we cannot trespass upon our limits in regard to its illustrious founder by giving an account of his European career, but must confine it to North America. It may seem singular that there are not a few well-read people who do not even know that George Fox was a visitor to the "North American Plantations," as this country was called. He came over in the year 1672, and the volume from which we quote has this to say of his travels and labors here.

We left George Fox going over to the Eastern Shore. In a day or two he set out for New England. He labored there, then returned to Maryland, held meetings on both sides of the Bay, and on the fifth of November set sail for Virginia from Patuxent River. In three days they came to Nancemund (Nansemond). Fox reached it by going down Patuxent River, down Chesapeake Bay and up Nansemond River. Here a great meeting was held. To this meeting came one Col. Dewes, "with several officers and magistrates, who were much taken with the declaration of truth." Then Fox "hastened towards Carolina; yet had several meetings by the way, wherein we had good service for the Lord: one about four miles from Nancemum water, which was very precious; and there was a men's and a women's meeting settled, for the affairs of the church. Another very good meeting we had at William Yarrow's, at Pagan Creek, which was so large that we were fain to be abroad, the house not being big enough to contain the people. A great openness there was, the sound of truth spread abroad, and had a good favor in the hearts of people: the Lord have the glory forever!"

"After this," Fox continues, "our way to Carolina grew worse, being much of it plashy, and pretty full of great bogs and swamps; so that we were commonly wet to the knees, and lay abroad a-nights in the woods by a fire: saving one of the nights we got to a poor house at Summertown [Somerton], and lay by the fire." The whole of this itinerary can be traced pretty clearly; coming down the Chesapeake and sailing up Nansemond River, as we have seen, Fox and his companions, Robert Widders, James Lancaster and George Pattison, probably took horse before they reached the Widow Wright's. They entered North Carolina by way of Somerton, Va., and went by canoe down Bennett's Creek, called by Fox Bonner's Creek, into "Macocomocock river," which is doubtless the modern Chowan, to the house of Hugh Smith, "where people of other professions came to see us (no Friends inhabiting that part of the country)." This house was probably situate in the western part of the present county of Chowan. "Then passing down the river Maratick in a canoe, we went down the bay Connie-oak [Edenton] to a captains who was loving to us and lent us his boat (for we were much wetted in the canoe, the water plashing in upon us). With this boat we went to the governor's; but the water in some places was so shallow, that the boat, being loaded, could not swim; so that we put off our shoes and stockings, and waded through the water a pretty way." The Governor's residence was probably near Edenton. Fox says he and his wife received them "lovingly," but they found a sceptic in the person of a certain doctor, who "would needs dispute with us," declaring that the light and the spirit of God were not in the Indians, and who "ran out so far that at length he would not own the Scriptures."

"We tarried at the Governor's that night; and next morning he very courteously walked with us about two miles through the woods, to a place whither he had sent our boat about to meet us. Taking leave of him, we entered our boat and went about thirty miles to Joseph Scot's, one of the representatives of the country [probably in Perquimans, near Pasquotank County]. There we had a sound, precious meeting; the people were tender, and much desired after meetings. Wherefore at an house about four miles further, we had another meeting; to which the Governor's secretary came, who was chief secretary of the province, and had been formerly convinced."

Fox also went among the Indians and spoke to them by an interpreter, and "having visited the north part of Carolina, and made a little entrance for the truth among the people there, we began to return again towards Virginia, having several meetings in our way, wherein we had good service for the Lord, the people being generally tender and open. . . . In our return we had a very precious meeting at Hugh Smith's . . . . the people were very tender, and very good service we had amongst them. . . . The ninth of the tenth month we got back to Bonner's Creek . . . . having spent about eighteen days in the north of Carolina.

"Our horses having rested, we set forward for Virginia again, traveling through the woods and bogs as far as we could well reach that day, and at night lay by a fire in the woods. Next day we had a tedious journey through bogs and swamps, and were exceedingly wet and dirty all the day, but dried ourselves at night by a fire. We got that night to Sommertown. . . . Here we lay in our clothes by the fire as we had done many a night before. Next day we had a meeting; for the people . . . . had a great desire to hear us; and a very good meeting we had among them, where we never had one before." After traveling about a hundred miles from Carolina into Virginia they were again among Friends. They spent about three weeks in Virginia, mostly among Friends. They had large and precious meetings. At the Widow Wright's "many of the magistrates, officers and other high people came. A most heavenly meeting we had; wherein the power of the Lord was so great, that it struck a dread upon the assembly, chained all down, and brought reverence upon the people's minds." The parish priest threatened to interfere, "but the Lord's power . . . . stopped him . . . . The people were wonderfully affected with the testimony of truth. . . . Another very good meeting we had at Crickatrough, at which many considerable people were, who had never heard a Friend before; and they were greatly satisfied, praised be the Lord! We had also a very good and serviceable meeting at John Porter's which consisted mostly of other people, in which the power of the Lord was gloriously seen and felt, and it brought the truth over all the bad walkers and talkers; blessed be the Lord!"

During the last week of his stay Fox spent time and pains correcting evils that had come into the Society and in "working down a bad spirit that was got up in some," and then, "having finished what service lay upon us at Virginia, the thirtieth of the tenth month [30 December, 1672] we set sail in an open sloop for Maryland."

Thus ended the only visit of George Fox to Virginia and Carolina. It was his good fortune to see his Society organized and prospering in each. In Virginia the number of Friends was more than doubled by his preaching, while "a large convincement" was upon many others who had not yet professed. The connection between these bodies and the English societies was close. An exchange of letters began. Fox sent copies of Edward Burrough's *Words* to Col. Thomas Dewes at Nansemond; to Major-General Bennett; to Lieutenant-Colonel Waters, in Accomack; to Justice Jordan, near Accomack, in Potomac; to the Governor of Carolina, and others. There was soon, no doubt, some sort of union between the meetings in Virginia and Carolina, but this has not been at any time an organic one, for the Quakers of North Carolina steadily fought against the idea of being absorbed by their Virginia neighbors. There has always been unity of thought and feeling between the Society in the two States and their history is one.

QUAKERISM IN VIRGINIA.

As the existence of Quakerism in Virginia on an extensive scale, prior to and long after the American Revolution, admits of no dispute an account of its introduction in Virginia and other Southern States is eminently demanded. The record shows that Massachusetts was the first American colony in which Quakerism was preached. The second seems to have been Virginia, although there is little difference in the time of its appearance in this colony and in Maryland. The person to plant the standard of Quakerism in the South was Elizabeth Harris, a native of London. Of her personal history we know little. She entered Virginia in 1656, and arrived in England on her return about July, 1657, "in a pretty condition." Bowden says "her religious labors were blessed to many in that province, who were sincere seekers after heavenly riches, and she was instrumental in convincing many of the primitive and spiritual views of the Christian religion professed by Friends."

We may say that, Virginia was first settled by the English, May 13, 1607. Under the preaching of an English woman, Elizabeth Harris, in 1656, the first Friends' meetings were established. Friends were no more welcome here than among their brother Englishmen in Massachusetts. The current extravagant stories concerning them were believed, and they were evidently thought to be a very dangerous class of people. In 1660, Virginia enacted the following law concerning them: "Whereas, there is an unreasonable and turbulent sort of people commonly called Quakers, who, contrary to law, daily gather unto themselves unlawful assemblies and congregations of the people. . . . It is enacted that no master or commander of a ship or other vessel do bring into this colony any person or persons called Quakers, under the penalty of one hundred pounds sterling, to be levied upon him and his estates by order of the governor and council or the commissions in the several counties where such ships shall arrive; that all such Quakers as have been questioned, or shall hereafter arrive, shall be apprehended wherever they shall be found, and they be imprisoned, without bail or mainprise, till they do abjure this country, or put in security with all speed to depart this colony and not return again. And if any should dare to presume to return hither after such departure, to be proceeded against as contemners of the laws and magistracy, and punished accordingly and caused again to depart the country, and if they should the third time be so audacious and impudent, they are to be proceeded against as follows: That no person shall entertain any of the Quakers who have heretofore been questioned by the governor and council, or which shall hereafter be questioned, nor permit in or near his house any assembly of the Quakers, under penalty of one hundred pounds sterling; that commissioners and officers are hereby required and authorized, as they will answer the contrary at their peril, to take notice of this act, to see it fully effected and executed, and that no person do presume on their peril to dispose of or publish their books, pamphlets, or libels bearing the title of their tenets and opinions."

In the early settlement of Virginia, Friends as well as others took up large tracts of land, and many of them settled near where Richmond, Winchester and Norfolk now are. Tradition tells us of one who took up 40,000 acres of land, another 4,000. We hear of one Pleasants, who owned many slaves, and was determined to have one thousand. At one time he held nine hundred and ninety-nine, but he failed to reach the full thousand before the Friends of Virginia decided that it was unrighteous to hold their fellow-men in bondage. By this decision he was very much annoyed. A committee went to visit him on account of his slave-owning, but he would not leave his field to meet them, so they waited patiently until he came to dinner. He then had their horses put in the stable and invited them to dine with him with true Friendly hospitality. But when dinner was over, he wished to hasten back to the field with his sable farm hands. The committee finally induced him to tarry for a season of waiting before the Lord. For some time they sat in silence, and then arose, saying if he would have their horses brought they would now proceed on their way. They departed without once mentioning the object of their visit; but he knew for what they came and was obliged to think about it. When upon his bed that night he said he dreamed that he died and was about to pass through the gateway of heaven, when a little darkey lad closed the gate, and he was not allowed to enter. He said he did not intend to be kept out of heaven by the darkeys, so the next morning he summoned the blacks and told them they were all free from that day. He arranged for those who wished to remain with him to work for wages, and said that with about half the number of servants his business was more profitable than before.

By the year 1817, all Friends in Virginia had freed their slaves. As in North Carolina, so in Virginia, the principles of Friends, for some time before the late Civil War, were so at variance with the prevailing sentiment around them that most of them moved West, so that at the time the war began, there were in the State only a few small remnants of meetings that met to worship God after the manner of Friends. One of these small meetings was in the vicinity of Winchester, which city has been made famous as the centre of important military operations during the Revolution as well as during the Civil War.

From the above it will be seen that while Virginia is second to Massachusetts as to the advent of Quakerism, there is no dispute as to the date in which the Old Dominion first heard the gospel as propounded by the good people nor the name of the good woman who did so. It may be noted that no allusion is made to the erection of any church building, although there were many converts. In all probability, as the Quakers were then under the ban, they held their meetings in private houses of Friends.

As to the antiquity of claimants as to first churches, we find on page 23 of the volume from which we just quoted the following:

Again, on the 12th of November, 1663, Hill found another Quaker meeting at the residence of Richard Russell, and summoned some 35 persons, including John Porter, Sr., and John Porter, Jr., to court. Ten days later Hill discovered a Quaker meeting on the ship Blissing, at anchor in the southern branch of Elizabeth river, and summoned John Porter, Jr., who was speaking; James Gilbert, master of the ship; Mrs. Mary Emperor, and others, to court. December 15 they were fined 200 pounds of tobacco each, this being their first trial. On the same day others were fined 50 pounds each for absenting themselves from public worship, and the grand jury presented John Porter, Jr., and Mrs. Mary Emperor and others for attending a meeting on that day at the house of Mrs. Emperor. The trial for the offense of November 12 occurred on February 14 following. John Porter, Jr., and Mrs. Mary Emperor were fined 500 pounds of tobacco each, for it was their second offense; Richard Russell was fined 5,000 pounds of tobacco for permitting the meeting to be held at his house, and the others were fined 200 pounds of tobacco each, as it was their first offense. The trial tor the meeting held at the house of Mrs. Emperor on December 15 also came off then. Mrs. Emperor and John Porter, Jr., were ordered to be sent out of the colony, it being their third correction. Ann Godby was fined 500 pounds of tobacco, it being her second correction, and others were fined 200 pounds, as it was their first. The sentence of transportation passed against Porter and Mrs. Emperor was not carried out. They were persons of influence in the county, and as there was no profit to the informer in their transportation the sentence was probably allowed to die of itself. Hill's term as sheriff expired in 1664, and there was no further persecution of Quakers in this county until 1675.

If we accept this account in its ecclesiastical sense then we may say that the Quaker Church was established in Virginia in the year 1662. Coming directly to the building of Meeting-Houses in Virginia the first one recorded was Buffkin's, on the east or Virginia side of Nansemond River. This house was 20x20, the inside was ceiled, and the floor was laid with planks and was fitted with pews and seats. It cost 3688 pounds of tobacco, of which the main contributors were John Murdah, 530 pounds; Robert Jordan, 580 pounds; Ben Small, 520; John Porter, 500 pounds, and John Hollowell, 350. Another house, 25x20, was built on the west branch of Nansemond in 1692, and so important was the question of *nails* that it was recorded that Francis Bridle gave them. They were all hand-made, or, as we say, "wrought nails." There were meeting-houses in Virginia before this, no doubt, but we have no record of them. Among the names recorded we find the following: Pleasants, Terrell, Howard, Woodson, Watkins, Porter, Ellyson, Jordan, Binford, Cate, Hunnicutt, Crew, Clarke, Munford and many others, which figure largely on the roll of Cedar Creek, Golansville and other churches. If you add to this list a few other names that we find more frequently in the eastern counties, such as Ricks, it will be seen that many of their descendants are prominent to-day.

Continuing the Virginia record, we find that the Quakers, after having gained a footing in eastern Virginia, branched out and established meetings in Loudoun and Frederick Counties, but whether they had Meeting-Houses as such or met at private houses the record at this early date does not state. It may be noted, however, that the meeting in east Virginia, although the oldest, were the first to decline, Quakers having entirely disappeared from Norfolk County before 1700.

CHAPTER II.

QUAKERISM IN NORTH AND SOUTH CAROLINA.

When Quakerism was thus expanding toward the west in Virginia, a similar but independent movement was going on in North Carolina toward the south. The first Quaker counties of North Carolina were Perquimans and Pasquotank. Here it was planted by Edmundson and Fox in 1672. Migrations from these original seats of the faith began as early as 1703. The movement crossed Albemarle Sound and went south. By the middle of the century there were Quakers in Hyde, Beaufort, Craven, Carteret, Jones, Bladen and Lenoir counties. They probably had meetings for worship in all of these counties.

In Carteret county, Core Sound Monthly Meeting was set up in 1733. It was probably the oldest in the section and its records have been preserved. In 1747 Quakers in Carteret were strong enough to send one of their number to the Assembly. But in 1771 Core Sound Monthly Meeting was small, for it seems that most of its members had moved farther into the interior of the State. At the end of the last century the principal families of Quakers in the meeting bore the names of Stanton, Williams, Harris, Brown, Howard, Mace, Thomas, Davis, Arnold, Hollowell, Horn, Overman, Dew, Bogue, Bishop, Bundy, Borden, Parker, Chadwick, Hellen, Scott, Physioc, and Cartright.

In 1748 we find mention of a monthly meeting on Falling Creek, then in Dobbs, now in Lenoir county. This monthly meeting was probably not far from the present town of Kinston, and continued here until January 6, 1772, when it was the judgment of Friends that, since most of the Friends about the Meeting-House on Lower Falling Creek had died or had moved away, the monthly meeting should be held at Richard Coxe's, near Upper Falling Creek. In July, 1772, it was said that Friends had settled on several branches of Contentnea Creek, and as they were distant from meeting, it was agreed to put a first day's meeting at Arthur Bryant's, and "at a monthly meeting held at Great Contentney, the 12th of the 9th mo., 1772," it was also agreed that the monthly meeting should be transferred to Arthur Bryant's. From this time the Falling Creek Monthly Meeting disappears and Great Contentnea takes its place. It was at the time of its organization farther from the sea-coast than any other monthly meeting in North Carolina. It was known later as Contentnea Monthly Meeting. We find among its members in the eighteenth century the following names: Beeman, Overman, Bogue, Hollowell, Cox, Pike, Pearson, Hall, Mayo, Wooten, Edgerton, Arnold, Copeland, Bundy, Morris, Doudna, and Outland. From these names we are led to infer that connection with the meetings in Carteret County to the east and Northampton county on the north was close.

Perhaps we can illustrate the expansion of Quakerism in eastern Virginia and eastern North Carolina in no better way than by quoting the journal of William Reckitt, who visited these meetings in 1756-57. He says of the meetings in Virginia: "I visited all the little handfuls scattered up and down in these parts, and often had service in families. I met with Samuel Spavold, who likewise was much engaged in the service of truth. His labor of love in the work of the gospel was indeed great in this part of the world; those of other societies being much reached by his ministry."

Reckitt then set forward to North Carolina; held meetings at Piney Woods, Wells, Old Neck, and Little River, all in Perquimans county; lodged with Thomas Nicholson, the author; probably did not go into Pasquotank county, but turned to the west, accompanied by Joshua Fletcher and Francis Nixon. He says, "I then set forward towards a wilderness country, where the inhabitants were very thin. . . . . Our first meeting after we left Perquimans was at John Coupeland's. . . . There were but few friends, but people of other societies came in, who had notice; amongst whom was an officer of the army . . . ." The first established meeting they reached was at Fort River (Roanoke?), "where a meeting had been recently settled, of such as had been convinced." They then came to Henry Horn's in Edgecombe county, who had been convinced from among the Baptists, for the inhabitants of this section belonged principally to that faith; then they came to a small meeting at Neuse in Wayne county, and then ninety miles to the meeting at Core Sound. The destination of Reckitt was to the Friends in South Carolina. "The first meeting we had after we left Core Sound, was at Permeanus Hauton's who gave us an invitation to his house, and sent to give notice to his neighbors, though some lived several miles distant. We got to his house about the time the meeting was appointed, where we found seats placed, and every thing in such convenient order for a meeting, as I thought I had seldom seen. His rooms being little, he had placed seats in his court yard, and under the windows, that I believe all could sit and hear without the least troubling one another; and indeed I thought his labor and good inclination were blessed, for a solid time it was, and I found openness to declare the truth amongst them. . . . We staid one night at Wilmington, the capital town in North Carolina; but it being their general court time and the privateers having brought in prizes, the people's minds were in great commotions, so that I could find no room nor freedom to have a meeting, though several called Quakers lived there, but held no meeting, except when strangers came." They crossed a branch of Cape Fear River and then went to Carver's Creek. "Here was a small gathering of Friends. We staid their first day meeting over, and then went to Dan's [Dunn's] Creek, where we found another gathering of such as call themselves Friends, but had been much hurt, and scattered in their minds from the true shepherd, by an enemy that had sown tares."

We find Quakerism planted in South Carolina in much the same manner as it was in North Carolina, but inasmuch as letters written from the scene are more interesting than a dry historical record, we will quote a letter written by Samuel Fothergill, a missionary from Charleston, S. C., February 13th, 1755. He says:

"Since I wrote you from Waynoak, [Va.], I have visited all the residue of Virginia and North Carolina, and last night arrived here, and have had a meeting here this day, amongst a poor miserable handful of professors, and believe I must visit all their families before I can easily leave this place. I expect to be in Georgia, 150 miles south of this place, sometime next week, and then return northwards, 800 miles, upon a line, without much stop, except seven meetings which I left as I came southwards.

"On the 2d instant, after a ride of fifty miles, we were obliged to lie in the woods all night.

"I have this day had a large, good meeting, to my satisfaction; but the meeting house being small was inconvenient. Most of the principal inhabitants attended, and I expect the use of the Baptist meeting house on first day evening, to take leave of the inhabitants of this place, who have given general instances of their regard.

"George Whitfield passed through this town a few days ago, to

Georgia, having travelled very hard from Philadelphia, to get to his flock before we came amongst them.

"The state of the church is generally low, and exceedingly so in this place; there is very little of the form, and much less of the power, of truth amongst them. My heart has been bowed into strong concern, and close labor for and with them, and hope for some little reviving of secret care in particular; but alas, many seem awakened for a time, and sink afresh into lukewarmness." In the same letter he says: "I have now been to the extent of my visit southward, being 120 miles further than any Friend hath travelled on religious account, and am setting my face northward. I propose another public meeting in this place to-morrow, and then to leave." He was also invited to visit the Sea Islands, and expected to do it, but "found a prohibition." These people seemed "desirous the testimony should be exalted by others, but won't lend a hand. . . . . When we left Charleston we had near 450 miles to ride to the next settlement of Friends, through a country little inhabited, and in which accommodations were scarce enough, though we made shift to get into some cabin or other at nights, but had not my clothes off for several nights successively, or any things at times to lie down upon but a bear skin or boards."

It will be of interest to us to see the names of some of the persons who were the leaders in this extensive migration, for their children became prominent in the Society in North Carolina, and their grandchildren went to the West and became equally prominent there. From Warrington Monthly Meeting, Pa., there were twenty-three arrivals; among them were Isaac and Peter Cox, Peter Nathan and Zacharias Dicks, Isaac Pidgen, John Beeson, Joseph Ozburn, Isaac Jones, Jacob and Abram Elliott, Thomas Kendall, William Reynolds, James and Aaron Frazer. Eight came from Bradford Monthly Meeting; among them were Ebenezer Worth, Phineas, John and Richard Mendenhall; while another Richard Mendenhall, William Reynolds, and Thomas Dennis, Jr., came from New Garden, Pa.; eleven came from Cedar Creek Monthly Meeting, Va., including Philip Hoggatt, William and Zachariah Stanley, Robert, John and William Johnson; eight from Caroline Monthly Meeting, Joseph Hoggatt, Stringman and Nathan Stanley, Talton and James Johnson; eight from Hopewell and six from Fairfax; from Hopewell came Richard, Isaac, Nathaniel and John Beeson,

Benjamin Brittain, John Beals, James Langley, Joseph Hiatt; from the neighboring Fairfax came George Hiatt, William Kersey, Micajah Stanley, William Ballinger; Joseph Unthank and family came from Richland, Bucks county, Pa.; James Brown, James Johnson came from East Nottingham, then in Pennsylvania, now in Maryland. The westward movement from the eastern North Carolina meetings was begun from Perquimans Monthly meeting by Henry, Jacob and Joseph Lamb, who came up in 1760, and thus set in motion a movement that was to attain large proportions fifty years later.

The names given in the above lists do not represent all the Quaker settlers who came to central North Carolina between 1751 and 1770, it gives only representatives of certain families that have since attained considerable distinction in the section and who first made this and the surrounding Quaker settlements a success. They represented some of the oldest and best Quaker families in Pennsylvania. The New Garden settlers were soon reinforced by other immigrants who also came from old Quaker stock. These were the settlers from Nantucket Island, Mass. This movement began in 1771, and Libni Coffin was the first Nantucket man to arrive at New Garden.

We get some particulars from the life of Elijah Coffin: "The island of Nantucket being small, and its soil not very productive, a large number of people could not be supported thereupon. . . . The population of the island still increasing, many of the citizens turned their attention to other parts, and were induced to remove and settle elsewhere, with a view to better their condition as to provide for their children, etc. A while before the Revolutionary war, a considerable colony of Friends removed and settled at New Garden, in Guilford county, North Carolina, which was then a newly settled country. My grandfather [William] Coffin [1720-1803] was one of the number that thus removed. His removal took place, I believe, in the year 1773." Again, Obed Macy, writing of the period about 1760, says that because of the failure of the whale fishery some went to New Garden, N. C., others to Nova Scotia and Kennebec: "Very few of whom benefited themselves, and some, after a few years' stay, returned." Again, about the outbreak of the Revolution, because of the derangement of their business by the war, others went to New York and North Carolina.

THE STOPPAGE OF SOUTHERN MIGRATION.

In 1780 two-thirds of the inhabitants of Nantucket were Quakers. We find among their leaders the Coffins, Starbucks, Folgers, Barnards and Husseys. Some of these became leaders in the Carolina migration, which was particularly large, 1771-75. During this period of five years there were no less than forty-one certificates recorded at New Garden Monthly Meeting from Nantucket out of a total of fifty certificates received. In this number there were eleven families, and it included many families that have since been prominent in that section of the State. We find among these immigrants Libni Coffin, William (Jr.), William, Barnabas, Seth (and wife), Samuel (and family), Peter and Joseph Coffin; Jethro Macy, David, Enoch, Nathaniel, Paul (and family), Matthew (and five children) and Joseph Macy; William, Gayer, Paul (and family) and William Starbuck; Richard, William, Stephen, and Stephen Gardner; Tristrim, Francis and Timothy Barnard; Daniel Francis and Jonah Worth; John Wickersham; William Reece; Jonathan Gifford; Reuben Bunker; Nathaniel Swain; Thomas Dixon.

This southward migration stopped almost as suddenly as it began. This was caused by the war of the Revolution. In 1775 there were eight certificates from Nantucket. In 1776 there was but one. In that year the migration from Virginia begins again with an occasional belated settler from Delaware or Maryland. But it never attained important proportions. During the seventeen years, 1783-1800, there were thirteen certificates received, less than one a year; some came from Nantucket, the most from Pennsylvania, but these were partly counterbalanced by the five certificates granted to parties who returned to their old homes.

It seems accurate to say that all of these new meetings had practically attained their full growth by the outbreak of the Revolution. Migration from the northward was steady until then. It then ceased largely, and from that time the meetings were kept up by the natural increase, not by the new arrivals.

It is quite interesting to record here what a good Quaker brother says as to the superiority of the North Carolina brand to that of Virginia.

The superiority of Carolina Friends over Virginia Friends, both in temporal and spiritual affairs, is also shown clearly by Hugh

Judge, who visited Southern Quakers in 1784. In speaking of his travels in the Hopewell section of Virginia he says: "We arrived there safely; but though it was a poor place, it was much better than the former, for we got a tolerably good bed, and corn blades for our horses; but they had no bread, milk, cheese nor butter for us. I asked whether we could have some water boiled, which they did in a large kettle, for they were entire strangers to tea and tea-tackling, having nothing of the kind. However, getting some hot water, I made some tea in a quart mug; and, having tea and sugar as well as bread and meat with us, we fared pretty well on our own.

"Set out before sunrise, and called at several places before we could get any breakfast, or anything for our horses to eat. At length we obtained some corn blades for them, and a broken kettle to boil water for ourselves a breakfast. So sorrowfully poor is the situation and condition of many of the inhabitants of old Virginia that travelers are hardly beset to get a little refreshment; yet they abound with negroes."

When South Carolina is reached there is found to be no essential difference in the evolution and development of the meetings in the northern and central part of the State, save that immigrants coming into this province, 1760-75, unlike those in Virginia and North Carolina, found some Quaker meetings already established in their line of march. Two of these, Pee Dee and Gum Swamp, were in Marlborough county, S. C. "The Friends there," says Reckitt, "though their circumstances in the world were but low, treated us very kindly. Their love to truth and diligence in attending meetings are worthy of notice; for they had nigh one hundred miles to go to the monthly meeting they belonged to, and I was informed very seldom missed attending it." These Friends "were truly glad to see us, they being seldom visited."

Another Quaker meeting on their line was that at Wateree. It was in, or near, Camden, in Kershaw county. It was also known as the Fredericksburg or Camden meeting. Mary Peisley and Catherine Peyton visited it in 1753. They found the Society very low as to religious experience, but "some of the youth were under a divine visitation, which afforded comfort and encouragement." Reckitt visited them in 1757, and says "several of the Friends from Ireland had been settled about six or seven years."

They seem to have grown rapidly, for in 1755 we find Wateree mentioned as a monthly meeting, but whether it was established by North Carolina Yearly Meeting we do not know. In 1757 we find that certificates were taken from New Garden to Wateree, and in 1761 parties returned to New Garden. In 1762 they were visited by William Hunt of North Carolina. So far as any evidence to the contrary is to be found, this monthly meeting, as well as other meetings in South Carolina, at first led a purely independent existence. They were congregational as far as government goes, and it seems some did not elect at first to come under North Carolina Yearly Meeting. Up to this time all South Carolina Quakers seem to have come by the sea route. Charleston, Edisto, Wateree, were all of the same character in this respect. But when the southward migration swept over North Carolina and reached South Carolina these older meetings became less important relatively, and their connection with North Carolina Yearly Meeting becomes more distinct as the immigrants become more powerful. In 1768 Fredericksburg Monthly Meeting was joined to the Western Quarter of North Carolina Yearly Meeting, and was held at Bush River, which was a settlement mostly of parties who had come overland from the north. In 1770 a committee was appointed to investigate the state of these Friends. They recommended the settlement of a monthly meeting at Bush River, in Newberry County, which was done, and that Fredericksburg Monthly Meeting "should return to the Wateree until further orders." This was also done, and from this time Bush River increases while Fredericksburg decreases. It dragged its slow length along through the Revolution and was laid down about 1782. Job Scott was there in 1789. "I had a very small, yet precious meeting at Camden, S. C., where no member of our Society liveth, except one very ancient woman; though once there was a settled meeting of Friends there." To this meeting there had come the families of Lamb, Parkins, Cox, Smith, Thomas, Pierson, Gant.

There seems to have never been more than one Quaker center in Georgia. Quakers were particularly favored under the Georgia charter, but it is not probable that any Friends appeared in the colony early enough to avail themselves of the advantages offered. Samuel Fothergill was the first Quaker preacher to visit Georgia. This was in 1755. "I went thence [Charleston] to Georgia, and had a large meeting in the court-house, and some opportunities in the inn where I lodged, to some service, though there were not any there who bore our name." The vagueness of this letter leaves us in doubt as to the sections visited.

The first effort at Quaker settlement was in 1758. In that year "Certain Quaker families entered the province and formed a settlement about seven miles above Augusta upon a tract of land known to this day as the Quaker Spring. The territory within which they fixed their abodes had been formerly owned by a tribe of Indians called the Savannahs. Thence were they expelled by the Uchees, who occupied adjacent lands. Peacefully inclined as they were, these Quakers hoped to dwell in amity with the neighboring Indians. While engaged in clearing lands and in building comfortable homes they were alarmed by the intelligence that the Cherokees were on the eve of invading the white settlements. Without pausing to ascertain the truth of the report, they hastily abandoned the country, leaving behind them no trace of their short occupancy save a spring and a slender memory."

The next effort was more successful. On the third of July, 1770, the General Assembly of Georgia granted to Joseph Maddock (or Mattock) and Jonathan Still a tract of 40,000 acres of land in St. Paul's Parish, Columbia (now McDuffie) County, Ga., to be held in trust for the Quakers. Here they began the town of Wrightsborough, on Town Creek, sixteen miles from Appling, the county seat, and named it for Sir James Wright, Governor of the colony. The records date from 1773. In that year a preparative and a monthly meeting were organized in Wrightsborough township by representatives sent from New Garden. The certificates recorded show that the Quaker population was made up of settlers from South Carolina, North Carolina, Virginia, Pennsylvania, and Burlington in West New Jersey. The outlook for a speedy development of their settlement was very promising when Indian troubles in 1774 prevented further expansion. We have an account of this Indian incursion from one who was so close to the sufferers that it may be interesting to reproduce. It is written by Rachel Price (*nee* Kirk) in her *Account of the Kirk Family* (MS.). It tells how her sister, Tamar Kirk, married Phineas Mendenhall and removed with him to Guilford County, N. C. This was about 1763. The account continues: "I have retained the recollection of a young man of the name of John Wickersham, who was acquainted with my sister Mary. He went to Carolina some time after her, where they renewed their attachment and were married and settled there for a time, but the State of Georgia opened for settlement, inducing many to move there. My sisters and their families were both of them amongst those who went about 300 miles from their then settlement into the State of Georgia to a place settled by Joseph Mattock and Mattock's Settlement. There they lived in peaceable possession of their homes undisturbed by the natives for a considerable time until there was a new purchase made by the Government, with which the Indians seemed dissatisfied. My brothers-in-law, with others, bought land in it; as it was considered very good, many were induced to make settlements on it, to clear and sow it with grain, but the frequent incursions of Indians was cause of great discouragement to them, so that it was deemed best by many not to reside on it. They therefore left it, but when the grain that they had sown was ripe, they thought that they would go there and gather it, the distance not being far from their first settlement where they resided. Sister Tamer, her husband and three sons went for that purpose, leaving their two daughters behind at home. Early one morning sister went to milk a cow they had with them; while her hands were thus engaged a party of Indians were lying in wait, fired on them, put an end to her useful life, also killed her eldest son; the youngest they took captive, and kept him in captivity about two years. They adopted him and were kind to him, and when redemption was offered for him, he had become so much attached to them and to their manner of life, that it required some persuading to get him from them. The father and other son made their escape.

"This awfully trying circumstance made such an impression on the minds of sister Mary and husband that they came as soon as they could get away to North Carolina to their former settlement. In that neighborhood they lived for many years. . . . They of later years moved with their children and their families to Indiana, where they are settled."

There were then about twenty families in the Wrightsborough connection. They report at that time: "Meetings are middling well kept up and love and unity subsist in a middling good degree amongst us." But the Indian incursion caused the population to become unsteady, and many returned to the older colonies.

We find, however, a few who ventured that far South during the war of the Revolution. Daniel Williams went down from Pennsylvania in 1777 to Wrightsborough, and in 1778 writes back to the people of Pennsylvania: "I got liberty to move into an empty cabin near my uncle, where we staid about six or seven weeks. During our abode there I dealt with a man for 100 acres of land in the old purchase. There were about seven acres cleared, and a nice house just built thereon, and about 40 bearing peach trees planted out. We moved there near the beginning of the second month, and I fell to grubbing and clearing a piece of ground, and got five acres ready to plant in corn in pretty good season, and have ten acres now growing of likely corn. . . . Our country is exceedingly fertile, and takes but little to render it complete. One discouragement there is to the settlement of it, and that is the frequent incursions of the savages, who almost every year cause some part of the settlement to break, though it is hard to penetrate above two or three miles within the English boundaries. Though we have often heard it was their decision to cut us off, yet the interposition of the Divine Hand has hitherto frustrated their intentions when no human power seemed sufficient. Notwithstanding discouragements of this kind appear, yet it is truly astonishing to see with what rapidity the country is settled and improved; this country which 11 years ago was a wild uninhabited wilderness. There are several people here this fall that are much indisposed with a fever that is not common in this country, for we have generally good water and clear, wholesome air in the middle of summer. . . . I shall advise if any of our friends should incline to come out here soon, that they bring no more money with them than what will bring them out, for we have no scarcity of paper currency. I would be very desirous if brother Isaiah would send 10 or 12 lbs. of iron out by William Benson, for it is a very scarce article here and rates I believe at $2.00 the pound."

Georgia Friends were drawn from all the meetings to the northward almost without exception. We find among them the families of Farmer, Pugh, Stubb, Jones, James, Vernon, Moorman, Upton, Williams, Webb, Dixon, Seypold, Coppock, Brown, Hodge, Mendenhall.

The Georgia meetings reported to the Bush River Quarterly

Meeting, and this in turn to the North Carolina Yearly Meeting. In 1775 we find Georgia mentioned in the North Carolina Yearly Meeting records. South Carolina had been mentioned for the first time in 1770. The change in the center was soon felt; in 1777 came the proposition to remove the Yearly Meeting from the east; in 1786 request was that it be held at Centre, in Guilford County. It was held here the next year, and then alternated between the east and the west until 1812, when the last Yearly Meeting in northeastern North Carolina was held at Little River.

It is now possible for us to take a summary review of the results obtained thus far. The promise of an aggressive and rapid growth made in the youth of Quakerism was not fulfilled in its maturer years. This promise was particularly clear in North Carolina. During the seventeenth century the records show that the Society in that colony was quietly but steadily extending its outposts and was being strengthened by immigration and conversions. To such an extent was this true, that in 1716 Rev. Giles Rainsford writes to the S. P. G. that the "poor colony of North Carolina will be soon overrun with Quakerism and infidelity if not timely prevented by your sending over able and sober missionaries as well as schoolmasters to reside among them." But this almost phenomenal growth of the native element ceased soon after the Established Church became well organized. Quakers never played in North Carolina under royal government the part they had played under the government of the Proprietors. They were still less important, relatively, in Virginia. During the last third of the eighteenth century they obtained their fullest growth in each of the several States under consideration. Soon after the beginning of the nineteenth century their decline becomes visible. The period of highest and fullest growth has itself a period of depression. The Revolution, like the Civil War, was a time of suffering to the Quakers. Many left their ranks and were disowned to take part in the struggle for liberty, and the Society was much depleted. On the other hand, the convincements were much more numerous than they had been in former years. Despite all the care which Friends might use to keep unworthy and timid persons out of the Socity, the number of "war Quakers" was considerable, and the Society did not prosper for some years after the end of the war.

CHAPTER III.

THE REPLANTING OF SOUTHERN QUAKERISM.

In the preceding chapter an account of the decline of Southern Quakerism was given. In this we shall see it was replanted and became quite vigorous.

In the half-century included between 1732 and the close of the Revolution a new and vigorous element was injected into the life of Southern Quakerism. Most of these new settlers were from Pennsylvania, but some had delayed a few years in Maryland; some were from New Jersey, and some from Nantucket. Some were of English antecedents, but many were Pennsylvania Germans, and some were Welsh. The influence of these new settlers was so distinct and overwhelming that I have ventured to call this movement the replanting of Southern Quakerism, for had this movement not taken place, Quakerism would hardly be an appreciable factor in these States to-day.

These immigrants seem to have had but one motive in coming South. This motive was distinctly economic. Their movement is parallel to that of the Scotch-Irish. These two waves passed over the same ground at the same time, but the two did not intermingle, for the gentle and peace-loving Friend, who decried all war, avoided the holding of office, sought not his own, and put his abiding faith in the personal presence of God, free grace and the powers that be, had little in common with the restless, aggressive, fighting, ruling Scotch-Irish, or with the democratic but stern tenets of Calvinism.

About 1725 the vanguard of the Quaker movement appeared at Monocacy, Maryland. Here, like a true wave of Teutonic migration, it rested for a time. It reached Hopewell, Va., in 1732, and the next twelve or fifteen years were spent in subduing northern Virginia. In 1743 an advance-guard had gotten as far as Carver's Creek, in Bladen county, N. C. The next twenty years are marked by the swarms of Quakers that came pouring into the central sections of North Carolina, many of them falling by the wayside, however, in Campbell and Bedford counties, Va., where South River Monthly Meeting was organized in 1757. From about 1760 to the Revolution the horde passed through North Carolina and pressed into South Carolina and Georgia.

Like a true migration again, this movement did not take the form of an overflow, but of successive waves. Many parts of the line of march were comparatively or even absolutely free from Quakers. It is idle for us to speculate on the reasons why they settled in the particular sections they did. It is possibly due to that "invincible attraction" which Walter Bagehot points out as playing such an important part in the formation of national character. Some accidental advantage, perhaps the excellence of the soil, located the first immigrant, and the gregarious instinct did the rest.

It now becomes us to narrate the planting of these meetings more in detail.

The beginning of this new movement southward, the counterpart of the movement of the next century westward, is to be found in the Hopewell settlement in Frederick County, Va. About 1725, Friends from Salem, N. J., and Nottingham, then in Pennsylvania, but thrown by Mason and Dixon into Maryland, settled in the upper part of Prince George County, Md., near the Monocacy, a tributary of the Potomac. They were erected into a meeting by New Garden Monthly Meeting, Pa. In 1732 Alexander Ross and a company crossed the Potomac, and thus initiated the migration of which we are now to write. In that year they obtained a charter for 100,000 acres of land situated on Opequan Creek, a tributary of the Potomac in what is now Frederick County, Virginia. A settlement was begun here by Alexander Ross, Josiah Ballenger, James Wright, Evan Thomas and other Friends from Pennsylvania and Elk River, Md. A meeting called Hopewell, or Opeckon, was established the same year, and one called Providence in 1733. They were organized in 1735 into Hopewell Monthly Meeting, under the auspices and care of Chester Quarterly Meeting in Pennsylvania.

In 1733 other Friends removed from Bucks county, Penn., and settled in Fairfax, now Loudoun county, about ten miles south of the Potomac, east of the Hopewell settlement, and near where the town of Waterford now is. When these parties settled in northern Virginia there were no Quakers in this section, and few inhabitants. The meeting for worship of the Fairfax settlement was at first held in the house of Amos Janney, the first Quaker settler here. The Janneys became a large and influential family, produced among others the historian, Samuel McPherson Janney, and some of the name still reside in the county. The meeting was called Fairfax, and dates from 1733. A meeting-house was erected in 1741 and called by the same name. In 1744 Fairfax Monthly Meeting was established. This also became a branch of Chester Quarterly Meeting and Philadelphia Yearly Meeting.

These meetings soon attracted the watchful care of traveling Friends. John Fothergill visited them in 1736. The state of the Society in Virginia, he said, was "low and painful"; those advanced in years were, in general, "very insensible of true feeling, or suitable zeal for truth's advancement in themselves, their families or the church." John Churchman (1705-1775) went down in 1741 to see if the Friends at Fairfax "were in number and weight sufficient to have a meeting settled amongst them." He also visited the families on the Shenandoah and says, "I believe that the delight in hunting, and a roving idle life, drew most of them under our name to settle there."

The meetings in Loudoun, Fairfax and Frederick counties were never as distinctively Virginian as those farther south. They looked first to Philadelphia Yearly Meeting, and after 1789 to Baltimore Yearly Meeting. Their distance and the inconvenience in traveling were doubtless important factors in this division. Then, too, the origin of the settlers had its effect. They were an offspring of the Pennsylvania meetings and looked naturally to them.

These meetings in turn began to extend their boundaries. Various meetings were established in Frederick, Loudoun, Culpeper and the adjoining counties. In 1756 a meeting-house was built and a meeting settled at Goose Creek. In 1760 Crooked Run meeting was settled. A monthly meeting was established at Crooked Run in 1782, and one at Goose Creek in 1785; at Southland in 1789, or earlier; and at Alexandria in 1802 Migration from Pennsylvania to northern Virginia continued brisk until the Revolution. Day, Barrett, Beeson, Piggott, Sidwell, Kirk, White, Brown, Wilson, Ross, Johnson, Bailey, Carter, Ballenger, Pugh, Rees, Branson, Webb, and Wright, were the names of some of the families that came south from Pennsylvania and settled in this section. There were in this immediate section one quarterly and five monthly meetings, with twenty or more meetings for worship. There was much interchange between these meetings; as the settlers increased in numbers they took their certificates from the older meetings like Hopewell and Fairfax to the newer ones like Goose Creek. The meetings in this locality are now reduced to about eight. In the schism in 1828 a majority accepted the views of Hicks. The census of 1890 gives 96 as the number of Orthodox and 506 as the number of Hickside Friends in Fairfax, Frederick and Loudoun counties. Friends have entirely disappeared from the adjoining counties of Culpeper, Stafford and Orange, Va., as well as from Hampshire, Berkeley and Jefferson counties, W. Va., in all of which they had members during the last century.

We may safely conclude that the meetings in Campbell and Bedford, Pittsylvania and Halifax counties, Va., were built up almost entirely by this southward movement. There were two monthly meetings in this section, South River and Goose Creek. The former dates from 1757; the latter, which is not the same as the Goose Creek Monthly Meeting in the Hopewell Quarter, from 1794. These monthly meetings applied for a quarterly meeting. It was granted in 1797, and was known as Western Quarterly Meeting; but the number of Friends in the section decreased so much that Goose Creek Monthly Meeting was laid down in 1814 and the Western Quarterly meeting in 1817. South River Monthly Meeting survived the Virginia Yearly Meeting, and was laid down in 1858. These meetings lay in the direct path of southern immigration. I conclude that they received most of their increase from persons who got stranded, as it were, on the way South. But they were also a mixture of the native and foreign elements. The Clarks of Louisa and Albemarle counties, and the Terrells of Caroline, seem to have been in the Society before 1730, and had been turned toward Quakerism by the preaching of Joseph Newby of North Carolina. The Lynch family, from whom the city of Lynchburg is named, and who have also given us the term "lynch law," became members about 1752. It was the widow of Charles Lynch, died about 1753, Irishman and founder of the family, who organized the meetings in this locality. The Lynches, Davises, Johnsons, Cadwalladers, Douglasses, Anthonys, Holloways, Strattons, Fishers, Stantons, Moormans, Burgesses, Butlers, Pidgeons, Perdues, were some of the prominent Qaker families in Campbell and the adjoining counties.

At a later period the migration from northern Virginia became more frequent. Between 1775 and 1800 we find thirty parties, some with families, taking certificates from Fairfax and the northern Goose Creek Monthly Meetings to South River Monthly Meeting.

CHAPTER IV.

CAUSES OF THE DECLINE OF SOUTHERN QUAKERISM.

It is not our purpose in giving an account of Ye Quakers of Ye Olden Times to make one feature of the book more prominent than the rest. But inasmuch as the present generation knows but little about them, it is our aim to give a brief history of their origin, movements, doctrines and social life.

Having already given an outline of their advent into this State and others, it now remains to notice the causes of their decline. These are five-fold:

I. The removal of Friends to the West. This removal was itself the result of at least three causes. The Quakers were Teutons. The old love of adventure was strong in their breasts as it was in the breasts of those who did not accept their religious views. The influence of this spirit in extending the area of their settlements is acknowledged by John Churchman, John Griffith and other traveling ministers. It was the same spirit that had led to the discovery and settlement of America. It was an historic force. These Quakers, all unconsciously, were carrying out the spirit of their race. It was the same as the spirit which took the Angles and Saxons to Britain; which drove the Franks and later the Normans into Gaul; led the Ostrogoths into Italy, the Visigoths into Spain, and the Vandals to Africa. This was the first heart-beat, as von Ranke calls it. The second heart-beat leads the descendants of these same Teutons to the Holy Land on the Crusades; when their day was over the struggle was kept up in Spain against the Moors; and the discovery of America was one of the results of the fall of Grenada. (2) Along with this historic spirit went the economic spirit—a search for more land and better land than was then available in the older States, for the best lands had been exhausted by continuous crops, and fertilizers were not extensively used. To show that these two reasons led many to emigrate it is only necessary for us to velopment of Old England, or New England, or the Middle Colonies, or the Germany of to-day. (3) It may be an open question as to how many of these particular emigrants would have gone West had there been no slavery in the South. But that slavery did have an overwhelming influence in the case under discussion no one can deny.

II. Dissensions within the Society. As we have seen, the Hicksite schism divided and therefore weakened the Society in Northern Virginia.

III. Disownments for slight offenses, like marrying out of Society, and persistent efforts to force all men into the same narrow mould, which is so visible in the earlier records of the Society, have both cost it dear.

IV. Two elements have prevented the growth of the Society. On the one hand, its extreme spirituality has been a load on the Society. No body of Christians has come so near fulfilling, perhaps, the injunction to worship in spirit and in truth as have Friends. This deep spirituality is too high for most men. Their deficiencies must be supplied by forms and ceremonies. On the other hand, Quakers were the radicals of the Reformation. They abominated above all things the forms, ceremonies and rituals of the Roman Church; they were equally as uncompromising with those of the English Church. But in their very effort to escape from the Scylla of ritualism they fell into the Charybdis of stiffness and inflexibility. They developed forms and ceremonies of their own which were no less ritualistic than those of the Roman Church, and which were adhered to with such tenacity that the expression "rigid as a Quaker" became a by-word in the English-speaking world. To have no forms, no rites, no symbols, no liturgies is the root of Quaker forms. Their entire history is full of the adoption of external signs as the witness of the ministry of the spirit. Wearing sackcloth on the body and ashes on the head, as was sometimes done in early times, and a difference in dress, tell the very same story as the alb and cassock of the priest. The use of the thee and thou, the broad-brim hat, the curved coat, the sing-song tone of address, the wearing of hats in court, disownment of those who marry outside of Society, all point to the same effort to indicate a coming out from the world. These things so utterly insignificant by the side of the deep spirituality for which the Society has always stood, have been abandoned to a large extent. Quakers are not now generally known by their speech or their dress; but this was not the case until recent years, and the outsider, when first coming in contact with them, experienced, in many cases, a vague feeling of dread, and this feeling has repelled many who might have been attracted by their spirituality and by their strong insistence on moral character.

V. Aggressiveness of other denominations. The most careless perusal of the journals of the traveling Friends from the time of the Revolution will convince the reader that Friends were being absorbed, as it were, slowly and imperceptibly, into the greater body of their more aggressive and vigorous rivals, the Methodists and Baptists. The journalists note frequently that their congregations are made up principally of outsiders; when denominations are given they are almost always Methodists and Baptists. These attended their meetings, entertained their preachers and absorbed their members. The completeness of this can be seen clearly in the journal of Samuel M. Janney, who notes the fact that there had been Friends in Culpeper, Orange and Albemarle counties, Virginia, in the closing years of the eighteenth century; but in 1841-42 they had disappeared. The Methodists had taken their place.

It is true to say that Quakerism was absorbed in Virginia and North Carolina to a great extent by the Methodists. But it would be far from the truth to think that Quakerism thus disappeared leaving no trace behind. The influence which it has exerted on Southern Methodism has been very profound. It is probably accurate to call the Methodist Church the heir of the Quakers. Indeed it is entirely within the bounds of historical accuracy to say that the foundations of Methodism in Virginia and North Carolina were laid by Edmundson and Fox rather than by Whitefield and Robert Williams. The beginnings of Methodism are much nearer 1672 than 1772. Methodism was a return toward the forms of primitive Quakerism. With them, as with the Methodists a century later, religion took the form of excessive emotion. The convicted sinner shook from head to foot; there were many groans and sighs and tears; then a sudden change, with a "sweet sound of thanksgiving and praise." In other words, the Quakerism of the

Revolutionary period was beginning to lose that aggressive and exuberant vitality that characterized it at the time of the death of Fox. It was sinking into that quietism which had characterized English Friends since the beginning of the eighteenth century. The continued enthusiasm of American Friends explains why the system retained its aggressive vitality and grew in numbers for almost a century after English Quakers had reached their maximum in numbers. When this spirit disappeared American Quakerism began to lose numbers relatively. The early Methodists were simply leading their Quaker hearers back to the good old days of the past.

The relations between Southern Quakers and Southern Methodists have usually been very cordial. Quakers seldom abandon outright the scenes of former habitations. They have returned to them in after years, have found few of their own members still alive, but have received a warm welcome at the hands of Methodists and others. Thus, although their last meeting in Pasquotank county, N. C., was laid down in 1854, they continued to visit and to preach among the Methodists there for nearly a generation. In the same way Friends left Carteret county, N. C., for the West, 1830-40, and regular services were suspended then, but Friends visited the section until their own meeting-house had perished from decay. They then held meetings in private houses or in the Methodist church, which was always open to them. A touching story is told of the three or four Quaker families who still lived in the section. One took up his residence in the meeting-house until he could erect a dwelling, and as long as the meeting-house stood this man and the two or three other families met regularly on Wednesdays and Sundays for silent worship.

CHAPTER V.

THE CREED OF THE QUAKERS.

While the religious belief of these quaint but Godly people has a "Thus saith the Lord" to buttress it, yet there are some articles of their faith which are so much at variance with the practices, if not the principles, of latter day Christians, that it will be of interest to notice them. Hence, we do so.

We make the following extracts from the *Southern Friend,* Richmond, Va., edited by John B. Crenshaw:

GREAT TENETS OF THE QUAKERS.

The Quakers hold four principles, which I shall distinguish by the name of Great Tenets. These are considered as arising out of the implied or positive injunctions of christianity, and were insisted upon as essentials on the formation of the society. The first of these is on the subject of Civil Government.

Civil Government had existed long before the appearance of christianity in the world. Legislators since that era, as they have imbibed its spirit, so they have introduced this spirit more or less into their respective codes. But no nation has ever professed to change its system of jurisprudence, or to model it anew, in consequence of the new light which christianity has afforded; neither have the alterations been so numerous in any nation, however high its profession of christianity with respect to laws, as to enable us to say that there is any government in the known world, of christian origin, or any government wholly upon the principles of the gospel.

If all men were to become real christians, civil government would become less necessary. As there would be then no offences, there would be no need of magistracy or of punishment. As men would then settle any differences between them amicably, there would be no necessity for courts of law. As they would then never fight, there would be no need of armies. As they would then consider their fellow creatures as brethren, they would relieve them as such, and there would be no occasion of laws for the poor. As men would then have more solicitude for the public good, and more large and liberal notions than at any former time, they would of themselves conceive and raise all necessary public institutions and works. Government then is not so necessary for real christians. It is necessary principally, as the apostle says, for evil doers. But if it be chiefly necessary for evil doers, then governors ought to be careful how they make laws, which may vex, harrass, and embarrass christians, whom they will always find to be the best part of their communities, or, in other words, how they make laws, which christians, on account of their religious scruples, cannot conscientiously obey.

It is a tenet of the Quakers, on the subject of government, that the civil magistrate has no right to interfere in religious matters, so as either to force any particular doctrines upon men, or to hinder them from worshiping God in their own way, provided that, by their creeds and worship, they do no detriment to others. The Quakers believe, however, that christian churches may admonish such members as fall into error, and may even cut them off from membership, but this must be done not by the temporal, but by the spiritual sword.

This tenet the Quakers support, first, by reason. Religion, they say, is a matter solely between God and man, that is, between God and that man who worships him. This must be obvious, they conceive, because man is not accountable to man for his religious opinions, except he binds himself to the discipline of any religious society but to God alone. It must be obvious again, they say, because no man can be a judge over the conscience of another. He can know nothing of the sincerity or hypocrisy of his heart. He can be neither an infallible judge, nor an infallible corrector of his religious errors. "The conscience of man," says Barclay, "is the seat and throne of God in him, of which he alone is the proper and infallible judge, who, by his power and spirit, can rectify its mistakes." It must be obvious again, they say, from the consideration that, if it were even possible for one man to discern the conscience of another, it is impossible for him to bend or control it. But conscience is placed both out of his sight and of his reach. It is neither visible nor tangible. It is inaccessible by stripes or torments. Thus, while the body is in bondage, on account of the religion of the soul, the soul itself is free, and, while it suffers under torture, it enjoys the divinity, and feels felicity in his presence. But if all these things are so, it cannot be within the province either of individual magistrates or of governments, consisting of fallible men, to fetter the consciences of those who may live under them. And any attempt to this end is considered by the Quakers as a direct usurpation of the prerogative of God.

This tenet the Quakers adopt again on a contemplation of the conduct and doctrines of Jesus Christ and of his apostles. They find nothing in these which can give the least handle to any man to use force in the religious concerns of another. During the life of Jesus Christ upon earth, it is no where recorded of him that he censured any man for his religion. It is true that he reproved the Scribes and Pharisees, but this was on account of their hypocrisy, because they pretended to be what they were not. But he no where condemned the devout Jew, who was sincere in his faith. But if he be found no where to have censured another for a difference in religious opinions, much less was it ever said of him that he forced him to the adoption of his own. In the memorable instance, where James and John were willing to have called fire from Heaven, to burn those who refused to receive him, he rebuked them by an assurance that "they knew not what spirit they were of." And, with respect to his doctrines, nothing can be more full to the point than his saying, that "his kingdom was not of this world," by which he meant that his dominion was wholly of a spiritual nature, and that men must cast off all worldly imaginations, and become spiritually minded, before they could belong to him. But no application of outward force, in the opinion of the Quakers, can thus alter the internal man. Nor can even the creeds and doctrines of others produce this effect, except they become sanctioned by the divine influence on the heart.

Neither is it recorded of any of the apostles, that they used any other weapons than those of persuasion and the power of God in the propagation of their doctrines, leaving such as did not choose to follow them to their own way. They were explicit also in stating the spiritual nature of Christ's kingdom, from whence an inference similar to the former is deducible, namely, that no compulsory interference can be effectual in matters of religion. And St. Paul in particular, tells the Corinthians, that, in his spiritual services to them, he does not consider himself "as having any dominion over their faith, but as helpers of their joy.

But if neither Jesus Christ, who was the author of that religion which many civil governments have established, nor the apostles, who afterwards propagated it, forced their doctrines upon other men, or hindered them by force from worshipping in their own way, even though the former could have called legions of angels to his support, it certainly does not become weak, ignorant, and infallible men, because they are placed in the situation of governors, to set up their own creeds as supreme, and to throw penalties and restrictions in the way of the religious exercise of others.

But if governors, contrary to the example of Jesus Christ and of his apostles, should interfere in religious matters, and impose laws upon the governed, of which, as christians, they cannot but disapprove, then the Quakers are of opinion that the governed ought always to obey the laws of Jesus Christ, rather than the laws of any governors, who are only men. Thus when Peter and John were commanded by the rulers of the Jews to speak no more in the name of Jesus, they dared not yield obedience to their commands, reasoning thus, "Whether it be right in the sight of God to hearken unto you more than unto God, judge ye."

And as the governed in such case ought, in obedience to God, the Supreme Ruler of the Universe, and the King of Kings, to refuse a compliance with the laws of their own governors, so they ought to be prepared patiently to submit to the penalties which are annexed to such refusal, and on no account, if just representations made in the meek and quite spirit of their religion, are not likely to be effectual, to take up arms or resist them by force. And this doctrine they ground, first, on the principle that it is not only more noble, but more consistent with their duties as christians, to suffer, than to give growth to the passions of revenge, or by open resistance to become the occasion of loss of life to others. And, secondly, on the example of Jesus Christ, and of the apostles and primitive christians, all of whom patiently submitted to the pains and penalties inflicted upon them by the governments of their respective times for the exercise of their religion.

A second tenet, which the Quakers hold, is, that it is unlawful for christians to take a civil oath.

Many and grievous were the sufferings of he Quakers, in the early part of their history, on account of their refusing to swear before the civil magistrate. They were insulted, fined, and imprisoned. Some of the judges too indulged a rancour against them on this account, unworthy of their high office, which prescribed justice impartially to all. For when they could not convict them of the offences laid to their charge, they administered to them the oath of allegiance, knowing that they would not take it, and that confiscation of property and imprisonment would ensue. But neither ill usage, nor imprisonment, nor loss of property, ever made any impression upon the Quakers, so as to induce them to swear in judicial cases, and they continued to suffer till the legislature, tired out with the cries of their oppression, decreed, that their affirmation should in all cases except criminal, or in that of serving upon juries, or in that of qualifications for posts of honor or emolument under government, be received as equivalent to their oath. And this indulgence towards them is continued to them by law to the present day.

The Quakers have an objection to oaths, as solemn appeals to God, because they are unnecessary.

It is an old saying among the Quaker writers, that "truth was before all oaths." By this they mean, there was a time when men's words were received as truths, without the intervention of an oath. Ancient fable, indeed, tells us that there were no oaths in the golden age, but that, when men departed from their primitive simplicity, and began to quarrel with one another, they had recourse to falsehood to substantiate their own case, after which it became necessary that some expedient should be devised, in the case of disputes, for the ascertaining the truth. Hence Hesiod makes the god of oaths the son of Eris or of contention. This account differs but little from that of Polybius, who says, that the use of oaths in judgment was rare among the ancients, but that, as perfidy grew, oaths increased.

And as it is a saying of the Quakers that truth "was before all oaths," so they believe that truth would be spoken if oaths were done away with. Thus, that which is called honor by the world will bind men to the truth, who perhaps know but little of religion. But if so, then he, who makes christianity his guide, will not be found knowingly in a falsehood, though he be deprived of the opportunity of swearing.

But if it be true, that truth existed before the invention of oaths, and that truth would still be spoken, even if all oaths were abolished, then the Quakers say, that oaths are not so necessary as some have imagined, because they have but a secondary effect in the production of the truth. This conclusion they consider also as the result of reason. For good men will speak truth without an oath, and bad men will hardly be influenced by one. And where oaths are regarded, it is probable that truth is forced out of men, not so much because they consider them as solemn appeals to God, as that they consider the penalties, which will follow their violation; so that a simple affirmation, under the same pains and penalties, would be equally productive of the truth.

The Quakers consider oaths again as very injurious to morality. For, first, they conceive it to be great presumption in men to summon God as a witness in their trifling and earthly concerns.

They believe, secondly, that if men accustom themselves to call upon God on civil occasions, they render his name so familiar to them that they are likely to lose the reverence due to it, or so to blend religious with secular considerations, that they become in danger of losing sight of the dignity, solemnity and awfulness of devotion. And it is not an unusual remark, that persons most accustomed to oaths, are the most likely to perjury. A custom house oath has become proverbial in our own country. I do not mean by this to accuse mercantile men in particular, but to state it as a received opinion, that, where men make solemn things familiar, there is danger of their moral degradation. Hence the Quakers consider the common administration of oaths to have a tendency that is injurious to the moral interests of men.

This notion relative to the bad tendency of oaths, the Quakers state to have prevailed even in the Gentile world. As heathen philosophy became pure, it branded the system of swearing as pernicious to morals. It was the practice of the Persians to give each other their right hand as a token of their speaking the truth. He who gave his hand deceitfully, was accounted more detestable than if he had sworn. The Scythians, in their conference with Alexander the Great, addressed him thus: "Think not that the Scythians confirm their friendship by an oath. They swear by keeping their word." The Phrygians were wholly against oaths. They neither took them themselves, nor required them of others. Among the proverbs of the Arabs this was a celebrated one, "Never swear, but let thy word be yes or no." So religious was Hercules, says Plutarch, that he never swore but once. Clinias, a Greek philosopher and a scholar of Pythagoras, is said to have dreaded an oath so much, that, when by swearing he could have escaped a fine of three talents, he chose rather to pay the money than do it, though he was to have sworn nothing but the truth. Indeed, throughout all Greece the system of swearing was considered as of the most immoral tendency, the very word, which signified "perjured," in the Greek language meaning, when analysed, "he that adds oath to oath," or "the taker of many oaths."

But, above all, the Quakers consider oaths as unlawful for christians, having been positively forbidden by Jesus Christ.

The words, in which they conceived this prohibition to have been contained, they take from the sermon on the Mount.

"Again, ye have heard, that it hath been said by them of old time, Thou shalt not forswear thyself, but shalt perform unto the Lord thine oaths."

"But I say unto you, swear not at all, neither by heaven, because it is God's throne."

"Nor by the earth, for it is his footstool: neither by Jerusalem, for it is the city of the great King."

"Neither shalt thou swear by thy head, because thou canst not make one hair white or black."

"But let your communication be yea, yea; nay, nay: for whatsoever is more than this cometh of evil."

The next of the great tenets which the Quakers hold, is on the subject of war. They believe it unlawful for christians to engage in the profession of arms or indeed to bear arms under any circumstances of hostility whatever. Hence there is no such character as that of a Quaker soldier. A Quaker is always able to avoid the regular army, because the circumstances of entering into it is a matter of choice. But where he has no such choice, as is the case in the militia, he either submits, if he has property, to distraints upon it, or, if he has not, to prison.

The Quakers ground the illicitness of war on several passages, which are to be found in the New Testament. I shall not quote all the texts they bring forward, but shall make a selection of them on this occasion.

Jesus Christ, in the famous sermon which he preached upon the mount, took occasion to mention specifically some of the precepts of the Jewish law, and to inform his hearers that he expected of those. who were to be his true disciples, that they would carry these to a much higher extent in their practice under the new dispensation, which he was then affording them. Christianity required a greater perfection of the human character than under the law. Men were not only not to kill, but not even to cherish the passion of revenge. And "whereas it was said of old, an eye for an eye, and a tooth for a tooth, I say unto you, says Christ, that ye resist not evil: but whosoever shall smite thee on thy right cheek, turn to him the other also. And farther on in the same chapter, he says, "Ye have heard that it hath been said, Thou shalt love thy neighbor, and hate thine enemy: But I say unto you, love your enemies, bless them that curse you, do good to them that hate you, and pray for them that despitefully use you and persecute you. For if ye love them which love you, what reward have you? do not even the Publicans the same? Be ye therefore perfect, even as your Father which is in heaven is perfect." Now the Quakers are of opinion that no man can receive this doctrine in his heart and assist either offensively or defensively in the operations of war.

Other passages, quoted by the Quakers in favor of their tenet on war, are taken from the apostles Paul and James conjointly.

The former, in his second epistle to the Corinthians, says, "For though we walk in the flesh, we do not war after the flesh: For the weapons of our warfare are not carnal, but mighty through God to the pulling down of strong holds, to the casting down imaginations, and every high thing that exalteth itself against the knowledge of God, and bringing into captivity every thought to the obedience of Christ." From hence the Quakers argue that the warfare of christianity, or that which christianity recognizes, is not carnal, but spiritual, and that it consists in the destruction of the evil imaginations, or of the evil lusts and passions of men. That is no man can be a true soldier of Christ unless his lusts are subdued, or unless the carnal be done away by the spiritual mind. Now this position having been laid down by St. Paul, or the position having been established in christian morals, that a state of subjugated passions is one of the great characteristic marks of a true christian, the Quakers draw a conclusion from it by the help of the words of St. James. This apostle, in his letter to the dispersed tribes, which were often at war with each other, as well as with the Romans, says, "From whence come wars and fightings among you? Come they not hence even of your lusts that war in your members?" But if wars come from the lusts of men, then the Quakers say that those who have subdued their lusts can no longer engage in them or in other words, that true christians, being persons of this description, or being such, according to St. Paul, as are redeemed out of what St. James calls the very grounds and occasions of wars, can no longer fight. And as this proposition is true in itself, so the Quakers conceive the converse of it to be true also; for if there are persons, on the other hand, who deliberately engage in the wars and fightings of the world, it is a proof that their lusts are not yet subjugated, or that, though they may be nominal, they are not yet arrived at the stature of true or of full grown christians.

A third quotation, made by the Quakers, is taken from St. Paul exclusively. "Now if any man have not the spirit of Christ, he is none of his." That is, if men have not the same disposition which Jesus Christ manifested in the different situations of his life, the same spirit of humility and forbearance, and of love, and of forgiveness of injuries, or if they do not follow him as a pattern, or if they do not act as he would have done on any similar occasion, they are not christians. Now they conceive, knowing what the spirit of Jesus was by those things which have been recorded of him, that he could never have been induced or compelled, by any earthly consideration or power, to have engaged in the wars of the world. They are aware that his mission, which it became him to fulfil, and which engrossed all his time, would not have allowed him the opportunity of a military life. But they believe, independently of this, that the spirit which he manifested upon earth would have been of itself a sufficient bar to such an employment. This they judge from his opinions and his precepts. For how could he have taken up arms to fight, who enjoined in the new dispensation that men were not to resist evil; that they were to love their enemies, that they were to bless those who cursed them, and to do good to those who hated them? This they judge also from his practice. For how could he have lifted up his arm against another, who, "when he was reviled, reviled not again;" and who, in his very agony upon the cross, prayed for his persecutors, saying, "Father, forgive them, for they know not what they do." But if Jesus Christ could not have been induced or compelled to have engaged in a profession which would have subjected him to take away the life of another, so neither can any christian, "for if a man have not the spirit of Christ, he is none of his."

An amusing as well as interesting story, which has a bearing upon this tenet, is told of a minister among Friends of more recent date, in a volume entitled "Southern Heroes."

Owing to his popularity and activity in the temperance work, Eli Jones was elected by a large majority to the State Legislature of Maine, in 1854. The election was very unexpected to him, as he had not sought the place; but having been chosen largely on account of

JOHN CARTER

ALLEN U. TOMLINSON

JOHN B. CRENSHAW

ISHAM COX

his temperance principles, he said he would see what he could do "to help put new teeth into the old law," and much credit is due to him for the existence of the "Maine Liquor Law."

When the time came to be sworn in as a member of the House, Eli Jones alone kept his seat while the others swore to do their duty. Then he arose and "affirmed" to the governor that he would faithfully perform the duties of his office.

Although he worked on important committees and was diligent in other duties of his office, he never addressed the House. Some of the members who knew his ability arranged a plan to call forth a speech from him. In the course of the session it became necessary to appoint a Major-General to the second division of the Maine militia. In 1838, Maine had undertaken by force of arms to assert her right to a region near her northern boundary, claimed by both her and Canada. There was much mustering of troops at the capital, and fully ten thousand soldiers marched through the deep snow and fierce cold to drive the enemy from Aroostook County. Though they were brave and ready for battle, happily no blood was shed, and peace was wisely made. But the "Aroostook War" became famous as a subject of banter, and many jokes were made at the expense of the officers. The old nursery rhyme was quoted:

"The King of France, with twice ten thousand men,
Marched up the hill, and then—marched down again."

Primarily for these two reasons—to urge Eli Jones to his feet, and to joke the former officers by appointing a Quaker, an avowed peace advocate—he was unanimously chosen to fill the vacancy of Major-General.

The nomination was so entirely unexpected by Eli Jones that he was at first perplexed by the situation. He saw that much was at stake, and that wisdom and caution were needed. Having his horse at Augusta, he drove that night to his home at Dirigo, fifteen miles away, chiefly, perhaps, to discuss the situation with his beloved Sibyl and the Friends most suitable for counsel. After talking far into the night with his brother-in-law, James Van Blarcom, he walked the floor alone until the new day was dawning.

Upon reaching Augusta again, he found the occasion far more important than he had anticipated. The news had spread that the Quaker was to speak in regard to his appointment, and the Hall of the Representatives was crowded. Not only were most of the members of the Senate present, but many other citizens. The subject of the appointment was introduced, and Eli Jones spoke in substance as follows:

"Whatever my ambitions may have been in times past, my aspirations have never embraced such an office as this as an object of desire. I can assure the House that my election as Major-General was an honor wholly unexpected. It is true that when the governor announced to the House the existence of the vacancy, a member privately remarked to me, 'I shall vote for you;' but I replied, declining the honor, and proposed to return the compliment.

"To my mind there is something ominous in this occurrence. I regard it as one of the developments of the times. Who of us, when assembled ten years ago, in quiet and retired places, to affix our signatures to pledges of abstinence from intoxicating drinks, would have believed that in 1855 we should be elected to the seats we now occupy, amid the overwhelming rejoicings of the people, and pledged to support the Maine Law? Who that at that time had visited the plantations of the South and seen the slave toiling under the lash of the taskmaster, would have believed that in 1855 the people of the larger portion of this great land would have roused with stern determination to subdue the encroachments of the slave power, and have pledged themselves never to cease their labors until the wrongs of slavery should be ameliorated—nay, *more,* until slavery itself should be abolished?

"Still more wonderful! Who would have believed that the State of Maine, which a few years since gloried in an Aroostook expedition, and was noisy with military training and the noise of arms, would, in 1855, exhibit the spectacle of a peaceable member of the Society of Friends being elected to the post of Major-General of a division of the militia, and that, too, by the representatives in their legislative capacity?

"But I have endeavored to regulate my own conduct by the principle that legislation should not go very far in advance of public sentiment, and it seems to me that this election may possibly be ahead of that sentiment. I therefore submit this suggestion in all candor.

"It is generally understood that I entertain peculiar views in respect to the policy of war. If, however, I am an exponent of the views of the Legislature on that subject, I will cheerfully undertake to serve the State in the capacity indicated. With much pleasure I shall stand before the militia of the second division and give such orders as I think best. The first would be, 'Ground arms.' The second would be, 'Right about face; beat your swords into plowshares and your spears into pruning-hooks, and learn war no more." I should then dismiss every man to his farm and to his merchandise, with an admonition to read daily at his fireside the New Testament, and ponder upon its tidings of 'Peace on earth, good will toward men.'

"If, on the other hand, it should be determined that my election is a little in advance of the times, I am willing, as a good citizen, to bow to the majesty of the law, and, as a member of the Legislature, to consult its dignity and decline the exalted position tendered me by the House—and I will now decline it. With pleasure I now surrender to the House this trust and the honor, and retire to private life."

This speech was delivered amid interruptions of loud applause, and made a great sensation throughout the State; and not in Maine only, but it was commented on by many of the newspapers, and appeared in the columns of English journals.

The fourth and last tenet of the Quakers is on the subject of the unlawfulness of a pecuniary maintenance of a gospel ministry.

In explaining this tenet, I am aware that I am treading upon delicate ground. The great majority of christians have determined that the spiritual laborer is worthy of his hire; that if men relinquish the usual occupations by which a livelihood is obtained, in order that they may devote themselves to the service of religion, they are entitled to a pecuniary maintenance; and that, if they produce a rich harvest from what they sow, they are of all men, considering their usefulness to man to be greater in this than in any other service they can render him, the most worthy of encouragement and support. I am aware also of the possibility of giving offence to some in the course of the explanation of this tenet. To these I can only say, that I have no intention of hurting the feelings of any; that in the church there are those whom I esteem and love, and whom of all others I should be sorry to offend. But it must be obvious to these, and indeed to all, that it is impossible for me in writing a history of the manners and opinions of the Quakers, to pass over in silence the tenet that is now before me; and if I notice it, they must be sensible that it becomes me to state fully and fairly all the arguments which the Quakers give for the difference of opinion, which they manifest from the rest of their fellow citizens, on this subject.

It does not appear then, the Quakers say, by any records that can be produced, that Jesus Christ ever received any payment for the doctrines which he taught, neither does it appear, as far as his own instructions, which are recorded by the evangelists, can be collected on this subject, that he considered any pecuniary stipend as necessary or proper for those who are to assist in the promotion of his religion.

Jesus Christ, on the erection of his gospel ministry, gave rules to his disciples how they were to conduct themselves in the case before us. He enjoined the twelve, before he sent them on this errand, as we collect from St. Matthew and St. Luke, that, "as they had received freely, so they were to give freely; that they were to provide neither gold, nor silver, nor brass in their purses, nor scrip, nor other things for their journey; for the workman was worthy of his meat." And, on their return from their mission, he asked them, "When I sent you without purse, and scrip, and shoes, lacked ye anything? And they said nothing. Then said he unto them, But now he that hath a purse let him take it, and likewise his scrip."

In a little time afterwards, Jesus Christ sent out other seventy as disciples, to whom he gave instructions similar to the former, that they should not take scrip, clothes, and money with them. But to these he said additionally, that wheresoever they were received, they were to eat such things as were given them; but where they were not received, they were to go their way, and say, Even the dust of your city, which cleaveth on us, we do wipe off against you." And as on that occasion he compared the ministers of his gospel to the laborers, whom a man sends to the harvest, he told them they were at liberty to eat what was set before them, because the laborer was worthy of his hire.

This the Quakers conceive to be the substance of all that Jesus Christ taught upon this subject. They go therefore next to St. Paul for a farther elucidation of it.

They are of opinion that St. Paul, in his epistle to Timothy, and to the Corinthians, and Galatians, acknowledges the position, that the spiritual laborer is worthy of his hire.

The same apostle, however, says, "that if any would not work, neither should he eat." From this text the Quakers draw two conclusions, first, that when ministers of the gospel are idle, they are not entitled to bodily sustenance; and, secondly, that those only who receive them are expected to support them. The same apostle says also, "Let him that is taught in the word communicate unto him that teacheth in all good things," but he no where says, "to him that teacheth not."

But though men, who faithfully spend their time in preaching the gospel, are entitled to bodily maintenance from those who receive them, yet St. Paul, the Quakers say, as far as his own practice was concerned, thought it more consistent with the spirit of christianity, and less detrimental to its interests to support himself by the labor of his own hands, than to be supported by that of others. And he advises others to do the same, and not to make their preaching chargeable, "not because, says he, we have not power, but to make ourselves an ensample to you to follow us."

This power the Quakers consider ministers of the gospel to abuse, who make their preaching chargeable, if by any means they can support themselves; for St. Paul says farther, "what is my reward then? Verily that, when I preach the gospel, I may make the gospel of Christ without charge, that I abuse not my power in the gospel." Thus the apostle, they conceive, looks up to God and not to men for the reward of his spiritual labors. And the same apostle makes it a characteristic of the false teachers, that they make merchandize of their hearers.

It is objected to the Quakers on this occasion, that St. Paul received relief from the brethren at Philippi, as well as from others, when he did not preach. But their reply is, that this relief consisted of voluntary and affectionate presents sent to him in circumstances of distress. In this case the apostle states, that he never desired these gifts, but that it was pleasant to him to see his religious instruction produce a benevolence of disposition that would abound to their account.

St. Peter is the only other person who is mentioned in the New Testament as speaking on this subject. Writing to those who had been called to the spiritual oversight of the churches, he advises as follows: "Feed the flock of God, which is among you, taking the oversight thereof not by constraint but willingly, not for filthy lucre, but of a ready mind, neither as being lords over God's heritage, but being examples to the flock. And when the chief Shepherd shall appear, ye shall receive a crown of glory that fadeth not away." Upon these words the Quakers make three observations: that ministers should not make a gain of the gospel; that they should look to God for their reward, and not to men; and that Peter himself must have preached like St. Paul, without fee or reward, or he could not consistently have recommended such a practice to others."

We may add here that the denomination known among us today as Primitive Baptists hold to the same tenet as the Quakers in respect to paying preachers a stated salary.

These four tenets it may be remarked are the causes why Quakers have been so bitterly and relentlessly persecuted. There are two great motives which influence unregenerate man more than aught else. They are "interest" and "appetite." Quakerism assailed both and persecution was inevitable.

CHAPTER VI.

THE DRESS OF THE QUAKERS.

We shall now see why the Quakers are considered quaint. Voltaire says, "Dress changes the manners," to which the Quakers make answer that Regeneration changes the dress, that of a savage into one of decency, that of a christian into one of simplicity.

Quoting from the same volume, the author has this to say:

I have now explained, in a very ample manner, the moral education and discipline of the Quakers. I shall proceed to the explanation of such customs as seem peculiar to them as a society of christians.

The dress of the Quakers is the first custom of this nature that I propose to notice. They stand distinguished by means of it from all other religious bodies. The men wear neither lace, frills, ruffles, swords, nor any of the ornaments used by the fashionable world. The women wear neither lace, flounces, lappets, rings, bracelets, necklaces, ear rings, nor anything belonging to this class. Both sexes are also particular in the choice of the color of their clothes. All gay colors such as red, blue, green, and yellow, are exploded. Dressing in this manner, a Quaker is known by his apparel through the whole kingdom. This is not the case with any other individuals of the island, except the clergy; and these, in consequence of black garments worn by persons on account of the death of their relations, are not always distinguished from others.

I know of no custom among the Quakers which has more excited the curiosity of the world, than this of their dress, and none in which they have been more mistaken in their conjectures concerning it.

In the early times of the English history, dress had been frequently restricted by the government. Persons of a certain rank and fortune were permitted to wear only clothing of a certain kind. But these restrictions and distinctions were gradually broken down, and people, as they were able and willing, launched out into unlimited extravagance in their dress. The fifteenth and sixteenth centuries, and down from thence to the time when the Quakers first appeared, were periods particularly noticed for prodigality in the use of apparel, there was nothing too expensive or too preposterous to be worn. Our ancestors, also, to use an ancient quotation, "were never constant to one color or fashion two months to an end." We can have no idea by the present generation, of the folly in such respects, of these early ages. But these follies were not confined to the laity. Affectation of parade, and gaudy clothing, were admitted among many of the clergy, who incurred the severest invectives of the poets on that account. The ploughman, in Chaucer's Canterbury Tales, is full upon this point. He gives us the following description of a priest:

"That hye on horse wylleth to ride,
In glytter ande gold of great arraye,
'I painted and pertred all in pryde,
No common knyght may go so gaye;
Chaunge of clothying every daye,
With golden gyrdles great and small,
As boysterous as is bere at baye;
All suche falshed mote nede fall."

To this he adds, that many of them had more than one or two mitres, embellished with pearls, like the head of a queen, and a staff of gold set with jewels, as heavy as lead. He then speaks of their appearing out of doors with broad bucklers and long swords, or with baldries about their necks, instead of stoles, to which their basellards were attached.

"Bucklers brode and sweardes longe,
Baudryke with baselards kene."

He then accuses them of wearing gay gowns of scarlet and green colors, ornamented with cut work, and for the long pykes upon their shoes.

But so late as the year 1652 we have the following anecdote of the whimsical dress of a clergyman. John Owen, Dean of Christ church, and vice-chancellor, of Oxford, is represented as wearing a lawn band, as having his hair powdered and his hat curiously cocked. He is discribed also as wearing Spanish leather boots with lawn tops, and snake bone band strings, with large tassels, and a large set of ribbands, pointed at his knees with points or tags at the end. And much about the same time, when Charles the second was at Newmarket, Nathaniel Vincent, doctor of divinity, fellow of Clarehall, and chaplain in ordinary to his majesty, preached before him. But the king was so displeased with the foppery of this preacher's dress, that he commanded the duke of Monmouth, then chancellor of the university, to cause the statutes concerning decency of apparel among the clergy to be put into execution, which was accordingly done. These instances are sufficient to show that the taste for preposterous and extravagant dress must have operated like a contagion in those times, or the clergy would scarcely have dressed themselves in this ridiculous and censurable manner.

But although this extravagance was found among many orders of society at the time of the appearance of George Fox, yet many individuals had set their faces against the fashions of the world. These consisted principally of religious people of different denominations, most of whom were in the middle classes of life. Such persons were found in plain and simple habits notwithstanding the contagion of the example of their superiors in rank. The men of this description generally wore plain round hats with common crowns. They had discarded the sugar-loaf-hat, and the hat turned up with a silver clasp on one side, as well as all ornaments belonging to it, such as pictures, feathers, and bands of various colors. They had adopted a plain suit of clothes. They wore cloaks, when necessary, over these. But both the clothes and the cloaks were of the same color. The color of each of them were either drab or gray. Other people who followed the fashions, wore white, red, green, yellow, violet, scarlet and other colors, which were expensive, because they were principally dyed in foreign parts. The drab consisted of the white wool undyed, and the grey of the white wool mixed with black, which was undyed also. These colors were then the colors of the clothes, because they were the least expensive, of the peasants of England, as they are now of those of Portugal and Spain. They had discarded also, all ornaments, such as of lace, or bunches of ribands at the knees, and their buttons were generally of alchymy, as this composition was then termed, or of the same color as their clothes.

The grave and religious women also, like the men, had avoided the fashions of their times. These had adopted the cap and the black hood for their head-dress. The black hood had been long the distinguishing mark of a grave matron. All prostitutes, so early as Edward the third, had been forbidden to wear it. In after times it was celebrated by the epithet of venerable by the poets, and had been introduced by painters as the representative of virtue. When fashionable women had discarded it, which was the case in George Fox's time, the more sober, on account of these ancient marks of its sanctity, had retained it, and it was then common among them. With respect to the hair of grave and sober women in those days, it was worn plain, and covered occasionally by a plain hat or bonnet. They had avoided by this choice those preposterous head dresses and bonnets, which none but those who have seen paintings of them, could believe ever to have been worn. They admitted none of the large ruffs, that were then in use, but chose the plain handkerchief for their necks, differing from those of others, which had rich point and curious lace. They rejected the crimson satin doublet with black velvet skirts, and contented themselves with a plain gown, generally of stuff, and of a drab, or grey, or buff, or buffin color, as it was called, and faced with buckram. These colors, as I observed before, were the colors worn by country people; and were not expensive, because they were not dyed. To this gown was added a green apron. Green aprons had been long worn in England, yet at the time I allude to, they were out of fashion, so as to be ridiculed by the gay. But old fashioned people still retained them. Thus an idea of gravity was connected with them; and therefore religious and steady women adopted them as the grave and sober garments of ancient times.

It may now be observed that from these religious persons, habited in this manner, in opposition to the fashions of the world, the primitive Quakers generally sprung. George Fox himself wore the plain grey coat that has been noticed, with alchymy buttons, and a plain leather girdle about his waist. When the Quakers therefore first met in religious union they met in these simple clothes. They made no alteration in their dress on account of their new religion. They prescribed no form or color as distinguishing marks of their sect, but they carried with them the plain habits of their ancestors into the new society, as the habits of the grave and sober people of their own times.

CHAPTER VII.

THEIR FORMS OF SPEECH.

Another peculiarity of the Quakers is their language, especially in regard to the pronoun "thou." That our readers may fully understand why they use this form of speech, we again quote from the same lucid author.

As the Quakers are distinguishable from their fellow-citizens by their dress, as was amply shown in a former chapter, so they are no less distinguishable from them by the peculiarities of their language.

George Fox seemed to look at every custom with the eye of a reformer. The language of the country, as used in his own times, struck him as having many censurable defects. Many of the expressions, then in use, appeared to him to contain gross flattery, others to be idolatrous, others to be false representatives of the ideas they were intended to convey. Now he considered that christianity required truth, and he believed therefore that he and his followers, who professed to be christians in word and deed, and to follow the christian pattern in all things, as far as it could be found, were called upon to depart from all censurable modes of speech, as much as they were from any of the customs of the world, which christianity had deemed objectionable. And so weighty did these improprieties in his own language lie upon his mind, that he conceived himself to have had an especial commission to correct them.

The first alteration, which he adopted, was the use of the pronoun thou. The pronoun you, which grammarians had fixed to be of the plural number, was then occasionally used, but less than it is now, in addressing an individual. George Fox therefore adopted thou in its place on this occasion, leaving the word you to be used only where two or more individuals were addressed.

George Fox however was not the first of the religious writers, who had noticed the improper use of the pronoun you. Erasmus employed a treatise in showing the propriety of thou when addressed to a single person, and in ridiculing the use of you on the same occasion. Martin Luther also took great pains to expunge the word you from the station which it occupied, and to put thou in its place. In his Ludus, he ridiculed the use of the former by the following invented sentence, "Magister, Vosestis iratus?" This is as absurd, as if he had said in English, "Gentlemen, art thou angry."

But though George Fox was not the first to recommend the substitution of thou for you, he was the first to reduce this amended use of it to practice. This he did in his own person, wherever he went, and in all the works which he published. All his followers did the same. And, from his time to the present, the pronoun thou has come down so prominent in the speech of the society, that a Quaker is generally known by it at the present day.

The reader would hardly believe, if historical facts did not prove it, how much noise the introduction or rather the amended use of this little particle, as reduced to practice by George Fox, made in the world, and how much ill usage it occasioned the early Quakers. Many magistrates, before whom they were carried in the early times of their institution, occasioned their sufferings to be greater merely on this account. They were often abused and beaten by others, and sometimes put in danger of their lives. It was a common question put to a Quaker in those days, who addressed a great man in this new and simple manner, "why you ill bred clown do you thou me?" The rich and mighty of those times thought themselves degraded by this mode of address, as reducing them from a plural magnitude to a singular, or individual, or simple station of life.

"The use of thou," says George Fox, "was a sore cut to the proud flesh, and those who sought self-honor."

George Fox, finding that both he and his followers were thus subject to much persecution on this account, thought it right the world should know, that, in using this little particle which had given so much offence, the Quakers were only doing what every grammarian ought to do, if he followed his own rules. Accordingly a Quaker-work was produced, which was written to show that in all languages thou was the proper and usual form of speech to a single person, and you to more than one. This was exemplified by instances taken out of the scriptures, and out of books of teaching in about thirty languages. Two Quakers of the names of John Stubbs and Benjamin Furley, took great pains in compiling it; and some additions were made to it by George Fox himself, who was then a prisoner in Lancaster castle.

This work, as soon as it was published, was presented to King Charles the second, and to his council. Copies of it were also sent to the Archbishop of Canterbury, the Bishop of London, and to each of the universities. The King delivered his sentiments upon it so far as to say, that thou was undoubtedly the proper language of all nations. The Archbishop of Canterbury, when he was asked what he thought of it, is described to have been so much at a stand, that he could not tell what to say. The book was afterwards bought by many. It is said to have spread conviction wherever it went. Hence it had the effect of lessening the prejudices of some, so that the Quakers were never afterwards treated, on this account, in the same rugged manner as they had been before.

But though this book procured the Quakers an amelioration of treatment on the amended use of the expression thou, there were individuals in the society who thought they ought to put their defence on a better foundation, by stating all the reasons, for there were many besides those in this book, which had induced them to differ from their fellow citizens on this subject. This was done both by Robert Barclay and William Penn in works, which defended other principles of the Quakers, and other peculiarities in their language.

One of the arguments, by which the use of the pronoun thou was defended, was the same as that on which it had been defended by

Stubbs and Furley, that is, its strict conformity with grammar. The translators of the Bible had invariably used it. The liturgy had been compiled on the same principle. All addresses made by English christians in their private prayers to the Supreme Being, were made in the language of thou, and not of you. And this was done because the rules of the English grammar warranted the expression, and because any other mode of expression would have been a violation of these rules.

But the great argument (to omit all others) which Penn and Barclay insisted upon for the change of you, was that the pronoun thou, in addressing an individual, had been anciently in use, but that it had been deserted for you for no other purpose than that of flattery to men; and that this dereliction of it was growing greater and greater, upon the same principle, in their own times. Hence as christians, who were not to puff up the fleshly creature, it became them to return to the ancient and grammatical use of the pronoun thou, and to reject this growing fashion of the world. "The word you," says William Penn, "was first ascribed in the way of flattery, to proud Popes and Emperors, imitating the heathens' vain homage to their gods, thereby ascribing a plural honor to a single person, as if one Pope had been made up of many gods, and one Emperor of many men; for which reason you, only to be addressed to many, became first spoken to one. It seemed the word thou looked like too lean and thin a respect; and therefore some, bigger than they should be, would have a style suitable to their own ambition."

Another alteration that took place in the language of the Quakers, was the expunging of all expressions from their vocabulary, which were either superfluous or of the same flattering tendency as the former.

In addressing one another, either personally or by letter, they made use of the word friend, to signify the bond of their own union, and the character, which man, under the christian dispensation, was bound to exhibit in dealings with his fellow-man. They addressed each other also, and spoke of each other by their real names. If a man's name was John, they called him John; they talked to him as John, and added only his surname to distinguish him from others.

In their intercourse with the world they adopted the same mode of speech, for they addressed individuals either by their plain names, or they made use of the appellations of friends or neighbors.

They rejected the word sir or madam, as then in use. This they did, because they considered them like the word you, as remnants of ancient flattery, derived from the papal and anti-christian ages; and because these words still continued to be considered as titles of flattery, that puffed up people in their own times. Howell, who was before quoted on the pronoun thou, is usually quoted by the Quakers on this occasion also. He states in his history, that "sir and madam were originally names given to none but the king, his brother and their wives, both in France and England. Yet now the ploughman in France is called sir and his wife madam; and men of ordinary trades in England sir and their wives dame, which is the legal title of a lady and is the same as madame in French. So prevalent hath pride and flattery been in all ages, the one to give and the other to receive respect."

The Quakers banished also the word master, or mister as it is now pronounced, from their language, either when they spoke concerning any one, or addressed any one by letter. To have used the word master to a person, who was no master over them, would have been, they considered, to have indicated a needless servility, and to have given a false picture of their own situation, as well as of those addressed.

Upon the same or similar principles they hesitated to subscribe themselves as the humble or obedient servants of any one, as is now usual, at the bottom of their letters. "Horrid apostacy," says Barclay, "for it is notorious that the use of these compliments implies not any design or service." This expression in particular they reprobated for another reason. It was one of those which had followed the last degree of impious services and expressions, which had poured in after the statues of the emperors had been worshipped, after the titles of eternity and divinity had been ushered in, and after thou had been exchanged for you, and it had taken a certain station and flourished among these. Good christians, however, had endeavored to keep themselves clear of such inconsistencies. Casaubon has preserved a letter of Paulinus, Bishop of Nola, in which he rebukes Sulpicius Severus for having subscribed himself "his humble servant." A part of the letter runs thus: "Take heed, hereafter, how thou, being from a servant called unto liberty, doth subscribe thyself servant to one who is thy brother and fellow servant; for it is a sinful flattery, not a testament of humility, to pay those honors to a man and to a sinner, which are due to the one Lord, one Master and one God."

The Quakers also banished from the use of their society all those modes of expression which were considered as marks or designations of honor among men. Hence, in addressing any peer of the realm, they never used the common formula of "my lord," for, though the peer in question might justly be the lord of many possessions, and tenants, and servants, yet he was no lord over their heritages or persons. Neither did they ever use the terms excellency, or grace, or honor, upon similar occasions. They considered that the bestowing of these titles might bring them under the necessity of uttering what might be occasionaly false. "For the persons," says Barclay, "obtaining these titles, either by election or hereditarily, may frequently be found to have nothing really in them deserving them, or answering to them, as some, to whom it is said, 'your excellency may have nothing of excellency in them, and he who is called your grace may be an enemy to grace, and he who called your honor may be base and ignoble.'" They considered also, that they might be setting up the creature, by giving him the titles of the Creator, so that he might think more highly of himself than he ought, and more degradingly than he ought of the rest of the human race.

But, independently of these moral considerations, they rejected these titles, because they believed that Jesus Christ had set them an example by his own declarations and conduct on a certain occasion. When a person addressed him by the name of good master, he was rebuked as having done an improper thing. "Why," says our Saviour, "callest thou me good? There is none good but one, that is God." This censure they believed to have been passed upon him, because Jesus Christ knew, that when he addressed him by this title, he addressed him, not in his divine nature or capacity, but only as a man.

But Jesus Christ not only refused to receive such titles of distinction himself in his human nature, but on another occasion exhorted his followers to shun them also. They were not to be like the Scribes and Pharisees, who wished for high and eminent distinctions, that is, to be called Rabbi Rabb of men; but, says he, "be ye not called Rabbi, for one is your master, even Christ, and all ye are brethren;" and he makes the desire which he discovered in the Jews, of seeking after worldly instead of heavenly honors, to be one cause of their infidelity towards Christ, for that such could not believe, as received honor from one another, and sought not the honor which cometh from God only; that is, that those persons, who courted earthly honors, could not have that humility of mind, that spirit that was to be of no reputation in the world, which was essential to those who wished to become the followers of Christ.

These considerations, both those of a moral nature and those of the example of Jesus Christ, weighed so much with the early Quakers that they made no exceptions, even in favor of those of royal dignity or of the rulers of their own land. George Fox wrote several letters to great men. He wrote twice to the king of Poland, three or four times to Oliver Cromwell, and several times to Charles the second; but he addressed them in no other manner than by their plain names or by simple titles, expressive of their situations as rulers or kings.

These several alterations, which took place in the language of the early Quakers, were adopted by their several successors and are in force in the society at the present day.

Another alteration, which took place in the language of the Quakers, was the disuse of the common names of the days of the week, and those of the months of the year.

The names of the days were considered to be of heathen origin. Sunday had been so called by the Saxons, because it was the day on which they sacrificed to the sun. Monday on which they sacrificed to the moon. Tuesday to the god Tuisco. Wednesday to the god Woden. Thursday to the god Thor, and so on. Now when the Quakers considered that Jehovah had forbidden the Israelites to make mention even of the names of other gods, they thought it inconsistent in christians to continue to use the names of heathen idols for the common divisions of their time, so that these names must be almost always in their mouths. They thought, too, that they were paying a homage, in continuing the use of them, that bordered on idolatry. They considered also as neither Monday nor Tuesday nor any other of these days were days in which these sacrifices were now offered, they were using words which conveyed false notions of things. Hence they determined upon the disuse of these words, and to put other names in their stead. The numerical way of naming the days seemed to them to be the most rational and the most innocent. They called therefore Sunday the first day, Monday the second, Tuesday the third, and so on to Saturday, which was of course the seventh. They used no other names but these, either in their conversation or in their letters.

Upon the same principles they altered the names of the months also. These, such as March and June, which had been so named by the ancient Romans because they were sacred to Mars and Juno, were exploded because they seemed in the use of them to be expressive of a kind of idolatrous homage. Others again were exploded because they were not the representatives of the truth. September, for example, means the seventh month from the storms. It took this seventh station in the calendar of Romulus, and it designated there its own station as well as the reason of its name. But when it lost its place in the calendar by the alteration of the style in England, it lost its meaning. It became no representative of its station nor any representative of the truth, for it still continues to signify the seventh month, whereas it is made to represent, or to stand in the place of the ninth. The Quakers therefore banished from their language the ancient names of the months, and, as they thought they could not do better than they had done in the case of the days, they placed numericals in their stead. They called January the first month, February the second, March the third, and so on to December, which they called the twelfth. Thus the Quaker calendar was made up by numerical distinctions, which have continued to the present day.

Another alteration, which took place very generally in the language of the Quakers, was the rejection of the word saint when they spoke either of the apostles, or of the primitive fathers. The papal authority had canonized these. This they considered to be an act of idolatry, and they thought they should be giving sanction to superstition, if they continued the use of such a title, either in their speech or writings. After this, various other alterations took place according as individuals among them thought it right to expunge old expressions, and to substitute new; and these alterations were adopted by the rest, as they had an opinion of those who used them, or as they felt the propriety of doing it. Hence new phrases came into use, different from those which were used by the world on the same occasions; and these were gradually spread till they became incorporated into the language of the society. Of these the following examples may suffice.

It is not usual with Quakers to use the words lucky or fortunate, in the way in which many others do. If a Quaker had been out on a journey, and had experienced a number of fine days, he would never say that he had been lucky in his weather. In the same manner if a Quaker had recovered from an indisposition, he would never say, in speaking of the circumstance, that he had fortunately recovered, but he would say, that he had recovered, and "that it was a favor." Luck, chance, or fortune are allowed by the Quakers to have no power in the settlement of human affairs

It is not usual with Quakers to beg ten thousand pardons, as some of the world do, for any little mistake. A Quaker generally on such an occasion asks a person's excuse.

The Quakers never make use of the expression "christian name." This name is called christian by the world, because it is the name given to children in baptism, or in other words, when they are christened, or when they are initiated as christians. But the Quakers are never baptized. They have no belief that water baptism can make a christian, or that it is any true mark of membership with the christian church. Hence a man's christian name is called by them his first name, because it is the first of the two, or of any other number of names that may belong to him.

The Quakers, on meeting a person, never say "good morrow," because all days are equally good. Nor in parting with a person at night, do they say "good evening," for a similar reason, but they make use of the expression of "farewell."

I might proceed, till I made a little vocabulary of Quaker expressions; but this is not necessary, and it is not at all consistent with my design. I shall therefore only observe, that it is expected of Quakers, that they should use the language of the society; that they should substitute thou for you; that they should discard all flattering titles and expressions; and that they should adopt the numerical, instead of the heathen names, of the days and months. George Fox gave the example himself in all these instances. Those of the society who depart from this usage are said by the Quakers to depart from "the plain language."

The Quakers were certainly a consistent people and carried this jewel wherever they went—in the palace of the rich as well as the cottage of the poor. The same reasons which led them to discard the use of "you" for "thou," also led them to keep their hats on when in the presence of those to whom their taking them off would be a mark of honor to which they were not entitled. An amusing instance of this occurred in the case of Fox himself.

When George Fox, and two other friends, were brought out of Launceston gaol, to be tried before judge Glynn, who was then chief justice of England, they came into court with their hats on. The judge asked them the reason of this, but they said nothing. He then told them that the court commanded them to pull off their hats. Upon this George Fox addressed them in the following manner: "Where, says he, did ever any magistrate, king or judge, from Moses to Daniel, command any to pull off their hats when they came before them in their courts, either amongst the Jews, who were God's people, or among the heathen? And if the law of England doth command any such thing, show me that law, either written or printed." Judge Glynn upon this grew angry, and replied that "he did not carry his law books upon his back." But says George Fox, "tell me where it is printed in any statute book, that I may read it." The judge in a very vulgar manner, ordered him away, and he was accordingly taken away, and put among thieves. The judge, however, in a short time afterwards ordered him up again, and, on his return, put to him the following question. "Come," says he, "where had they hats from Moses to Daniel? Come, answer me. I have you fast now." George Fox replied, that "he might read in the third chapter of Daniel, that the three children were cast into the fiery furnace by Nebuchadnezzar's command, with their coats, their hose, and their hats on." The repetition of this apposite text stopped the judge from any further comments on the custom, and he ordered him and his companions to be taken away again. And they were accordingly taken away and they were thrust again among thieves. In process of time, however, this custom of the Quakers began to be known among the judges, who so far respected their scruples as to take care that their hats should be taken off in future in the courts.

These omissions of the ceremonies of the world, as begun by the primitive Quakers, are continued by the modern. They neither bow nor scrape, nor pull off their hats to any, by way of civility or respect, and they carry their principles like their predecessors, so far, that they observe none of these exterior parts of politeness even in the presence of royalty. The Quakers are in the habit on particular occasions of sendings deputies to the king. And it is remarkable that his present majesty always sees them himself, if he be well, and not by proxy. Notwithstanding this, no one in the deputation ever pulls off his hat. Those, however, who are in waiting in the anti-chamber, knowing this custom of the Quakers, take their hats from their heads before they enter the room where the king is. On entering the room they neither bow nor scrape nor kneel, and as this ceremony cannot be performed for them by others, they go into the royal presence in a less servile, or more dignified manner, than either the representatives of sovereigns or those who have humbled nations by the achievements of great victories.

In the company of the Quakers a circumstance sometimes occurs, of so peculiar a nature, that it cannot be well omitted in this place. It sometimes happens that you observe a pause in the conversation. This pause continues. Surprised at the universal silence now prevailing, you look around and find all the Quakers in the room apparently thoughtful. The history of the circumstance is this. In the course of the conversation the mind of some one of the persons present has been so overcome with the weight or importance of it, or so overcome by inward suggestions or other subjects, as to have given himself up to meditation, or to passive obedience to the impressions upon his mind. This person is soon discovered by the rest on account of his particular silence and gravity. From this moment the Quakers in company cease to converse. They become habitually silent, and continue so, both old and young, to give the apparently meditating person an opportunity of pursuing uninterruptedly the train of his own thoughts. Perhaps, in the course of his meditations, the subject that impressed his mind gradually dies away and expires in silence. In this case you find him resuming his natural position, and returning to conversation with the company as before. It sometimes happens, however, that in the midst of his meditations he feels an impulse to communicate to those present the subject of his thoughts, and breaks forth, seriously explaining, exhorting and advising, as the nature of it permits and suggests. When he has finished his observations, the company remain silent for a short time, after which they converse again as before.

The Quakers are generally supposed to be a stiff and reserved people, and to be a people of severe and uncourteous manners. I confess there is something in their appearance that will justify the supposition in the eyes of strangers, and of such as do not know them; I mean of such as just see them occasionally out of doors, but do not mix with them in their own houses.

It cannot be expected that persons, educated like the Quakers, should assimilate much in their manners to other people. The very dress they wear, which is so different from that of others, would give them a stiff appearance in the eyes of the world, if nothing else could be found to contribute towards it. Excluded also from much intercourse with the world, and separated at a vast distance from it by the singularity of many of their customs, they would naturally appear to others to be close and reserved. Neither is it to be expected that those, whose spirits are never animated by music, or enlivened by the exhibitions of the theatre, or the diversions which others follow, would have other than countenances that were grave. Their discipline also, which calls them so frequently to important duties, and the dispatch of serious business, would produce the same feature. I may observe, also, that a peculiarity of gait, which might be mistaken for awkardness, might not unreasonably be expected in those, who had neither learned to walk under the guidance of a dancing master, nor to bow under the direction of the dominion of fashion. If those and those only are to be esteemed really polished and courteous, who bow and scrape, and salute each other by certain prescribed gestures, then the Quakers will appear to have contracted much rust, and to have an indisputable right to the title of a clownish and inflexible people.

I must observe however that these appearances, though they may be substantial in the estimation of those who do not know them, gradually vanish with those who do. Their hospitality in their own houses, and their great attention and kindness, soon force out of sight all ideas of uncourteousness. Their freedom also soon annihilates those of stiffness and reserve. Their manners, though they have not the polish surface of those which are usually attached to fashionable life, are agreeable when known.

There is one trait in the Quaker manners which runs through the whole society, as far as I have seen in their houses, and which is worthy of mention. The Quakers appear to be particularly gratified when those who visit them ask for what they want. Instead of considering this as rudeness or intrusion, they esteem it as a favor done them. The circumstance of asking, on such an occasion, is to them a proof that their visitors feel themselves at home. Indeed they almost always desire a stranger who has been introduced to them "to be free." This is their usual expression. And if he assures them that he will, and they find him asking for what he wishes to have, you may preceive in their countenances the pleasure which his conduct has given them. They consider him, when he has used this freedom, to have acted, as they express it, "kindly." Nothing can be more truly polite than that conduct to another, by which he shall be induced to feel himself as comfortably situated as if he were in his own house.

As the Quakers desire their visitors to be free, and to do as they please, so they do not fail to do the same themselves, never regarding such visitors as impediments in the way of their concerns. If they have any business or engagements out of doors, they say so and go, using no ceremony and but few words as an apology. Their visitors, I mean such as stay for a time in their houses, are left in the interim to amuse themselves as they please. This is peculiarly agreeable, because their friends know, when they visit them, that they neither restrain, nor shackle, nor put them to inconvenience. In fact it may be truly said that if satisfaction in visiting depends upon a man's own freedom to do as he likes, to ask and call for what he wants, to go out and come in as he pleases; and if it depends also on the knowledge he has, that, in doing all these things, he puts no person out of his way, there are no houses where people will be better pleased with their treatment than in those of the Quakers.

The Quakers, as a religious body, agree in the propriety of grace before their meals, that is, in the propriety of giving thanks to the author of every good gift for this particular bounty of his providence as to the articles of their daily subsistence, but they differ as to the manner and seasonableness of it on such occasions. They think that people who are in the habit of repeating a determined form of words, may cease to feel as they pronounce them, in which case the grace becomes an oblation from the tongue but not from the heart. They think also that if grace is to be repeated regularly, just as the victuals come, or as regularly and as often as they come upon the table, it may be repeated unseasonably, that is unseasonably with the state of the heart of him who is to pronounce it; that the heart of man is not today as it was yesterday, nor at this hour what it was at a former, nor on any given hour alike disposed; and that if this grace is to be said when the heart is gay, or light, or volatile, it ceases to be a devotional act, and becomes at least a superfluous and unmeaning if not a censurable form.

CHAPTER VIII.

INDUCTION AS MINISTERS.

The manner in which a person, male or female, is inducted into the ministry is also peculiar.

Any member has a right to rise up in the meetings for worship, and to speak publicly. If any one, therefore, should rise up and preach, who has never done so before, he is heard. The congregation are all witnesses of his doctrine. The elders, however, who may be present, and to whose province it more immediately belongs to judge of the fitness of ministers, observe the tenor of his discourse. They watch over it for its authority; that is, they judge by its spiritual influence on the mind, whether it be such as corresponds with that which may be persumed to come from the Spirit of God. If the new preacher delivers any thing that appears exceptionable, and continues to do so, it is the duty of the elders to speak to him in private, and to desire him to discontinue his services to the church. But if nothing exceptionable occurs, nothing is said to him, and he is allowed to deliver himself publicly at future meetings. In process of time, if, after repeated attempts in the office of the ministry, the new preacher should have given satisfactory proof of his gifts, he is reported to the monthly meeting to which he belongs. And this meeting, if satisfied with his ministry, acknowledges him as a minister, and then recommends him to the meeting of ministers and elders belonging to the same. No other act than this is requisite. He receives no verbal or written appointment or power for the execution of the sacerdotal office. It may be observed also, that he neither gains any authority, nor loses any privilege, by thus becoming a minister of the gospel. Except, while in the immediate exercise of his calling, he is only a common member. He receives no elevation by the assumption of any nominal title, to distinguish him from the rest. Nor is he elevated by the prospect of any increase to his worldly goods in consequence of his new office, for no minister in this society receives any pecuniary emolution for his spiritual labors.

When ministers are thus approved and acknowledged, they exercise the sacred office in public assemblies, as they immediately feel themselves influenced to that work. They may engage, also, with the approbation of their own monthly meeting, in the work of visiting such Quaker families as reside in the county, or quarterly meeting to which they belong. In this case they are sometimes accompanied by one of the elders of the church. These visits have the name of family visits, and are conducted in the following manner:

When a Quaker minister, after having commenced his journey, has entered the house of the first family, the individual members are collected to receive him. They then sit in silence for a time. As he believes himself concerned to speak, he delivers that which arises in his mind with religious freedom. The master, the wife, and the other branches of the family, are sometimes severally addressed. Does the minister feel that there is a departure in any of the persons present, from the principles or practice of the society, he speaks, if he believes it required of him, to these points. Is there any well disposed person under any inward discouragement, this person may be addressed in the language of consolation. All in fact are exhorted and advised as their several circumstances may seem to require. When the religious visit is over, the minister, if there be occasion, takes some little refreshment with the family, and converses with them; but no light or trifling subject is ever entered upon on these occasions. From one family he passes to another, till he has visited all the families in the district for which he had felt a concern.

A spirit of discernment and prophecy seems to have characterized the ministry of many preachers among Friends, and Mahlon Hockett was noted for speaking to that which was in the minds of others, and telling them of their misdeeds. On one occasion two ungodly men were discussing the manner in which they should spend the Sabbath morning, when one of them said, "Let's go and hear what old Mahlon has to say to-day." Accordingly they went to Springfield meeting. Soon after they entered, Mahlon, fastening his eyes upon them, arose and said, "Well, let's go and hear what old Mahlon has to say to-day." He thus gained their attention, and proceeded to preach a sermon which was blessed to the good of their souls.

On another occasion a woman entered, while he was preaching. He stopped a moment, looked at her, and remarked, "Go and carry home that filling, and thou shalt have peace of mind." He then proceeded with his subject. The woman took home the filling, which she had stolen from a neighbor for whom she had been weaving, confessed her sin, and became a changed character.

Two of the most remarkable prophecies concerning the civil war in this country were made by Joseph Hoag. He was born of Presbyterian parents, in New York, in 1762. He became a Friend and minister, and settled at Monkton, Vt. In 1820 he was traveling with a companion, on horseback, visiting the meetings of Friends in Pennsylvania. As they were riding he suddenly stopped his horse; looking around him and then down to the ground, he said to his friend, "My horse's feet are wading in blood, even to the fetlocks." Upon this very ground, forty-three years later, was fought the terrible battle of Gettysburg, July 1, 2 and 3, 1863.

Joseph Hoag's wonderful vision concerning the civil war and the abolition of slavery was widely published long before the war, but it should have a place here.

VISION OF JOSEPH HOAG.

"In the year 1803, probably the eighth or ninth month, I was alone in the fields and observed that the sun shone clear, but that a mist eclipsed the brightness of its shining. As I reflected upon the singularity of the event, my mind was drawn into silence the most solemn I ever remember to have witnessed, for it seemed as if all my faculties were laid low and unusually brought into deep solemnity. I said to myself, 'What can all this mean? I do not recollect ever before to have been sensible of such feelings,' and I heard a voice from Heaven say, 'This that thou seest which dims the brightness of the sun, is a sign of the present and coming times. I took the forefathers of this country from a land of oppression; I planted them here among the people of the forest; I sustained them; and while they were humble I blessed and fed them, and they became a numerous people; but they have now become proud and lifted up, and have forgotten Me who nourished and protected them in the wilderness, and are running into every abomination and evil practice of which the old countries are guilty; I have taken quietude from the land, and suffered a dividing spirit to come among them. Lift up thine eyes and behold.'

"And I saw them dividing in great heat. This division began in the church upon points of doctrine. It commenced in the Presbyterian Society and went through the various denominations, and in its progress and close its effect was nearly the same. Those who dissented went off with high heads and taunting language, and those who kept to the original sentiment appeared exercised and sorrowful. And when this dividing spirit entered the Society of Friends it raged in as high a degree as any I had before discovered; and as before, those who separated went away with lofty looks and taunting, censuring language, while those who kept to the ancient principles retired by themselves.

"It next appeared in the lodges of Free Masons, and it broke out like a volcano, insomuch that it set the country in an uproar for a length of time. Then it entered politics throughout the United States, and it did not stop until it produced civil war, and an abundance of human blood was shed in the combat. The Southern States lost their power, and slavery was annihilated from their borders."

No one day, in the estimation of the Quakers, can be made by human appointment either more holy or more proper for worship than another. They do not even believe that the Jewish Sabbath, which was by the appointment of God, continues in gospel times, or that it has been handed down by divine authority as the true Sabbath for christians. All days with the Quakers are equally holy, and all equally proper for the worship of God. In this opinion they coincide with the ever memorable John Hales. "For prayer, indeed," says this venerable man, "was the Sabbath ordained, yet prayer itself is Sabbathless, and admits of no rest, no intermission at all. If our hands be clean, we must, as our Apostle commands us, lift them up everywhere, at all times, and make every place a church, every day a Sabbath-day, every hour canonical. As you go to the market, as you stand in the streets, as you walk in the fields—in all these places you may pray as well, and with as good acceptance as in the church; for you yourselves are temples of the holy ghost, if the grace of God be in you, more precious than any of those which are made with hands."

Though, however, the Quakers believe no one day in the sight of God to be holier than another, and no one capable of being rendered so by human authority, yet they think that christians ought to assemble for the public worship of God. They think they ought to bear an outward and public testimony for God; and this can only be done by becoming members of a visible church, where they may be seen to acknowledge him publicly in the face of men. They think, also, that the public worship of God increases, as it were, the fire of devotion, and enlarges the sphere of spiritual life in the souls of men. "God causes the inward life," says Barclay, "the more to abound when his children assemble themselves diligently together, to wait upon him; so that as iron sharpeneth iron, the seeing the faces of one another, when both are inwardly gathered unto the life, giveth occasion for the life secretly to rise, and to pass from vessel to vessel; and as many candles lighted and put in one place do greatly augment the light and make it more to shine forth, so when many are gathered together into the same life, there is more of the glory of God, and his power appears to the refreshment of each individual; for that he partakes not only of the light and life raised in himself, but in all the rest. And therefore Christ hath particularly promised a blessing to such as assemble in his name, seeing he will be in the midst of them." For these and other reasons, the Quakers think it proper that men should be drawn together to the public worship of God; but if so, they must be drawn together at certain times. Now, as one day has never been, in the eyes of the Quakers, more desirable for such an object than another, their ancestors chose the first day in the week, because the apostles had chosen it for the religious assembling of themselves and their followers. And, in addition to this, that more frequent opportunities might be afforded them of bearing their outward testimony publicly for God, and of enlarging the sphere of their spiritual life, they appointed a meeting on one other day in the week in most places, and two in some others, for the same purpose.

They believe that no ground can be made holy, and therefore they do not allow the places on which their meeting houses are built to be consecrated by the use of any human forms.

Their meeting houses are singularly plain. There is nothing of decoration in the interior of them. They consist of a number of plain long benches with backs to them. There is one elevated seat at the end of these. This is for their ministers. It is elevated for no other reason than that their ministers may be the better heard.

The women occupy one-half of these benches, and sit apart from the men.

These benches are not intersected by partitions. Hence there are no distinct pews for the families of the rich, or of such as can afford to pay for them; for, in the first place, the Quakers pay nothing for their seats in their meeting houses; and, in the second, they pay no respect to the outward condition of one another. If they consider themselves, when out of doors, as all equal to one another in point of privileges, much more do they abolish all distinctions, when professedly assembled in a place of worship. They sit, therefore, in their meeting houses undistinguished with respect to their outward circumstances, as the children of the same great parent, who stand equally in need of his assistance; and as in the sight of Him who is no respecter of persons, but who made of one blood all the nations of men who dwell on all the face of the earth.

The Quaker ministers are not distinguishable, when in their places of worship, by their dress. They wear neither black clothes, nor surplices, nor gowns, nor bands. Jesus Christ, when he preached to the multitude, is not recorded to have put on a dress different from that which he wore on other occasions. Neither do the Quakers believe that ministers of the church ought, under the new dispensation, to be a separate people, as the Levites were, or to be distinguished on account of their office from other men.

CHAPTER IX.

THE SACRAMENT AND BAPTISM.

The Quakers, among other particularities, reject the application of water baptism, and the administration of the Sacrament of the Supper, as christian rites.

These ordinances have been considered by many as so essentially interwoven with christianity, that the Quakers, by rejecting the use of them, have been denied to be christians.

But whatever may be the difference of opinion between the world and the Quakers, upon these subjects, great indulgence is due to the latter on this occasion. People have received the ordinances in question from their ancestors. They have been brought up to the use of them. They have seen them sanctioned by the world. Finding their authority disputed by a body of men, who are insignificant as to numbers, when compared with others, they have let loose their censure upon them, and this without any inquiry concerning the grounds of their dissent. They know perhaps nothing of the obstinate contentions, nothing of the difficulties which have occurred, and nothing of those which may still be started on these subjects.

On the subject of the sacrament of Supper, similar difficulties have occurred.

Jesus Christ unquestionably permitted his disciples to meet together in remembrance of their last supper with him. But it is not clear that this was any other than a permission to those who were present, and who had known and loved him. The disciples were not ordered to go into all nations and to enjoin it to their converts to observe the same ceremony. Neither did the apostles leave any command by which it was enjoined as an ordinance of the christian church.

Another difficulty which has arisen on the subject of the Supper, is, that christians seem so little to have understood the nature of it, or in what it consisted, that they have had, in different ages, different views and encouraged different doctrines concerning it. One has placed it in one thing and another in another. Most of them, again, have attempted in their explanation of it to blend the enjoyment of the spiritual essence with that of the corporeal substance of the body and blood of Christ, and thus to unite a spiritual with a ceremonial exercise of religion. Grasping, therefore, at things apparently irreconcilable, they have conceived the strangest notions; and, by giving these to the world, they have only afforded fuel for contention among themselves and others.

In the time of the apostles, it was the custom of converted persons, grounded on the circumstances that passed at the Supper of the Passover, to meet in religious communion. They used, on these occasions, to break their bread and take their refreshment and converse together. The object of these meetings was to imitate the last friendly supper of Jesus with his disciples, to bear a public memorial of his sufferings and death, and to promote their love for one another. But this custom was nothing more, as far as evidence can be had, than that of a brotherly breaking of bread together. It was no sacramental eating. Neither was the body of Jesus supposed to be enjoyed, nor the spiritual enjoyment of it to consist in the partaking of this outward feast.

In the process of time, after the days of the apostles, when this simple custom had declined, we find another meeting of christians, in imitation of that at the Passover Supper, at which both bread and wine were introduced. This different commemoration of the same event had a new name given to it, for it was distinguished from the other by the name of Eucharist.

Another difficulty, but of a different nature, has occurred with respect to the Lord's Supper. This has arisen from the circumstance, that other ceremonies were enjoined by our Saviour in terms equally positive as this, but which most christians, notwithstanding, have thought themselves at liberty to reject. Among these the washing of feet is particularly to be noticed. This custom was of an emblematic nature. It was enjoined at the same time as that of the Lord's Supper, and on the same occasion. But it was enjoined in a more forcible and striking manner. The Sandimanians, when they rose into a society, considered the injunction for this ordinance to be so obligatory that they dared not dispense with it, and, therefore, when they determined to celebrate the Supper, they determined that the washing of feet should be an ordinance of their church. Most other christians, however, have dismissed the washing of feet from their religious observance. The reason given has principally been, that it was an eastern custom, and therefore local. To this the answer has been, that the Passover, from whence the Lord's Supper is taken, was an eastern custom also, but that it was much more local. Travelers of different nations had their feet washed for them in the east. But none but those of the circumcision were admitted to the Passover Supper. If, therefore, the injunction relative to the washing of feet be equally strong with that relative to the celebration of the Supper, it has been presumed that both ought to have been retained, and, if one has been dispensed with on account of its locality, that both ought to have been discarded.

In conclusion we will say, that, after having carefully read the record of this singular denomination, one cannot fail to be impressed with their loyalty to the teachings of the Bible, as they interpret it. If we were asked, What has Quakerism done for humanity? our answer would be, a great deal. First, The abandonment of African slavery through its teaching. Secondly, It has emphasized the great idea of the fatherhood of God, and the brotherhood of man. Lastly, It calls for "The Simple Life," antedating both in theory and practice the burden of this popular book for over two hundred and fifty years. Are not the teachings of such a church worthy of perpetuation? We think so. And what is more to the point, if the American or any other people wish to practice "The Simple Life," let them become conscientious Quakers, and no modern novel will be necessary to show them the way.

APPENDIX II.

A BRIEF VIEW

OF THE

DOCTRINES OF CHRISTIANITY*

AS SET FORTH IN HOLY SCRIPTURE

AND HELD BY THE

SOCIETY OF FRIENDS.

DECLARATION OF FAITH.

We believe in God, the Father Almighty, Maker of Heaven and earth, and of all things visible and invisible; and in Jesus Christ, His only Son, our Lord, by whom He created all things; and in the Holy Ghost, who proceedeth from the Father and the Son; and that these three, the Father, and the Son, and the Holy Ghost, are one in the Eternal Godhead.

OUR LORD JESUS CHRIST.

We believe that Jesus of Nazareth was conceived of the Holy Ghost and born of the Virgin Mary, and that He is the beloved and only-begotten Son of God, in whom the Father is well pleased. We believe that the eternal Word, who was with God, and was God, was made flesh and dwelt among men in the person of Him, our Lord and Saviour Jesus Christ. "In Him dwelleth all the fulness of the God-head bodily." He is the one perfect man, who hath fulfilled all righteousness, and who was in all points tempted like as we are, yet without sin.

We believe that He died for our sins, that He was buried, and rose again the third day, that He ascended into Heaven, and is on the right hand of God, angels and authorities and powers being made subject unto Him. He is the one Mediator between God and man, our Advocate with the Father, our High-Priest forever, who is able to save them to the uttermost that come unto God by Him, seeing He ever liveth to make intercession for them. He baptizes with the Holy Ghost. He is the Shepherd and Bishop of souls,

---

* Taken from the Book of Discipline of the New York Yearly Meeting.

the Head over all things to the Church, the King who reigns in righteousness, the Prince of Peace. By Him the world shall be judged in righteousness, for the Father judgeth no man, but hath committed all judgment unto the Son, that all men should honor the Son, even as they honor the Father. We believe in the Deity and manhood of our Lord Jesus Christ, and that His willing sacrifice upon the cross was the one propitiation and atonement for the sins of the whole world, wherein God hath declared His righteousness, that He might be just, and the justifier of him that believeth in Jesus. He is the Lamb of God, without blemish and without spot, with whose precious blood we are redeemed. The remission of sins which any partake of is only in and by virtue of that most satisfactory sacrifice, and no otherwise.

We reverently confess and believe that divine honor and worship are due to the Son of God, and that He is in true faith to be prayed unto, and the name of the Lord Jesus Christ called upon, as the primitive Christians did, and that we cannot acceptably offer up prayers or praises to God, nor receive a gracious answer or blessing from Him, but in and through His dear Son.

THE HOLY SPIRIT.

We believe that the Holy Ghost is in the unity of the Eternal Godhead, one with the Father and the Son; that He is the promise of the Father, whom Christ declared He would send in His name; that He is come and convicts the world of sin; that He leads to repentance toward God, and as the Gospel is known, to faith in the Lord Jesus Christ. Coming in the name and in the authority of the risen and ascended Saviour, the Holy Spirit is the most precious pledge of His continued love and care. He glorifies the Saviour, and takes of the things of Christ and gives them as a realized possession to the believing soul. He dwells in the hearts of believers according to the promise of the Saviour: "I will pray the Father, and He shall give you another Comforter, that He may abide with you forever." He opens to them the truths of the Gospel as set forth in Holy Scripture, and as they exercise faith, guides, sanctifies, comforts, and supports them.

His light must ever be distinguished, both from the conscience which He illumines, and from the natural faculty of reason, which, when unsubjected to His holy influences, is, in the things of God, very foolishness.

We believe that the qualification for the Lord's service in the enduement of power for His work is bestowed on His children through the reception and baptism of the Holy Ghost.

The Holy Spirit is the seal of reconciliation to the humble believer in Jesus, the earnest and the foretaste of the full communion and perfect joy which are reserved for them that endure unto the end.

THE HOLY SCRIPTURES.

It has ever been, and still is, the belief of the Society of Friends that the Holy Scriptures of the Old and New Testament were given by inspiration of God; that, therefore, the declarations contained in them rest on the authority of God Himself, and that there can be no appeal from them to any other authority whatsoever; that they are able to make wise unto salvation, through faith which is in Christ Jesus. "These are written that ye might believe that Jesus is the Christ, the Son of God; and that believing ye might have life through His name." The Scriptures are the only divinely authorized record of the doctrines which we are bound as Christians to accept, and of the moral principles which are to regulate our actions. No one can be required to believe as an article of faith any doctrine which is not contained in them, and whatsoever any one says or does contrary to the Scriptures, though under profession of the immediate guidance of the Holy Spirit, must be reckoned and accounted a delusion of the Devil.

MAN'S CREATION AND FALL.

It pleased God, in His wisdom and goodness, to create man out of the dust of the earth, and to breathe into his nostrils the breath of life, so that man became a "living soul," formed after the image and likeness of God, capable of fulfilling the divine law and of holding communion with his Maker. Being free to obey or to disobey, under the temptation of Satan, through unbelief, he fell into transgression, and thereby lost that spiritual life of righteousness in which he was created; and so death passed upon him as the inevitable consequence of his sin. As the children of fallen Adam, all mankind bear his image and partake of his nature; and until created anew in Christ Jesus by the regenerating power of the Holy Spirit, they are fallen, degenerated, and dead to the divine life.

But while we hold these views of the lost condition of man in the fall, we rejoice to believe that sin is not imputed to any until they transgress the divine law after sufficient capacity has been given to understand it, and that infants, though inheriting this fallen nature, are saved, in the infinite mercy of God, through the redemption which is in Christ Jesus.

JUSTIFICATION AND SANCTIFICATION.

"God so loved the world that He gave His only-begotten Son, that whosoever believeth in Him should not perish, but have everlasting life."

We believe that justification is of God's free grace, through which, upon repentance and faith, He pardons our sins and accepts us as righteous in His sight for the sake of the Lord Jesus Christ; that it is received, not because of our works, but of our acceptance of God's mercy in Christ Jesus; that through faith in Him and His atoning blood, the guilt of sin is taken away and we stand reconciled to God.

We believe that in connection with Justification is Regeneration; that, being reconciled to God by the death of His Son, we are saved by His life, a new heart is given and new desires, old things are passed away, and we become children of God through faith in Christ Jesus. Sanctification, or being made holy, is experienced in connection with Justification in so far that every pardoned sinner, on account of faith in Christ, is clothed with a measure of His righteousness and receives the promised Holy Spirit.

The provisions of God's grace are sufficient to deliver from the power of evil, as well as from the guilt of sin, and to enable His believing children always to triumph in Christ. This is to be experienced by faith: "according to your faith be it unto you." Whoever submits himself wholly to God, believing His promises, and exercises faith in Christ Jesus, will have his heart continually cleansed from all sin by His precious blood, and through the renewing, refining power of the Holy Spirit be brought into perfect conformity to the will of God, love Him with all his heart, mind, soul, and strength, and be able to say with the Apostle Paul: "The law of the spirit of life in Christ Jesus hath made me free from the law of sin and death." "This is the will of God, even your sanctification," and if any fall short of this experience, it is because they frustrate the grace of God.

THE RESURRECTION AND A FINAL JUDGMENT.

We believe, according to the Scriptures, that there shall be a Resurrection of the dead, both of the just and of the unjust, and that God hath appointed a day in which He will judge the world in righteousness by Jesus Christ, whom He hath ordained. For, as saith the apostle, "we must all appear before the judgment-seat of Christ, that every one may receive the things done in his body according to that he hath done, whether it be good or bad."

We believe that the punishment of the wicked, and the blessedness of the righteous, shall be alike everlasting; according to the declaration of our adorable Redeemer, to whom the judgment is committed, "These shall go away into everlasting punishment, but the righteous into life eternal."

BAPTISM.

"One Lord, one Faith, one Baptism."

"John answered, saying unto them all, I indeed baptize you with water; but one mightier than I cometh, the latchet of whose shoes I am not worthy to unloose: He shall baptize you with the Holy Ghost, and with fire."

We believe the one baptism of the Gospel dispensation is that of Christ, who baptizes His people with the Holy Ghost. The ordinances instituted by God under the law were typical. When Christ the great Antitype came and fulfilled the law, He took away the hand-writing of ordinances, "nailing it to His cross," and since He opened the new and living way which He hath consecrated for us through the Veil, that is to say His flesh, we have access by faith, and enter into the holiest by the blood of Jesus, without the intervention of priest or ordinance, or any mediation, but that of Him, the one Mediator.

We believe that He established no new rite or ordinance, and that the "one baptism" which now saveth, and which is essential to living membership in His Church, is that which He Himself administers as the glorious Minister of the sanctuary, the baptism of the Holy Spirit, as saith the apostle, "by one spirit are ye all baptized into one body." It is only under this baptism that any can be truly made members of the one family of the redeemed, or be taught to understand the new relation to which God has called them by His grace under this, the new and everlasting covenant.

THE SUPPER OF THE LORD.

We believe that the true Supper of the Lord is the Communion which His believing children are enabled to hold with Him, through the realization of the presence of the Lord Jesus Christ in their hearts, who hath cleansed them from all sin, through the offering of His body, and the shedding of His blood upon the cross.

This communion is described by Him in the words: "Behold, I stand at the door and knock; if any man hear my voice, and open the door, I will come in to him, and sup with him, and he with me."

We believe this experience to be essential to the life of the Christian. It is only in the strength of this communion that he can pursue his heavenward journey, or bring forth fruit unto holiness; for, saith our blessed Lord, "except ye eat the flesh of the Son of man and drink His blood, ye have no life in you."

PUBLIC WORSHIP.

"God is a Spirit, and they that worship Him must worship Him in spirit and in truth."

Worship is the adoring response of the heart and mind to the influence of the Spirit of God.

Having become His children through faith in the Lord Jesus Christ, it is our privilege to meet together and unite in the worship of Almighty God; to wait upon Him for the renewal of our strength, for communion one with another, for the edification of believers in the exercise of spiritual gifts, and for the declaration of the glad tidings of salvation to the unconverted who may gather with us. By the immediate operations of the Holy Spirit, the Head of the Church alone selects and qualifies those who are to present His messages, or engage in other service for Him, and hence we cannot admit of a formal arrangement of exercises, or commit them to any individual.

We believe that the worship of any heart or assembly most glorifies God which most perfectly responds to the promptings of His Spirit, whether it be in vocal service or in silent adoration.

THE MINISTRY.

We believe the preaching of the Gospel is one of the means divinely appointed for the spreading of the glad tidings of life and salvation through our crucified Redeemer, for the awakening and conversion of sinners, and for the comfort and edification of believers.

As it is the preorgative of the great Head of the Church alone to select and call the ministers of His Gospel, so we believe both the gift and the qualification to exercise it must be derived immediately from Him; and that, as in the primitive Church, so now also, He confers them on women as well as men, agreeably to the prophecy recited by the Apostle Peter: "It shall come to pass in the last days, saith God, I will pour out of my Spirit upon all flesh, and your sons and your daughters shall prophesy;" respecting which the apostle declares, "The promise is unto you and your children, and to all that are afar off, even as many as the Lord our God shall call." As this gift is freely received, so it is to be freely exercised, in simple obedience to the will of God.

The Apostle Paul, in speaking of his ministry, declares, "I neither received it of man, neither was I taught it, but by the revelation of Jesus Christ;" that the exercise of it was not in the words which man's wisdom teacheth; but which the Holy Ghost teacheth; and that his speech and his preaching was not with enticing words of man's wisdom, but in demonstration of the Spirit and of power; that the faith of his hearers might not stand in the wisdom of men, but in the power of God. Nothing but power from on high, renewedly furnished, can enable men to preach the Gospel.

While the Church cannot confer spiritual gifts, it is its duty to recognize and foster them, and to promote their efficiency by all the means in its power. And while, on the one hand, the Gospel should never be preached for money, on the other it is the duty of the Church to make such provision that it shall never be hindered for want of it.

PRAYER.

Prayer is the result of a feeling of need and dependence upon God. The condition of heart and mind which cries, in substance, "God be merciful to me a sinner," must precede pardon and remission of sins. At every stage prayer is essential to Christian life.

We believe that prayer and praise are indispensible to a growth in Grace, and for a qualification for those duties which devolve upon every Christian; that without these any religious experience which may have been gained will finally be lost.

Without prayer there can be no acceptable worship. It is therefore incumbent upon all Christians, in their meetings especially, to seek after Divine help to offer spiritual sacrifices, acceptable to God, by Jesus Christ. Vocal prayer uttered in response to the promptings of the Holy Spirit is an important part of public worship; and whenever God's people meet together in His name, they should reverently seek unto Him in united prayer.

We would encourage parents and heads of families to be faithful in the exercise of this privilege before their children or households. The qualification for such services may differ in degree from that which should be looked for on more public occasions. The sense of need, of parental responsibility, of the priceless value of the souls entrusted to our care, not only warrants but requires such acts of dedication, whilst our countless blessings claim the tribute of praise from thankful hearts.

We believe the spirit of prayer and thanksgiving will certainly be bestowed upon us if we duly ask for it; and thus to ask is a prayer which may safely be regarded as always in accordance with the Divine will. "If ye, then, being evil, know how to give good gifts unto your children, how much more shall your Heavenly Father give the Holy Spirit to them that ask Him."

"I will, therefore, that men pray everywhere, lifting up holy hands, without wrath and doubting."

TESTIMONIES CONCERNING WAR AND OATHS.

War.

"From whence comes wars and fightings among you? Come they not hence even of your lusts that war in your members?"

War conflicts with, and is a violation of, the principles, precepts, and injunctions of the Gospel, which breathe peace on earth and good-will toward men. It is entirely incompatible with the commands of our holy Redeemer: "I say unto you that ye resist not evil"—"Love your enemies, bless them that curse you, do good to them that hate you, and pray for them which despitefully use you and persecute you; that ye may be the children of your Father which is in heaven: for He maketh His sun to rise on the evil and on the good, and sendeth rain on the just and on the unjust."

We believe that the emphatic prayer of our Lord, "Forgive us our debts, as we forgive our debtors," and His declaration, "If ye forgive not men their trespasses, neither will your Father forgive your trespasses," continue of binding force. And we believe that no Divine injunction or command that is binding upon individuals, under the Christian dispensation, can be rendered void by any number of individuals in a collective capacity as nations or otherwise. The prophecy which fortold the coming of the Messiah declared him to be the Prince of Peace; and His birth was announced by the Heavenly anthem, "Glory to God in the highest, and on earth peace, good-will toward men."

Oaths.

With regard to Oaths, we believe that our Lord evidently forbade a kind of swearing which had been allowed before: "Ye have heard that it hath been said by them of old time, Thou shalt not forswear thyself, but shalt perform unto the Lord thine oaths; but I say unto you, swear not at all, neither by heaven, for it is God's throne, nor by the earth, for it is God's footstool, neither by Jerusalem, for it is the city of the Great King; neither shalt thou swear by thy head, because thou canst not make one hair white nor black; but let your communication be yea, yea, nay, nay: for whatsoever is more than these cometh of evil." And the Apostle James declared, "But above all things, my brethren, swear not, neither by heaven, neither by the earth, neither by any other oath; but let your yea be yea, and your nay nay, lest ye fall into condemnation."

We therefore consider the prohibition to include judicial oaths, and refuse for conscience' sake, either to administer or take an oath. In courts of law and in the authentication of documents, instead of taking an oath we make affirmation to the truth of that which we assert.

APPENDIX III.

DECLARATION OF FAITH.

As Stated in the Epistle of George Fox to the Governor of Barbadoes, 1671.

For the Governor of Barbadoes, with his Council and Assembly, and all others in power, both civil and military, in this island, from the people called Quakers.

Whereas, Many scandalous lies and slanders have been cast upon us to render us odious, as that we deny God, Christ Jesus, and the Scriptures of truth, etc.: This is to inform you that all our books and declarations, which for these many years have been published to the world, clearly testify the contrary; yet for your satisfaction we now plainly and sincerely declare that we own and believe in the only wise, omnipotent, and everlasting God, the Creator of all things in heaven and in earth, and the Preserver of all that He hath made; who is God over all, blessed forever; to whom be all honor, glory, dominion, praise, and thanksgiving, both now and for evermore. And we own and believe in Jesus Christ, His beloved and only-begotten Son, in whom He is well pleased; who was conceived by the Holy Ghost and born of the Virgin Mary; in whom we have redemption through His blood, even the forgiveness of sins; who is the image of the invisible God, the first-born of every creature, by whom were all things created that are in heaven and in earth, visible and invisible, whether they be thrones, dominions, principalities, or powers; all things were created by Him. And we own and believe that He was made a sacrifice for sin, who knew no sin, neither was guile found in His mouth; that He was crucified for us in the flesh without the gates of Jerusalem; and that He was buried, and rose again the third day by the power of His Father for our justification; and that He ascended up into heaven, and now sitteth at the right hand of God. This Jesus, who was the foundation of the holy prophets and apostles, is our foundation; and we believe there is no other foundation to be laid but that which is laid, even Christ Jesus; who tasted death for every man, shed His blood for all men, is the propitiation for our sins, and not for ours only, but also for the sins of the whole world; according as

John the Baptist testified of Him when he said, "Behold the Lamb of God, which taketh away the sin of the world," John i, 29. We believe that he alone is our Redeemer and Saviour, the Captain of our salvation (who saves us from sin, as well as from hell and the wrath to come, and destroys the devil and his works); He is the seed of the woman that bruiseth the serpent's head, to wit, Christ Jesus, the Alpha and Omega, the First and the Last; He is (as the Scriptures of truth say of Him) our wisdom, righteousness, sanctification, and redemption; neither is there salvation in any other, for there is no other name under heaven given among men whereby we must be saved. He alone is the Shepherd and Bishop of our souls; He is our Prophet whom Moses long since testified of, saying, "A prophet shall the Lord your God raise up unto you of your brethren, like unto me; Him shall ye hear in all things, whatsoever He shall say unto you; and it shall come to pass that every soul which will not hear that Prophet shall be destroyed from among the people," Acts ii, 22, 23. He it is that is now come, "and hath given us an understanding, that we know Him that is true." He rules in our hearts by His law of love and of life, and makes us free from the law of sin and death. We have no life but by Him, for He is the quickening Spirit, the second Adam, the Lord from heaven, by whose blood we are cleansed, and our consciences sprinkled from dead works to serve the living God. He is our Mediator that makes peace and reconciliation between God offended and us offending; He being the Oath of God, the new covenant of light, life, grace, and peace, the author and finisher of our faith. This Lord Jesus Christ, the heavenly man, the Emmanuel, God with us, we all own and believe in; He whom the highpriest raged against and said He had spoken blasphemy; whom the priests and elders of the Jews took counsel together against and put to death; the same whom Judas betrayed for thirty pieces of silver, which the priest gave him as a reward for his treason; who also gave large money to the soldiers to broach an horrible lie, namely, "That His disciples came and stole Him away by night whilst they slept." After He was risen from the dead, the history of the Acts of the Apostles sets forth how the chief priests and elders persecuted the disciples of this Jesus for preaching Christ and His resurrection. This, we say, is that Lord Jesus Christ whom we own to be our life and salvation.

Concerning the Holy Scriptures, we believe that they were given forth by the Holy Spirit of God, through the holy men of God, who (as the Scripture itself declares, 2 Peter i. 21) spake as they were moved by the Holy Ghost. We believe they are to be read, believed and fulfilled (He that fulfils them is Christ), and they are "profitable for doctrine, for reproof, for correction, for instruction in righteousness, that the man of God may be perfect, thoroughly furnished unto all good works," 2 Tim. iii. 16, 17; and are able to make wise unto salvation, "through faith which is in Christ Jesus."

We believe the Holy Scriptures are the words of God, for it is said in Exodus xx. 1, "God spake all these words, saying," etc., meaning the Ten Commandments given forth upon Mount Sinai; and in Revelation xxii. 18, 19, saith John, "I testify unto every man that heareth the words of the prophecy of this book. If any man shall add unto these things." "And if any man shall take away from the words of the book of this prophecy" (not the word). So in Luke i. 20, "Because thou believest not my words;" and in John v. 47; xv. 7; xiv. 23; xii. 47. So that we call the Holy Scriptures, as Christ, the Apostles, and holy men of God called them—the words of God.

We declare that we esteem it a duty incumbent on us to pray with and for, to teach, instruct, and admonish those in and belonging to our families. This being a command of the Lord, disobedience thereunto will provoke His displeasure, as may be seen in Jeremiah x. 25: "Pour out Thy fury upon the heathen that know Thee not, and upon the families that call not upon Thy name." Now, Negroes, Tawnies, and Indians make up a very great part of the families in this island, for whom an account will be required by Him who comes to judge both quick and dead, at the great day of judgement, when every one shall be rewarded according to the deeds done in the body, whether they be good or whether they be evil—at that day, we say, of the resurrection both of the good and of the bad, of the just and the unjust, "when the Lord Jesus shall be revealed from heaven with His mighty angels in flaming fire, taking vengeance on them that know not God and obey not the Gospel of our Lord Jesus Christ; who shall be punished with everlasting destruction from the presence of the Lord, and from the glory of His power; when He shall come to be glorified in His Saints, and to be admired in all them that believe in that day." 2 Thess. i. 7, 10. See also 2 Peter iii. 3, 7.

APPENDIX IV.

PROMINENT FAMILIES.

THE DAVIS FAMILY.

It very often occurs in tracing a line of ancestors that an author comes into possession of documents not contemplated nor contained in official records. These contributions, possessing all the charms of variety, include also the value of original documents, are mainly owing to data in the possession of private families, descendants of those officially mentioned in the body of the book. The compiler of this history of "Our Quaker Friends of Ye Olden Times" is fortunate in this respect, for contributions from unexpected sources have come in to such an extent, as to make him feel the embarrassment of riches—so much so, that what to use and what to reject is the main question, for to use all would swell this volume to unwonted dimensions.

However, since the compilation of these sketches began, we have come into the possession of documents giving so fully and clearly the genealogy and necrology of several prominent families whose descendants are numerous to-day, that, as an item of additional interest to the book, we publish them in full

William Davis, Sr., son of John Davis and Susanna Smithson Davis, was born August 13, 1755. Married Mary Gosney, born January 15, 1755, located in Lynchburg. Both buried at South River. He died March 19, 1853.

Micajah Davis, Sr., located in Bedford county. William Davis, Jr., son of William Davis, Sr., born July 3, 1770, married Zalinda Lynch, daughter of John Lynch, the founder of Lynchburg. Both buried at Quaker Meeting House. John Davis, son of William Davis, Jr., was born September 24, 1774, married Hannah Anthony, daughter of Christopher Anthony, July 7, 1805. Removed to Cincinnatti in 1814, died August 13, 1830. Thomas Davis, born February 18, 1777, married Rachel Davis. Micajah Davis, Jr., son of Micajah Davis, Sr., born May 24, 1779, married Mary C. Gwatkin. John Davis, son of Micajah Davis, Jr., married Ann Jennings. Henry Davis, born November 21, 1779, married Sarah Anthony, July 10, 1811, died December 11, 1863. Susan Davis, born April 29, 1780, died unmarried. Elizabeth, born December 5, 1782, died unmarried. Benjamin Davis, born June 5, 1785, married

Catharine Gilbert, (date not given). Isaac Joseph Davis, born November 10, 1788, died unmarried. Mary Davis, born March 25, 1790, married Cornelius Pierce, (no date given). Nancy Davis, born October 26, 1792, married Peter Dudley, January 31, 1814. Louisa Davis, born March 4, 1795, died unmarried. Deborah Davis, born April 25, 1797, unmarried. Samuel and John and Sarah Lynch Davis, never married. Mary Annis Davis, born February 26, 1805, married Robinson Stabler, of Alexandria, Va., in November, 1828. Ann Maria Davis, born February 26, 1806, (these were twins), married Achilles Pugh, of Cincinnati, August 23, 1832, died February 14, 1877. Mary Jordan Davis, born October 10, 1808, married Caleb Taylor, of Cincinnati, January 1, 1830, died May 9, 1875. Samuel, (second) born August 12, 1809, married Rebecca Wallace, of Rushville, Ind., died July 2, 1887. Sarah Annis Davis, born March 8, 1811, married Hugh Smith, of Indianapolis, Ind., died in November, 1888. Charlotte, born February 21, 1813, died September 16, 1888. William, born March 23, 1815, died in 1837. John, born April 15, 1818, died in October, 1832. Charles, born July 11, 1820, died in 1836. Hannah Davis, born October 21, 1823, married Henry Stagg, of St. Louis, in 1842. All these, beginning with Mary Annis Davis, who married Achilles Pugh, of Cincinnati, were descendants of John Davis and Hannah Anthony, who moved to Cincinnati in 1814.

FAMILY OF SAMUEL DAVIS.—Married Anne Lipscombe, August 15, 1769, who located near Green Springs, Louisa county, who afterwards moved to Bedford county, where he died in 1779. First, Samuel Lipscombe Davis, who died young; second, George Dixon Davis, born June 10, 1805, and died in 1840. He married Mary A. Wills, March 4, 1840, and died in 1879. Fourth, John Thomas Davis, who married Margaret Preston (no dates given). All buried at Quaker Meeting House.

FAMILY OF THOMAS DAVIS.—Born February 18, 1877, and married Rachel Davis. Children: First, Annis Elizabeth, who married Pleasant Preston. Second, Micajah, who married, first, Mary E. Phillips, and then Sallie W. Seldon, who died in 1884. Third, Zalinda Lynch Davis, who married Frazier O. Stratton.

CHILDREN OF MICAJAH DAVIS.—Married Mary C. Gwatkin. First, William, who married a Miss Alexander, (first name not given). Second, Charles, died unmarried. Third, Samuel Gwatkin, unmarried. Fourth, John Gwatkin, unmarried. Fifth, Mary Annis, unmarried. Sixth, Margaret, unmarried. The family of this Micajah Davis, unless William Davis left issue by his marriage with Miss Alexander, became extinct.

CHILDREN OF JOHN DAVIS, WHO MARRIED ANN JENNINGS.—First, William Minor Davis, who married Nannie Hunter Eubank. Second, Christopher Davis, who married, but name of wife is not given. Third, Mary Jane Davis, who married John Henry.

CHILDREN OF HENRY DAVIS, born November 21, 1779, and married Sarah Anthony, July 10, 1811. First, Samuel Anthony Davis, married, but name of wife not given, died September 13, 1821. Second, William Henry Davis, born December 23, 1802, died August 6, 1803. Third, Mary, born July 26, 1804, married, but husband's name not given. Fourth, Charles, born November 30, 1806. Fifth, Sarah A. Davis, born January 9, 1811, married first, William Smith, and secondly, Rev. Franklin G. Smith, rector of St. Paul's Episcopal Church, Lynchburg, May 29, 1838, and moved to Columbia, Tennessee, in January, 1871. Sixth, James Davis, born September 16, 1813, married, but wife's name not given. Seventh, Robert Jordan Davis, born August 13, 1815, and married Ann Cabell, of Amherst county, Va. Eighth, Alexander Christopher Davis, born December 12, 1817, wife's name not given. Ninth, James Frederick Davis, born May 23, 1820, died in infancy. Tenth, Lucy Elizabeth Davis, born March 23, 1822, married William Tudor Yancey, dates of marriage and death not given.

CHILDREN OF MARY DAVIS, born March 25, 1790, who married Cornelius Pierce: Mary Pierce, who married Benjamin Brown; Susan, who married James D. Taylor; Louisa, who married Lunsford Lomax Loving Robinson, name of wife not given.

CHILDREN OF NANCY DAVIS, who married Peter Dudley: John W., who married Andalusia Fourqueron, both of whom died in 1878; Thomas Stevens, who died unmarried; Mary Elizabeth, who married Capt. Thomas W. Johns; Fanny Jane, who married James F. Payne; Nancy Davis, died in infancy; Peter L., who married Elizabeth Saunders; Henry D., died in San Francisco, unmarried; Louisa S., died in infancy; Deborah Ann, who married Rev. W. H. Kinckle in Lynchburg; Maria Rose, who married J. Edward Calhoun, and Robert L., no record.

CHILDREN OF SAMUEL DAVIS, son of Evan Davis, of Georgia, who moved to Kentucky: Hon. Jefferson Davis, U. S. Senator, Secretary of War, President of Confederate States, born in Christian county, 1808, first married Pocahontas Taylor, daughter of Gen. Zachary Taylor, secondly, Miss Elizabeth Hayes, died December 11, 1889.

CHILDREN OF ANN MARIA DAVIS, who married Achilles Pugh, of Cincinnati, Ohio, in 1832: Esther Pugh, born August 31, 1834, never married; John Davis Pugh, born March 10, 1838, married Laura Fay; Mary Taylor Pugh, born September 26, 1840, married John Widman, November 29, 1865; Achilles H., born November 24, 1846, married Mary L. Darr, June 14, 1875.

CHILDREN OF MARY JORDAN DAVIS, who married Caleb Taylor, of Cincinnati: Hanna Taylor, born September 2, 1832, married Murray Shipley, May 22, 1851, died November 19, 1871; William H., M. D., born December 25, 1836, married first, Charlotte French, December 17, 1861, secondly, Mary Haines, 1871, thirdly, Helen Collord, 1880; Elizabeth L. Taylor, born January 27, 1839, married George Dean, July 25, 1868; Ann M., born June 20, 1841, married E. L. Johnson, October 27, 1864.

CHILDREN OF SAMUEL DAVIS AND REBECCAH (WALLACE) DAVIS: John Wallace Davis, born in 1841, married in St. Louis; Charles H., married Florence Stagg, of St. Louis; Ellen H., born in 1844, married Charles Braithwait, of Kendall, England, living there now; Caleb T. lives in St Louis.

CHILDREN OF SARAH ANNIS DAVIS, who married Hugh Smith, of Indianapolis: Colonna Smith, who died young; Anna Mary Smith, unmarried.

CHILDREN OF HANNAH DAVIS, who married Henry Stagg, of St. Louis in 1842. First, Charles Henry, (no dates). Second, Virginia Isabella, married "Moses" Forbes. Third, William Stagg, married, living in Springfield, Mo. Fourth, Charlotte, nothing recorded. Fifth, Henry, nothing recorded.

CHILDREN OF GEORGE DIXON DAVIS, who married Mary Ann Wills, March 4, 1840. First, John W., born April 20, died May 18, 1869. Second, Thomas Dixon, born April 16, 1841. Third, Mary Virginia, born March 7, 1845, who married P. A. Krise, Lynchburg, Va., September 30, 1868. Fourth, Alice Smith, born

January 3, 1847. Fifth, George W., died in infancy. Sixth, Rachel Ellen, died young. Seventh, Samuel B., died in his 24th year. Eighth, Micajah Preston, born April 21, 1855, married Maude Mathews. Ninth, Creed Wills, born June 12, 1857, married Jennie Lybrook, August 18, 1885. Tenth, Richard Taylor, born August 23, 1863, died in infancy.

CHILDREN OF JOHN THOMAS DAVIS, who married Margaret Preston: First, Mary Elizabeth, who married Camillus Christian. Second, Margaret Preston. Third, Thomas, killed during Civil War.

CHILDREN OF ANNIS ELIZABETH DAVIS, who married Pleasant Preston. First, Samuel D., who married Miss Saunders. Second, Thomas S., who married Miss Nannie Preston. Third, Elizabeth, no record. Fourth, John B. Prof., Bowling Green, Ky. Fifth, George, lived and died in Lynchburg. Sixth, Pleasant, married, name not given.

CHILDREN OF MICAJAH DAVIS, who married, first, Ellen E. Phillips, secondly, Sallie W. Selden in 1884. First, Thomas Edward, lives in New Orleans, married Mollie Moore, of Texas. Second, Mary Annis, married W. W. Berry, died without issue. Third, Samuel Phillips, married Laura West, of Belleville, Ill. Fourth, John Micajah, married Jennie Phillips, of Memphis, Tenn.

CHILDREN OF ZALINDA LYNCH DAVIS, who married F. O. Stratton. First, Nannie R., married Dr. Marcellus Christian, of U. S. and C. S. navies. Second, Ellen Beaufort, married Rev. E. S. Gregory. Third, George Wadsworth, married Clara Hoffman.

CHILDREN OF WILLIAM MINOR DAVIS, who married Nannie Hunter Eubank. First, Thomas N. Davis, born May 7, 1842, married V. Blanche Thompson, February 11, 1874. Second, Jane Minor, changed to Jane Eubank.

CHILDREN OF CHRISTOPHER DAVIS. First, Margaret Newman Davis, married Charles P. Hendricks. Second, Friend W. Davis.

CHILDREN OF MARY JANE DAVIS, who married John Henry. First, John Henry. Second, William D. Henry. Third, Kinckle Henry, died in infancy.

CHILDREN OF MARY DAVIS, who married Cornelius Pierce. First, Mary Purce, married Benjamin Brown. Second, Susan, married James D. Taylor. Third, Louisa, who married L. L. Loving. Fourth, Robinson.

Grandchildren of Nancy Davis, who married Peter Dudley, January 31, 1814. First, Ellen Dudley, who married William A. Webb. Second, Eliza F., married W. L. Mallory. Third, Thomas R., who never married. W. R. Dudley, never married; John M. Dudley, never married; Andalusia married F. D. Tullidge; Nancy married John Taylor; Peter R., married Mary Shaw; George R., married Annie Bachman; James Saunders Dudley, married Helen Younger; William Henry Dudley, no record; Grace D. Kinckle, married W. S. Adams.

Grandchildren of Anna Maria Davis, who married A. D. Pugh, of Cincinnati. First, Achilles H., born March 13, 1876. Second, Therese Josephine, born October 21, 1879.

Grandchildren of Mary Jordan Davis, who married Caleb Taylor, of Cincinnati, in 1830. First, Mary L. Shipley, born October 23, 1883. Second, Anna Charlotte, born May 18, 1885.

[Note.—The name of Minor, which frequently is found in connection with the names of the Davises, is not a family name, but was first used as a designation to indicate minority, and was afterwards used as a middle name. In closing this list of the Davis family we have followed copy furnished the editor, and whatever mistakes may have been made, we flatter ourselves that this record for accuracy, at least, cannot be well surpassed in such a multitude of names. It will be noted also that the ancestry of such distinguished men as Jefferson Davis, Mark Hanna and many others reaching as far back as the third and fourth generations will be found in this list.]

THE JORDAN FAMILY.

No family in the state perhaps has a more undisputed and clearer line of descent, than that of Jordan. Beginning with Samuel Jordan, who was wrecked on the Vext Bermoothes in 1608, with Sir George Somers, arrived in Jamestown in 1609. Member of House of Burgesses, mentioned in census of 1623. Also two daughters by his wife Cicely, Mary and Margaret, aged two and four years. We have an almost unbroken record terminating with James Robert Jordan in 1872, a long period of 172 years, beginning with Thomas Jordan, his son.

Here is the record as we find it: Thomas Jordan, son of Samuel, born 1600; married; wife's name not given; was a soldier under

Yeardly; had a land grant 1624; a member of House of Burgesses. Then comes the following entry: Samuel, of 1632, and Robert killed by Indians in great massacre of 1622. They left the following children: Richard, living in 1679; had a son living in 1739; also John and Nicholas. Then comes Thomas Jordan, born in 1634, who married Margaret Brasheres, and died in 1699. He was a son of Thomas Jordan, who served under Yeardley. He left the following children: Thomas Jordan, born 6th of January, 1660, who married Elizabeth Burgh 1679; John, born 1663, married Margaret Burgh, 1688; James, 1665, married Elizabeth Ratcliffe, 1688; died 1695; Robert, born July 11th, 1688, Minister Society of Friends, married Christian Outland 1687, married again Mary Bolson 1690. Four other children, no names or dates given.

James Jordan (brother), born 11th month, 23d, 1665; married Ann Ratcliffe, 3d month, 29th, 1688. Children of same: first, John Jordan, born 1689; second, Elizabeth, married —— Scott; James (twin brother), born 1689, died 1782, aged 93.

The children by the marriages of Richard and James Jordan bring us in unbroken succession until we reach the official records of the Quaker churches given in the body of this book. Hence we close the record here at 1690, 215 years ago.

THE LYNCH, CLARK AND MOORMAN FAMILIES.

As might have been anticipated, these large and influential families, most of whom, with the exception of the Lynch family, were Friends, figure prominently in the history of Our Quaker Friends of Ye Olden Times. As is well known, the Lynch family came from Ireland and were Catholics.

Beginning with Col. Charles Lynch, of Lynch law fame, we have the following record. He was born in 1736, married Anna Terrell January 12, 1755; died October 29, 1796. His children: First, Charles, who married Sarah Adams, his first cousin. Second, Anselm, who married Mrs. Susan Baldwin (nee Miller), in 1799; he was born June 8th, 1764, died February 18, 1826. Third, Capt. "Staunton" John Lynch, born in 1767; married his first cousin, Anna Terrell, and died in Tennessee in 1840. Christopher, never married. Sally Lynch, married her first cousin, Capt. Chas. Lynch Terrell. Sarah Lynch, born in 1738; married Micajah Terrell in 1754, John Lynch, the reputed founder of Lynchburg, was born in 1740; married Mary Bowles; died in 1820, leaving a large family. First, Mattida (evidently Matilda), born in 1769; married Enoch Roberts 1789. Second, Zalinda, born February 6th, 1772; married William Davis, Jr., May 13, 1793. Third, Edward B., born in 1774; married Mary Terrell in 1796, and died in Waynesville. Sarah, born in 1777, died in 1704. John, born in 1779. Hannah, who died in 1817. Christopher, born 1782. Mary, born in 1784, married Alexander Liggatt. Charles Clark Lynch, born in 1787, died in 1814. Anselm, born in 1793, also died in 1814. Howard, born in 1796. William, married Jane Humphrey. Micajah, married Ann Moorman. Penelope, daughter of Christopher Lynch, who married Ann Ward, died unmarried. Recurring to the descendants of John Lynch, and beginning with Edward B. Lynch, who married Mary Terrell, we find the following list of children: Chas. Edward, born October 30, 1804; Christopher, born in 1807; Mary, born in 1808; Matilda, born in 1811, married Chas. Albert Withers; Elizabeth Ann, born in 1813, married Dr. Richard Pretlow, of Covington, Ky.

THE CLARK FAMILY.

Another family, with a well kept record, is that of the Clarks. Beginning with Micajah Clark, born September 16th, 1718, and Judith (Adams), his wife, we have an almost unbroken record for 187 years. To give this entire record, would require space sufficient for a volume in itself, and we must content ourselves with an abridgement to points of special interest, such as an account of their marriages into other prominent families of today, etc. We find then, that Elizabeth Clark, evidently a sister of Micajah Clark, born May 2, 1713, married Joseph Anthony, April 22, 1741, who died November 23, 1785. It is an interesting fact that Mark Anthony Haden, living near Evington, Campbell county, Virginia, and John Anthony, near Cascade, Virginia, are lineal descendants in the sixth generation of this Joseph Anthony. We also find the Anthonys and their descendants inter-married with the Moormans, the Lynches, Pendletons, Couches, Winstons, Davises, Terrells, Garlands, Randolphs and Baldwins. But as many of these facts are briefly related in the body of this book, we omit them here.

THE TERRELL FAMILY.

According to historical and traditional evidence, the family of Terrell is of Anglo-Norman origin, and was founded in England by Sir Walter Tyrrell, a Norman Knight, about 1066, when William the Conqueror took possession of that country. The ancient orthography of the name was Tyrell, Terrail, Tyrrell, etc., until the form of Terrell was adopted by our direct ancestors several centuries ago, and the name has generally been so spelled to the present day, though some of the branches use the form of Terrill.

From this old Anglo-Norman stock descended three brothers named William, James and John Terrell, of English birth, who, during the Protectorate of Oliver Cromwell, being Quakers and grievously persecuted on account of their religion, passed over into Ireland as English colonists "within the Pale," and after a temporary residence emigrated from thence to America, the date being some time between the years 1665 and 1700. William Terrell, the first ancestor of the family branch in this country, settled in the Colony of Virginia; one of the other brothers settled in North Carolina near Virginia, and the other brother is supposed to have settled in New England, but whether he founded a family in that Colony, or died without male issue, is not known. Another tradition is that the "three brothers" were sent to Virginia by King James the Second of England, about A. D., 1687, as explorers and huntsmen for the crown, and that they were each awarded for their services a royal grant of fifteen hundred acres of land in the counties of Hanover, Caroline and King George.

William Terrell, of the first generation married and had three sons: 1, David, Senior; 2, Henry, and 3, James.

David Terrell, Senior, of the second generation, was born in Virginia, where he married and had ten children, seven sons and three daughters. Of this family we have scarcely any record, except as to one son, viz:

Henry Terrell, called "the First" to distinguish him from his son of the same name. He was a member of the Society of Friends, a lawyer by profession, and very wealthy. He lived in Hanover and subsequently in Caroline county. He married Anna Chiles, of an eminent Virginia family, by whom he had nine children, four sons and five daughters. One of the sons, George Terrell, was a soldier of the Revolution and fought at Camden, S. C., under Gen. Gates. Another son was Thomas Terrell, 1st, (second of that name), who married Rebecca Peters, and many of their descendants removed to Ohio. Ursula married a Mr. Raglan, and Abagail married Col. Durrett, of Albemarle county, Virginia. We have scarcely any trace of Charles, Anna, Mary and Nancy. Another son was Henry Terrell, the 2d. He was of the 4th generation, and was born in Caroline county, in the year 1735, where he was brought up. He afterwards lived in Spottsylvania county. He married Mary Tyler, a daughter of Captain William Tyler, of Spottsylvania county, where they lived until the year 1787, when they emancipated their slaves and removed with their nine children to the District of Kentucky, and settled in Montgomery county. He was a pious member of the Society of Friends and the last of the immediate family who belonged to that sect. He died in Kentucky in 1811, in the seventy-sixth year of his age. The family record is very complete of all his children except as to Henry Chiles Terrell, George Terrell and their sisters, Mary and Elizabeth. Anna C. and Catharine died young. Richard Terrell lived many years in Natchez and New Orleans, and died in the last named city in 1845. Zachariah Terrell was a Captain of Kentucky troops under General Jackson at New Orleans, and died in Spencer county, Kentucky, in 1861. The other son bore the name of John Terrell. He was of the fifth generation, born in Spottsylvania county, Virginia, in 1772, and when about fifteen years old removed with his parents to Montgomery county, Kentucky, where he grew to manhood and became noted as an Indian fighter. He was a soldier in Colonel Hardin's regiment of Kentuckians and served in two expeditions against the Indians on the northern frontier under Generals Harmar and Wayne. He married Abba Allan, of Montgomery county, in 1797. She was a sister of Hon. Chilton Allan, of Kentucky, who afterward became a prominent lawyer and statesman in that State. John Terrell in the early part of this century lived for several years in Indiana Territory, and in 1807 was commissioned by Governor Harrison a Captain in the territorial militia service. In consequence of a severe wound which permanently disabled him, he moved back to Kentucky in 1810, and died in Louisville the next year. John Terrell and Abba Allan Terrell had eight children, five sons and three daughters, all of whom were born in

Kentucky (except Arch Allan Terrell who was born in Indiana Territory), and of them our records are full and complete. They were of the sixth generation, and are all dead except Aunt Maria (Hobbs), who is still living, in her seventy-ninth year, at Columbus, Indiana. The writer, W. H. H. Terrell, is of the seventh generation, and was born in Henry county, Kentucky, in 1827.

Of the Terrells of Caroline, one branch of the family moved to Campbell county, Virginia, for we find that as early as February 10th, 1754, Micajah Terrell married Sarah Lynch, sister of Col. Chas. Lynch, of Lynch law fame, while the doughty Colonel himself married Anna Terrell, Micajah's sister, January 12, 1755. We will remark in conclusion that marriages of first cousins were much more common in those days among the wealthy than at present, and there was a reason for it, as property in those days was mainly confined to land and slaves, and the great land-owners encouraged their children to intermarry with their cousins in order to keep the property in the family.

APPENDIX V.

COLONIAL CHURCH.

CEDAR CREEK, FAMOUS QUAKER MEETING HOUSE, PREY OF TIME.

One of the few remaining old colonial churches is Cedar Creek Quaker Church, which is situated in upper Hanover county, Virginia, near Montpelier post-office. It was constructed in the year 1770. Its architect and builder was a man named Kimbrough. Most of the material of which it is built was brought from England. The body is of brick, and the old-fashioned steep roof was formerly covered with shingles. It has large galleries on all sides. The main body contains two rooms, although it may be converted into one by a movable partition. In olden times it was the custom of this church for the ladies to sit in one room, and the men in the other. The body of the church is sixty by forty feet. The window blinds, doors, &c., are of solid heart pine plank. The old fashioned substantial woodwork on the interior is of heart pine, and is as sound as when placed there. All of this, of course, was sawed.

At one time the church had a large membership, and at the big meetings thousands would often gather here. Rev. Nathaniel C. Crenshaw and John Bacon Crenshaw were two of the prominent old pastors. With little hopes of this fast diminishing denomination ever again getting any foothold here, the church a short time ago was sold.

This old structure, which is an interesting landmark, and a model of ancient architecture, is situated amidst a gloomy forest of pine and cedar, which now grow almost up to its walls, and near it runs a stream of clear, sweet water, known as Cedar Creek.

[NOTE.—The South River meeting was established in 1757, and "laid down' 1858, and in 1902, the old building was sold to the Presbyterians, some of whose members are descended from the Quakers who once worshiped here.

Cedar Creek meeting was established in 1739, and "laid down" in about 1874. The meeting-house was built in 1797, and destroyed by forest fire in 1904.

Golansville meeting was established in 1739, and "laid down" in 1853. The building went to decay and the land reverted to the heirs of the Friend who gave the land.]

ONE HUNDRED YEARS AGO.

A Beautiful Poem on the Old Quaker Meeting House (South River).

[The poetic lines below will be appreciated by those who have visited the ruins of the old Quaker Meeting House not far from Lynchburg. The author of the poem, Mrs. Lucy Randolph Fleming, wife of Rev. Dr. R. H. Fleming, died July, 1900. The poem has been extensively copied. It originally appeared in *Harper's Bazar,* and is entitled, "The Old Meeting House, 1794-1894."]

The blue hills rise in stately strength,
  Streams ripple soft below,
As on those long-gone Sabbath days,
  One hundred years ago,

When in these crumbling, roofless walls,
  Where birds flit to and fro,
The Quaker fathers worshiped God
  One hundred years ago.

And word of truth, or praise, or prayer,
  In measured tone, and slow,
Was spoken as the Spirit moved
  One hundred years ago.

Here many a calm and saintly brow
  Seemed lit by Heaven's glow,
And caught the promised peace of God
  One hundred years ago.

Perhaps just here the sunshine fell
  On golden heads below,
Where children lifted patient eyes
  One hundred years ago.

Here youth and maidens primly sat
  In silent, decorous row,
But, as to-day, Love stole his glance
  One hundred years ago.

In ancient graves, where trailing vines
  And tender wild flowers grow,
Sleep those whose footsteps thither turned
  One hundred years ago.

Long have these altar fires been cold,
  And only ruins show
The temple holy to the Lord
  One hundred years ago.

But true and simple faith abides,
  Though centuries onward flow—
The fathers did not build in vain
Who reared this modest forest fane
  One hundred years ago.

APPENDIX VI.

THE DIARY OF JOHN B. CRENSHAW.

From "Southern Heroes."

Virginia Friends had become so reduced by emigration that the yearly meeting was laid down in 1844. At the close of the war there were only four small meetings left, viz., Black Creek, Somerton, Cedar Creek and Richmond. These formed what was then and is now known as the Virginia Half Year's Meeting. It belongs to Baltimore Yearly Meeting, as does Hopewell Meeting, near Winchester. Each of these meetings had its trying experiences, and the few men of legal age belonging to them were claimed by the strong hand of military law.

At Richmond meeting, John B. Crenshaw was the minister. He was born May 2, 1820, at the home occupied by him during the war. In 1860 he married his second wife, Judith Willets, who survives him. His father, Nathaniel C. Crenshaw, had been a soldier in the war of 1812, but becoming convinced of the principles of peace and the sinfulness of slavery, he joined the Society of Friends and became a minister. His life was several times threatened on account of his pronounced and freely expressed opinions. He was unwilling to receive slaves by inheritance, and suffered much on that account. It was said that he was the means of freeing more than three hundred slaves, and he lived to see all the colored people in this country free. He died in 1866 at a good old age.

John B. Crenshaw was much interested in church matters, and was a strong peace man. Five miles north of the city he had a pleasant home, and kept open house for all Friends traveling in the ministry or on other church service. Owing to his acquaintance and influence with men of authority, he was often called upon to aid Friends and Dunkards who were drafted or conscripted into the Southern army.

His widow has kindly given access to many letters and papers which show plainly how these unfortunate people depended upon his assistance, and looked to him to secure their release from prison or from the army. In many cases they did not look in vain. It is very apparent that they had great love for him and confidence in him. She states that he finally gave up his time almost exclusively to looking after the interests of these people. He labored by day and by night, often making long journeys, sometimes on foot, to visit the Friends who were sick, in prison, or in the army. Looking carefully into the merits of individual cases, and usually being able to present a clear case, the officials came to have great confidence in him, and for this reason and because of their regard for him as a Christian minister, they usually granted his requests. Besides the service thus rendered, his house was frequently for weeks the home of those whom he was serving.

For about two years he edited and published the "Southern Friend," which became a necessity, as the people were unable to secure the publications of their Northern brethren, and they were so often misunderstood and maligned in the public press that some means of being correctly represented before the people was quite important.

The committee that came from North Carolina in the interest of their members came to John B. Crenshaw's house and worked with his advice and assistance. Friends of North Carolina appreciated his services. He was cut off from Baltimore Friends, with whom he really belonged, and for the time being he was identified with North Carolina Yearly Meeting, and the Friends learned to esteem him very highly "for his works' sake," as well as on account of his general nature. He kept a diary, at least a part of the time, during his busy life in these trying times. Having liberty to quote therefrom, we make a few extracts, which will serve to give the reader some idea of his continued activity in the cause of peace and good will to men.

Under date of Fourth month 18th, 1861, he writes: "Attending the sittings of the Philadelphia Yearly Meeting. There is great excitement. Mobs going about forcing suspected persons to hoist the United States flag. It is indeed a very trying time, both in church and state."

"19th. Left Philadelphia about 11 p. m. We reached Baltimore on the 20th. Found the railroad bridge was burning. The cars we came in were promptly filled with soldiers, who went back and burned the bridges we had just crossed. We were left outside the city. Hired a carriage to the Washington depot. In Washington we found the Potomac boats in the hands of the government. We went to Alexandria, Va., by a boat which, on arrival, was seized by Governor Letcher of Virginia. Reached home safely, for which I trust we are truly thankful."

"28th. No heart to write, feeling too depressed with the condition of my beloved country. O Virginia! That thy counselors may in faith look to the only true God for guidance, is the prayer of my heart."

"5th month 29th. Father Crenshaw came down to try to get to Baltimore to the meeting for sufferings. We felt called to petition the powers that be, on behalf of peace."

"6th month 2d. Our poor little meeting nearly broken up."

"7th month 30th. I rode around the neighborhood to see if I could raise anything for the sick in Richmond. All that I saw promised to send something."

"7th month 31st. Visited four hospitals for the sick and wounded soldiers. Most of them comfortably situated, but many of them wounded and suffering much."

"8th month 14th. Again made collections for and visited the sick."

"10th month 7th. A long and interesting meeting, during which a document was issued setting forth the condition of Friends in the present distressed condition of the country."

"12th month 11th. Father asked permission of meeting to visit the Federal prisoners in the city; I to accompany him, should we get the permit from the proper authorities."

"12th month 22d. Father and I had a satisfactory meeting with the Federal officers, then with some of their men in Libby prison Richmond. On last Seventh-day I went to meet an appointment with the Massachusetts men. Had a very satisfactory meeting, and was urged to come again.

"1st month 23rd, 1862. Went with father to visit Federal prisoners, with some of whom we had a meeting. Some seemed serious, but others careless and noisy. Distributed Testaments and other books, which were gratefully received.

"1st month 30th. Again, with father, had some very interesting meetings with Federal prisoners. Distributed more Testaments. The men seemed grateful, and some manifested a very tender spirit."

"4th month 4th. Went with Isham Cox and others to attend meeting for sufferings held at Deep River. An exceedingly interesting occasion. The situation of young Friends subject to military call claimed most serious attention, and a memorial was prepared and a committee appointed to present it to their State Convention, now in session."

"4th month 16th. On reaching Richmond found Dr. Nicholson and Joseph Elliott awaiting me, and on the 18th father and I went with them to see the President. After waiting for hours we were informed that we could not see him before 9 p. m., at his residence, whither we repaired at that hour. Were politely received, but he positively refused to accede to the petition which we presented, requesting him to send a message to Congress recommending that Friends be released from military duty on account of religious scruples. He said he refused on the ground that it would be special legislation and open the door against us for further persecution in a future day."

"4th month 23d. Several balloons in sight, supposed to have in them Federals reconnoitering. About 6 a. m. we heard what seemed to be heavy firing at or near the head of Mechanicsville turnpike. There is a picket this afternoon at my bridge. Oh, that we may be able to maintain our principles as followers of the Prince of Peace!"

"4th month 24th. Went to Aunt Crenshaw's. They were expecting the Federal army about noon. We learn that several were killed in the skirmish this morning. A large number of Confederate soldiers camped on and around my farm, expecting to fight tomorrow."

"4th month 25th. Sent my wife and children to father's; so many soldiers coming in and out."

"4th month 26th. Quiet in this neighborhood today."

"4th month 28th. Went to meeting. The few Friends seemed glad indeed to see me. Hurried home on account of the soldiers. They are constantly wanting something, milk or something to eat and I supply them freely."

"4th month 29th. A large division of the army on the road. Gen. D. H. Hill has selected my house as his headquarters. The Crenshaw and Johnson batteries are camped in the woods back of my barn, and from there all across the country the woods are full of soldiers."

"4th month 30th. Busy all day waiting on the soldiers, who are constantly calling for something."

"5th month 31st. General Hill moved his headquarters to Vass, and General Gregg took up his at the house, having previously been below the hill."

"6th month 1st. Went to our little meeting. Saw many wounded brought from the battlefields of yesterday and today, in which it is supposed that more than two thousand Confederate soldiers were killed."

"6th month 4th. Continual crowd and care. A very stormy night. The poor soldiers must have suffered. My porches were full, and some of the sick were in the dwelling-house. Three houses in the woods full, and many lie in the barn and shelters. Many quite sick."

"6th month 4th. Many sick soldiers left in my house and outbuildings, some with measles and some with pneumonia."

"6th month 9th. Two of the sick dead."

"6th month 13th. Pressed my wagon today to carry off the sick. All gone from the house but one. One poor man buried today, making three here."

"6th month 23d. We hear much cannon firing here today, some so near we can see the smoke from the guns and see the shells burst."

"6th month 28th. Fighting continues. Many lives lost on both sides."

"6th month 29th. We hear that the Federals have been cut off from York river and driven across the Chickahominy."

"7th month 9th. Father and I at meeting at Jane Whitlock's house, our meeting-house having been taken possession of by the government." (The meeting-house was at that time at Nineteenth and Cary streets, one square distant from Libby prison.)

"8th month 8th. Whiting's division of the Confederate army encamped on our farm. Left next day, having taken some potatoes and fruit and stripped plank from many panels of the fence, etc. Upon the whole I think we have cause to be thankful that we are not more injured. The officers placed a guard over the orchard, potatoes and houses."

"8th month 27th. John Carter and Nereus Mendenhall here, to present a memorial from North Carolina Meeting for Sufferings to the Congress of the United States. A copy is placed on the desk of each member."

"8th month 28th. Went with Friends to see if we could get Thomas Elliott out of prison, but General Winder had received no reply from Petersburg, where he had sent for information. By appointment we met Miles, the chairman, and other members of the military committee of the House, to explain, as well as we could, our principles on war. They asked us many close questions, which I trust we were led to answer to their satisfaction, as they expressed themselves so at the close, and I feel that we have cause for gratitude for help received on that interesting occasion. We hear that the committee of the House has already united in recommending that Friends and Dunkards be exempted from military duty, etc."

"8th month 29th. General Winder released Thomas Elliott on condition that I would give receipt for him and have him forthcoming when called for. On the 31st he was called for, and I had to give bond for $500 for his return whenever called."

"10th month 1st. Letters from Dr. Mendenhall, asking my attention to the cases of several young men."

"10th month 15th. I failed to find the young men, but met at camp here a number of other young Friends."

"10th month 17th. Went to look up some young men. Jonathan Harris here for same purpose."

"10th month 18th. Went with J. Harris. We paid the tax for five Friends and three Dunkards $4000. Put in a petition for Jesse Gordon, who professes to be a Friend in principle. The Secretary of War agreed to pass him as a Friend, much to our relief."

"10th month 19th. The Friends and Dunkards from Camp Lee came to our little meeting today."

"10th month 20th. Jonathan Harris and I got off young Gordon at the war office. Met some of the Virginia Dunkards brought here as conscripts, some of whom had paid the $500 tax into the State treasury. At their request I drew up a petition to the Secretary of War asking that those who had paid the tax might be allowed to return home until the Legislature meets, when they hope to be allowed to draw the money from the State treasury to pay the Confederate treasury."

"10th month 22d. At Camp Lee found that the Friends had gone home, except young Gordon, who was too sick to go; also the North Carolina Dunkards. The Virginia Dunkards are not yet through with their cases."

"10th month 25th. We attended the meeting for sufferings of North Carolina Yearly Meeting. An interesting occasion. Committee appointed to consider the exemption law, and report. Friends seem very sweetly united in this time of trial and affliction. Friends cannot accept the provisions of the law as just, or as what they had a right to expect. A number have placed money in my hands for exemption."

"I have been engaged for several days assisting our friends Isham Cox and Allen U. Tomlinson in trying to get off some young Friends from military duty. Isham Cox stopped at a camp between Richmond and Petersburg to see his son-in-law Woody, whom, with his brother, we succeeding in getting off. Isham Cox had a very acceptable service in our meeting, and left next day for home, taking the Woody boys with him."

"12th month 10th. Took my wife in the buggy to camp near Drury's Bluff, where General Daniel is in command, to visit the young Friends. They have been kindly treated and not required to perform military duty. Thompson is expecting exemption on account of poor health; Stephen Hobson, hoping for release on the ground of being a miller; and General Daniel tells us that an order has been issued for the release of J. Harvey and S. Hobson."

"1st month 3d, 1863. Went to General Daniel's camp. The young Friends have left. Called at Drury's Bluff, but found no Friends there."

"1st month 16th. Isham Cox here to get Friends released from army and prison."

"1st month 17th. Engaged all day arranging for the release of six young Friends, for whom Isham Cox paid $3000."

"1st month 18th. Isham Cox gave us what seemed food convenient for us at meeting today. He takes cars tomorrow for camp near Fredericksburg."

"2d month 7th. Interceded for M. H. Bradshaw, not a Friend. Secretary of War agreed to pass him as a Friend. I paid the tax and brought him home with me."

"2d month 9th. Got Bradshaw a passport home. Petitioned Secretary of War in behalf of Calvin Perkins."

"2d month 19th. General Pickett's division of the army quartered here. A large portion in our woods. Colonel Brocton and aids stayed with us. All left at noon. Have burned a lot of wood and fencing."

"3d month 2d. Successful in having the Secretary of War pass as a Friend William A. Wells. Paid the tax for him and arranged for his discharge."

"3d month 5th. Went with Matthew Osborne to see about removing the remains of his son Jesse, who died at Oakwood in Eighth month last. The superintendent showed us what he said he was sure was the grave. Sent the coffin to Raper and Murray's to be packed for removal to North Carolina. On opening it, there was found only a skeleton, a little hair and some pieces of cloth."

"3d month 19th. Letter from Thomas Kennedy's wife saying that he was sent to Richmond."

"3rd month 21st. Went to Richmond to see about Thomas Kennedy. Learned that he had been sent North under a flag of truce."

"3d month 31st. Went to meet Christian Robertson and his son-in-law (Dunkards), to help them to get the former out of the army."

"4th month 1st. Isham Cox here to try to get some young men exempted."

"4th month 2d. Went with Isham Cox, and we succeeded in getting all these cases exempted from military duty, for which we are truly thankful."

"4th month 6th. I was favored to get the release of O. Gordon, and paid the tax for him."

"4th month 12th. Nathan Hunt, Jr., at our meeting today. Came home with me. I got a passport for him to Fredericksburg tomorrow."

"4th month 18th. Got a release for William P. Osborne. Learned that Christian Robertson's application was refused; but they offered him a detail to hospital work. Procured a furlough for C. Robertson (Dunkard) to go home for ten days. He has not applied for transfer to hospital duty."

"5th month 1st. C. Robertson has returned, true to his promise. Called at the war office, but found no decision in his case."

"5th month 2d. Took C. R. to get his furlough extended eight days. He went to Chimborazo hospital. His uncle came home with me."

"5th month 6th. Coming from meeting with J. Harris we learned that the Federals had been in strong force around father's, and taken all his horses. Got passport for J. Harris to go home."

"5th month 9th. Got an order to send Joseph Fell North; also a discharge for Eli Bird, who came home with me much rejoiced."

"5th month 14th. Went with Isham Cox to see Assistant Secretary of War on account of several persons who desire exemption by paying the tax imposed upon non-combatants."

"6th month 9th. Took C. Robertson to Richmond to the war office to see about his case. Got two Friends through and paid the tax for them."

"9th month 4th. Went with John Pretlow and William Bradshaw to make an effort for Bradshaw's release. Hope we have succeeded though it has to pass through a long routine yet."

"10th month 1st. Isham Cox and J. Harris came in about night from Orange Court House. Found the grave of John Hobson. His father much distressed."

"11th month 2d. Engaged with father preparing memorial to present to the Legislature, on exempting Friends from military duty."

"11th month 5th. The memorial was presented to the half-year's meeting, which adopted it with great unanimity, and directed 300 copies printed for distribution among the members of the Legislature. Friends parted in much love and unity, feeling that trials await us."

"11th month 14th. Detained until late before the military committee of House of Delegates, who treated me respectfully, but declined to do anything for Friends."

"11th month 15th. Went to see Judge Campbell, who wished to see me about the Hockett boys. He offers to send them North. Wrote to their father for advice."

"11th month 21st. A defense which I wrote in reply to an attack on non-combatants appeared in the 'Whig' today."

"12th month 7th. The Secretary of War decided against T. R. Vestal. I asked for a special interview in regard to his case. T. R. Vestal is poorly."

"12th month 11th. William Cox here to get me to assist him in the case of William Overman."

"12th month 12th. Received orders for the release of C. Robertson and John Reynolds."

"12th month 21st. Went to Camp Lee and paid $500 to Captain Maynard as exemption tax for my son, Nathaniel B. Crenshaw."

"12th month 26th. Procured an order to send A. G. Fell North, and an order to discharge A. G. Rush from the army. I paid tax for him in 6th month last, but he did not get his discharge."

"12th month 28th. Lazarus Pearson came to see about Overman."

. . . .

John B. Crenshaw's diary for the year 1864 is missing, but the year was spent in a continuation of the same arduous work as the extracts given indicate. A few quotations from the diary of 1865 may here be given.

"1st month 4th. At the enrolling office I was handed an exemption as a minister."

"2d month 1st. Went with David Moffitt before the Secretary of the Navy, and succeeded in securing the release of his son from the Confederate States navy."

"2d month 3d. Went to see about the cases of several Friends who were suffering for the non-performance of military duties."

"2d month 14th. Got an early start to see the Advocate General and several other officers. Saw W. T. Haley, H. Ford and Milliken. Obtained a recommendation from Hale's officers for his discharge. Returned to Petersburg very weary, having walked nearly twenty miles."

"2d month 16th. On my way to Richmond met James Hockett, Nathan Spencer and N. Farlow going toward my home. They came by appointment of their monthly meeting to look after Friends in the army."

"2d month 17th. Waiting on Friends, he found Seth Laughlin died on the eighteenth of last month. Blair still sick."

"2d month 20th. Went to father's. Found them more cheerful than expected from all that we had heard. The Federals took all of his horses and most of his provisions. Father is trying to use some of the broken-down horses and mules the Federals left on his place."

On the first of Fourth month John B. Crenshaw and his daughter, now the wife of Josiah Leeds of Philadelphia, went to his father's, sixteen miles away, to attend meeting for worship at Cedar Creek on the Sabbath, where occasional appointments were made after the meeting had ceased to be regularly held. The next day, April 2d, Jefferson Davis and his cabinet, and many prominent citizens of Richmond, left the capital of the fast-waning Confederacy. With the few troops remaining in the city, they hurriedly took their departure for a more southern point, for safety from the approaching Northern troops. While John B. Crenshaw had been attending meeting with the little company in the country, a Friend minister from England was attending the city meeting, and on arriving home that evening they found him as a guest. The diary continues:

"J. J. Neave, a minister from England, at my home. Early in the morning we heard heavy explosions, the blowing up of the magazines, and we learn that the Federals are in the city. J. J. Neave and I drove to the city and called on our Friends, whom we were glad to find composed. On coming out we were stopped by colored pickets, but they let us pass home. Warwick's mills and a large space around destroyed by the Confederates burning the tobacco warehouses."

"4th month 5th. Called on a number of Friends, among them Judge Campbell, with whom I had a most interesting interview. I rejoice that he remained in the city, believing that he will be very useful in restoring order. Went to see some of my neighbors. Servants everywhere very unsettled. One of my neighbors, Colonel J. B. Young, grossly insulted by the colored troops. His silver, etc., stolen, but was soon restored by an officer. Lawless men are taking horses, etc."

"4th month 8th. J. J. Neave and I were not allowed to go into the city. A number of the neighbors called to ask advice. The fright and harassment from robbers continues. At the request of the neighbors I drew up a statement of the manner in which the soldiers are robbing and insulting the people, and presented it to General Wirtzel, to whom I was introduced by Judge Campbell. The general promised to issue orders to repress the disorders.'"

"4th month 12th. Had to get a pass to go home. Colored

pickets at our toll-gate. We all renewed our allegiance to the United States."

"4th month 14th. Colored troops sent off and arrangements made to protect this section with white troops."

"4th month 18th. Went with numbers to get their passes."

"4th month 26th. Went with Allen U. Tomlinson to affirm his allegiance to the United States. Got a pass to go to my home."

"6th month 2d. Had a long interview with Judge Campbell's wife with reference to his present condition as a prisoner."

"6th month 3d. Writing a memorial to President Johnson on behalf of Judge Campbell."

"6th month 5th. Father and I had a consultation with Judge Campbell's wife. Met F. Ruffin and Colonel Ray in reference to memorial certificate, etc. Judge Lyons introduced us to Governor Pierpont, who received us courteously and gave father Willets a permit to visit the penitentiary and jails of the State, with request that he would report the result."

"6th month 25th. After meeting, read to our Friends the memorial in behalf of Judge Campbell. I was unanimously requested to sign it in behalf of Friends in Virginia."

"6th month 29th. Father Crenshaw started this morning for Washington with the memorial in behalf of Judge Campbell."

. . . .

Here ends the diary, but we know that John B. Crenshaw continued in good works until the tenth of Fifth month, 1889, when he passed from works to rewards.

INDEX.

CPSIA information can be obtained at www.ICGtesting.com
Printed in the USA
LVOW101103100613

337816LV00008B/33/P